Abby's Drawing

by

Abigail Kisiwaa Owusu

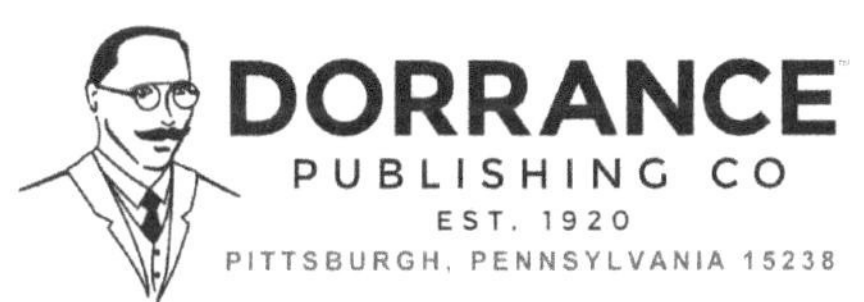

Dorrance Publishing Co
585 Alpha Drive
Suite 103
Pittsburgh, PA 15238
Visit our website at *www.dorrancebookstore.com*

ISBN: 978-1-6442-6185-9
eISBN: 978-1-6442-6436-2

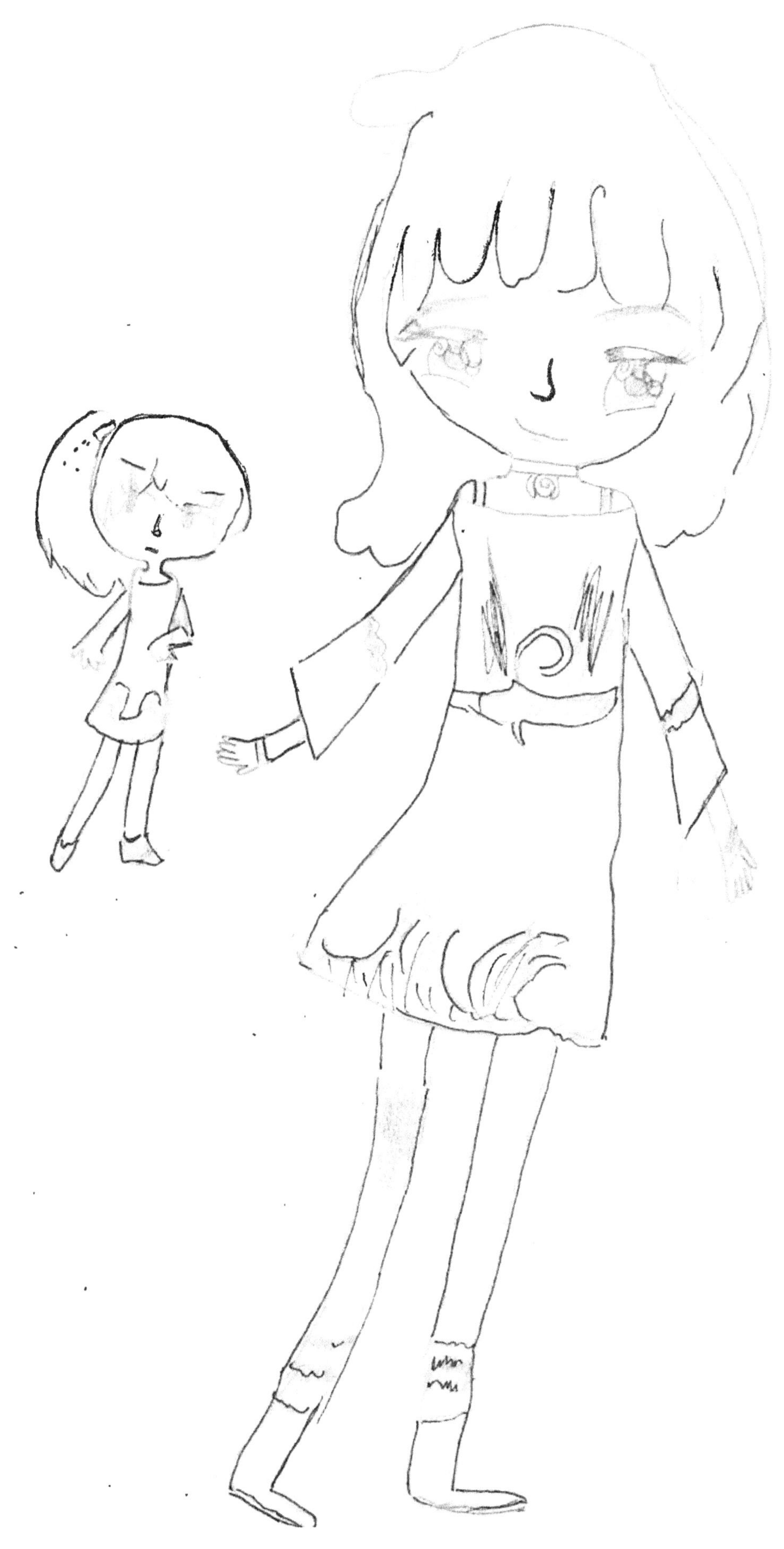

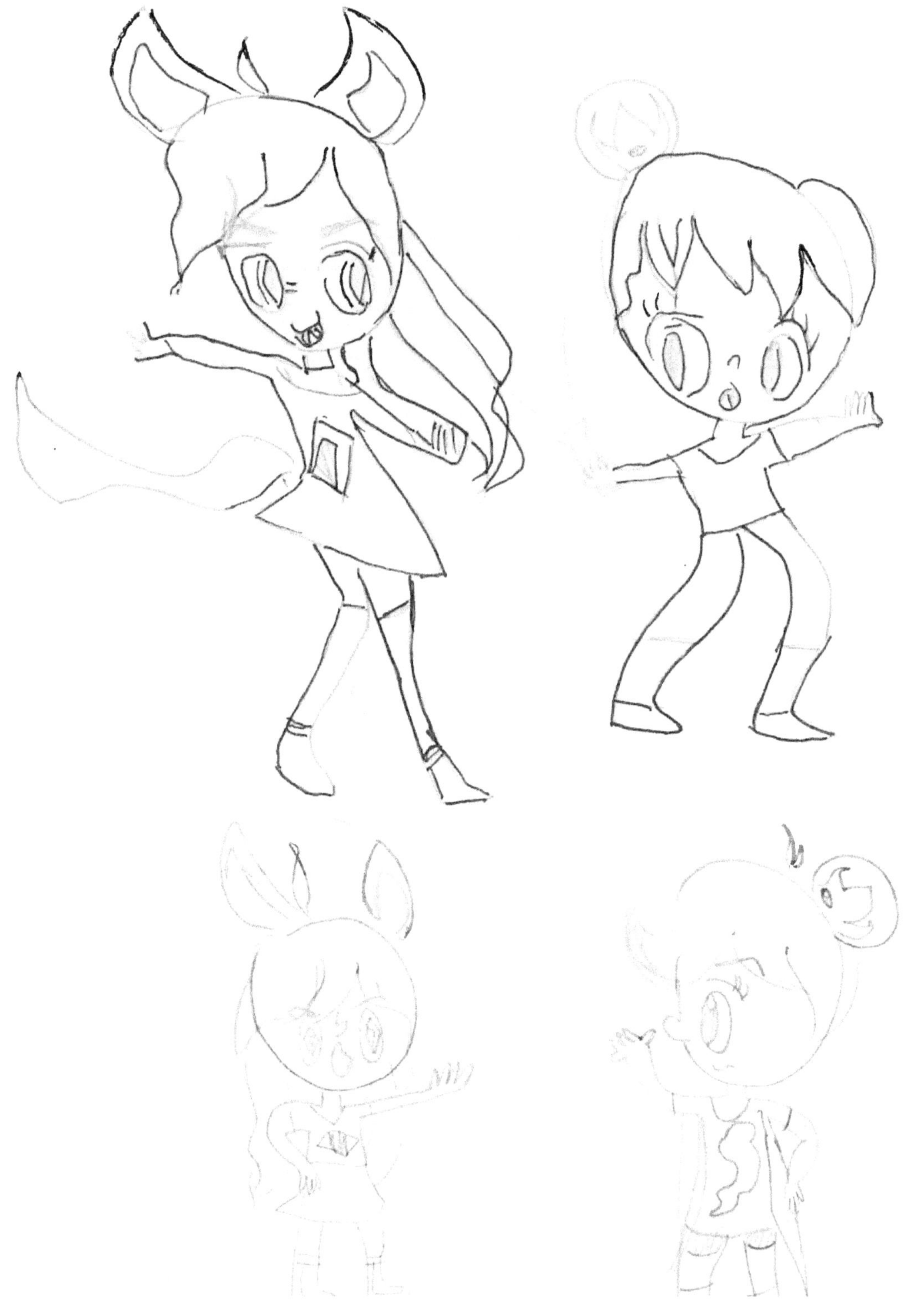

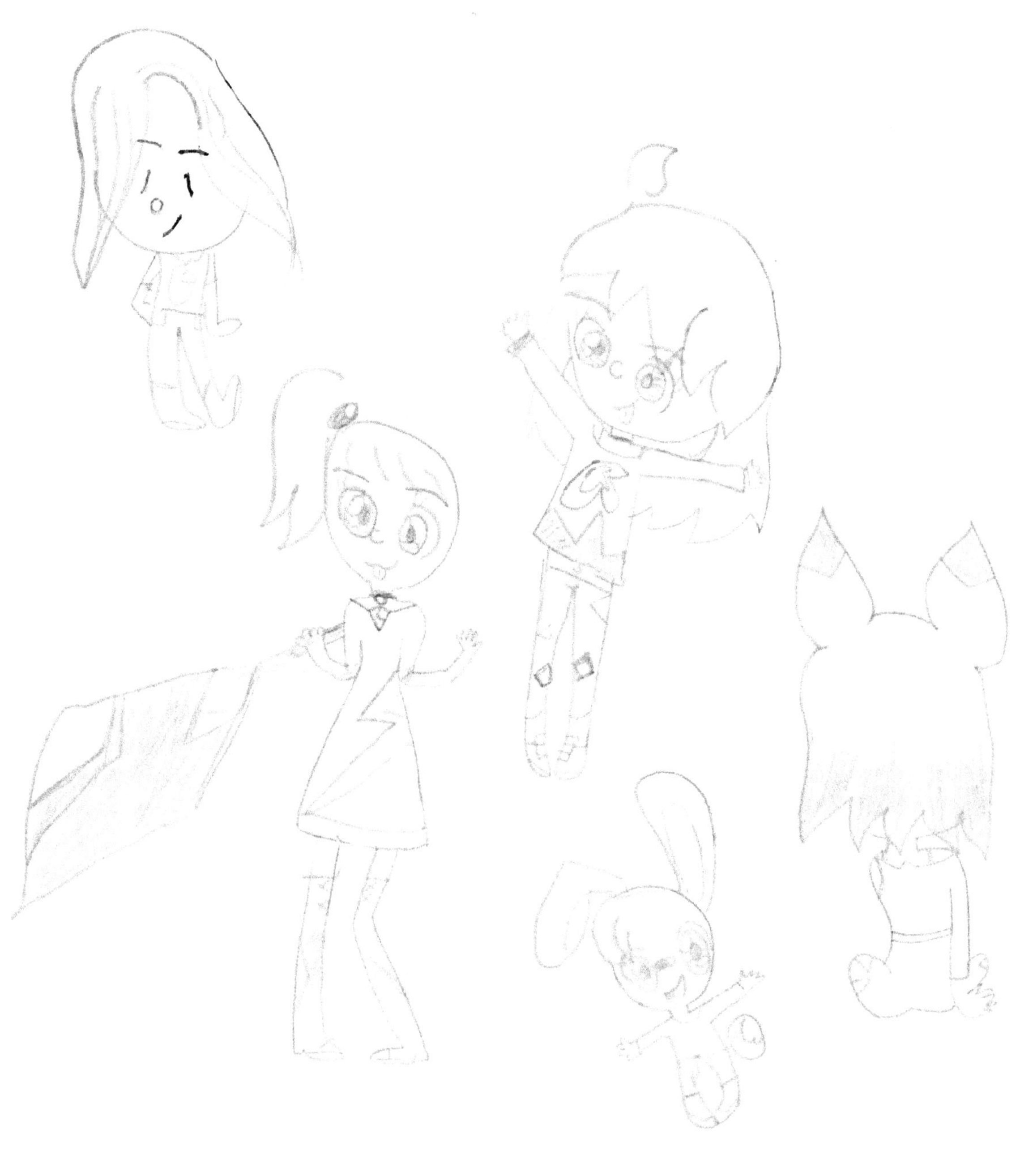

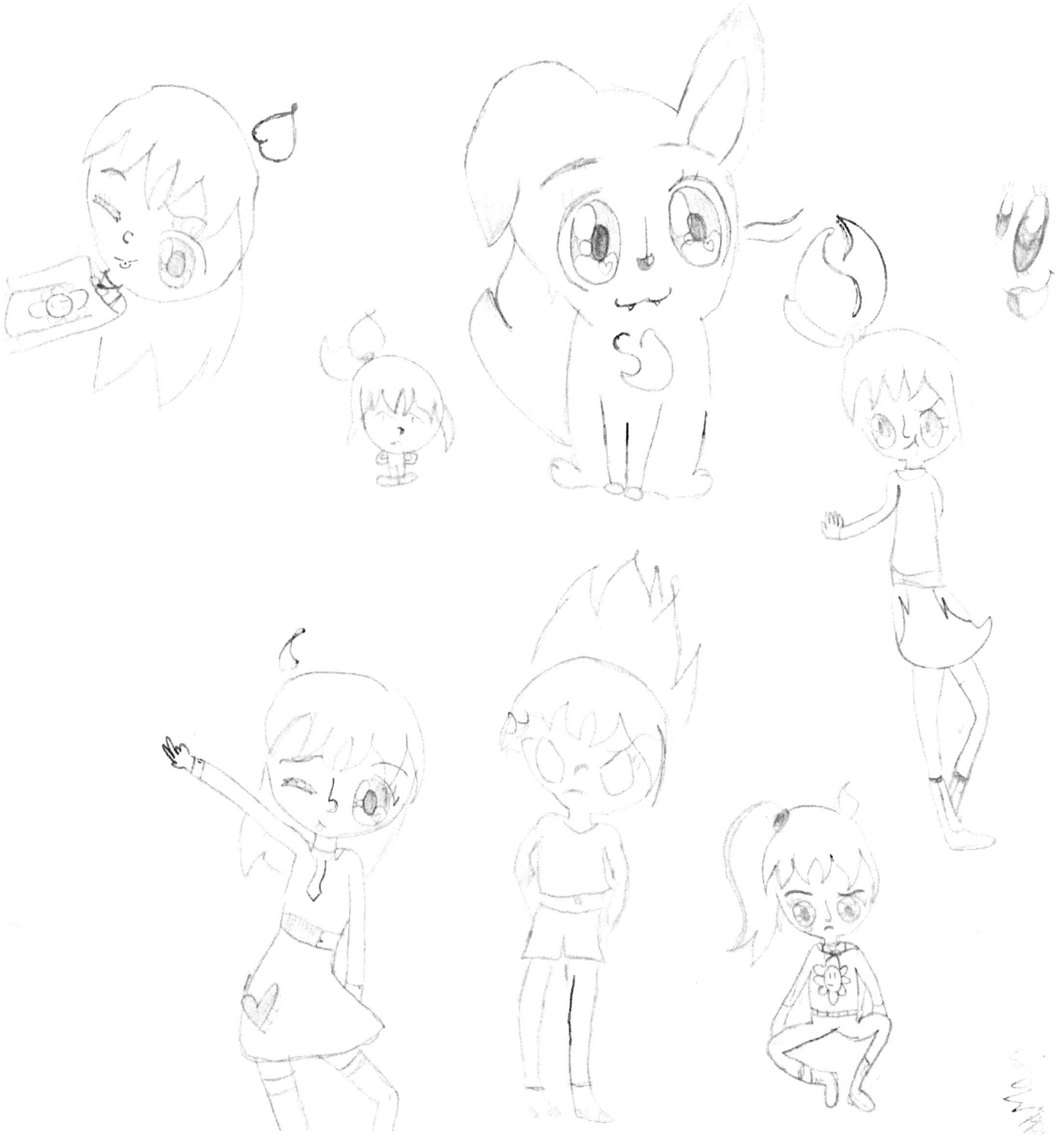

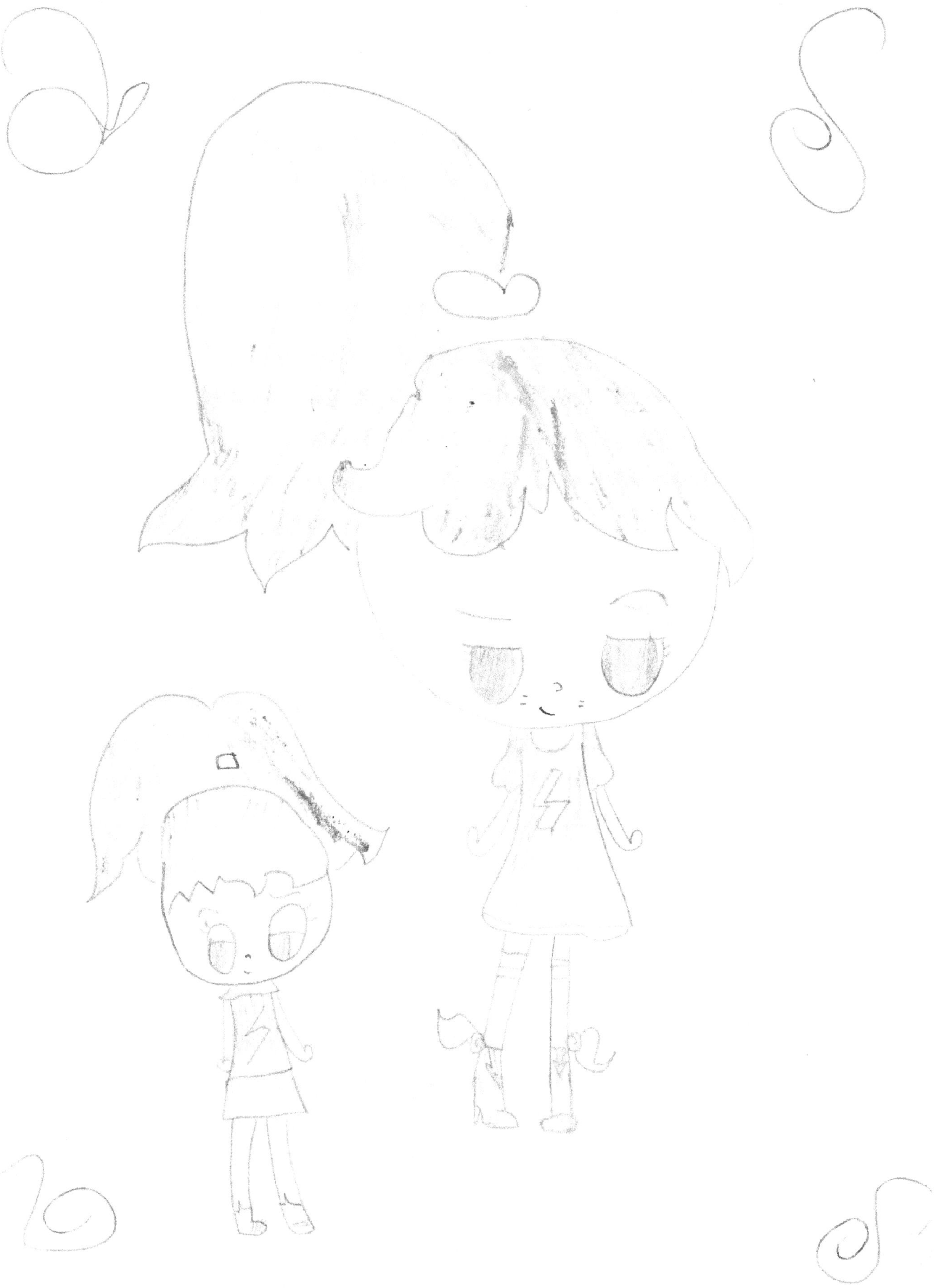

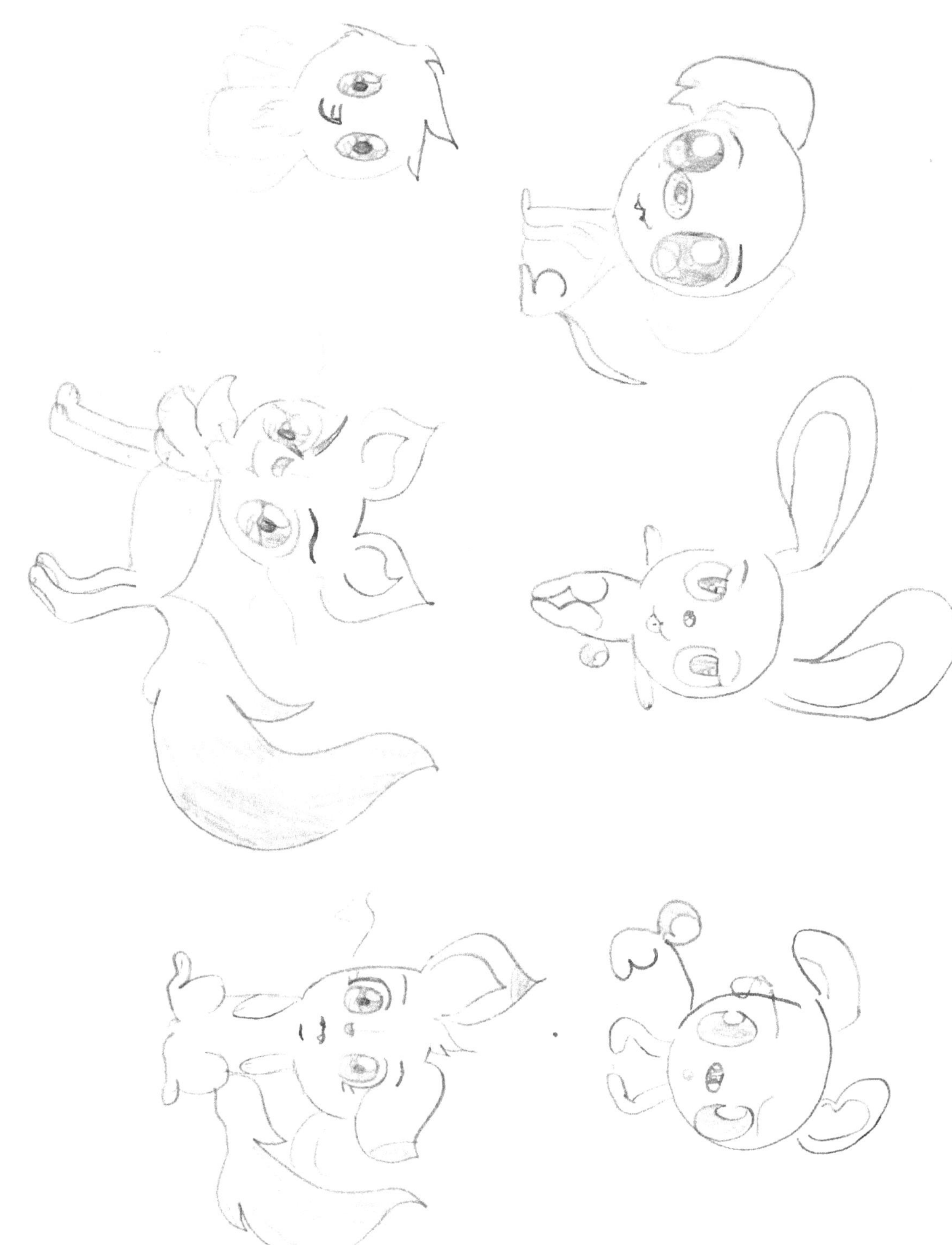

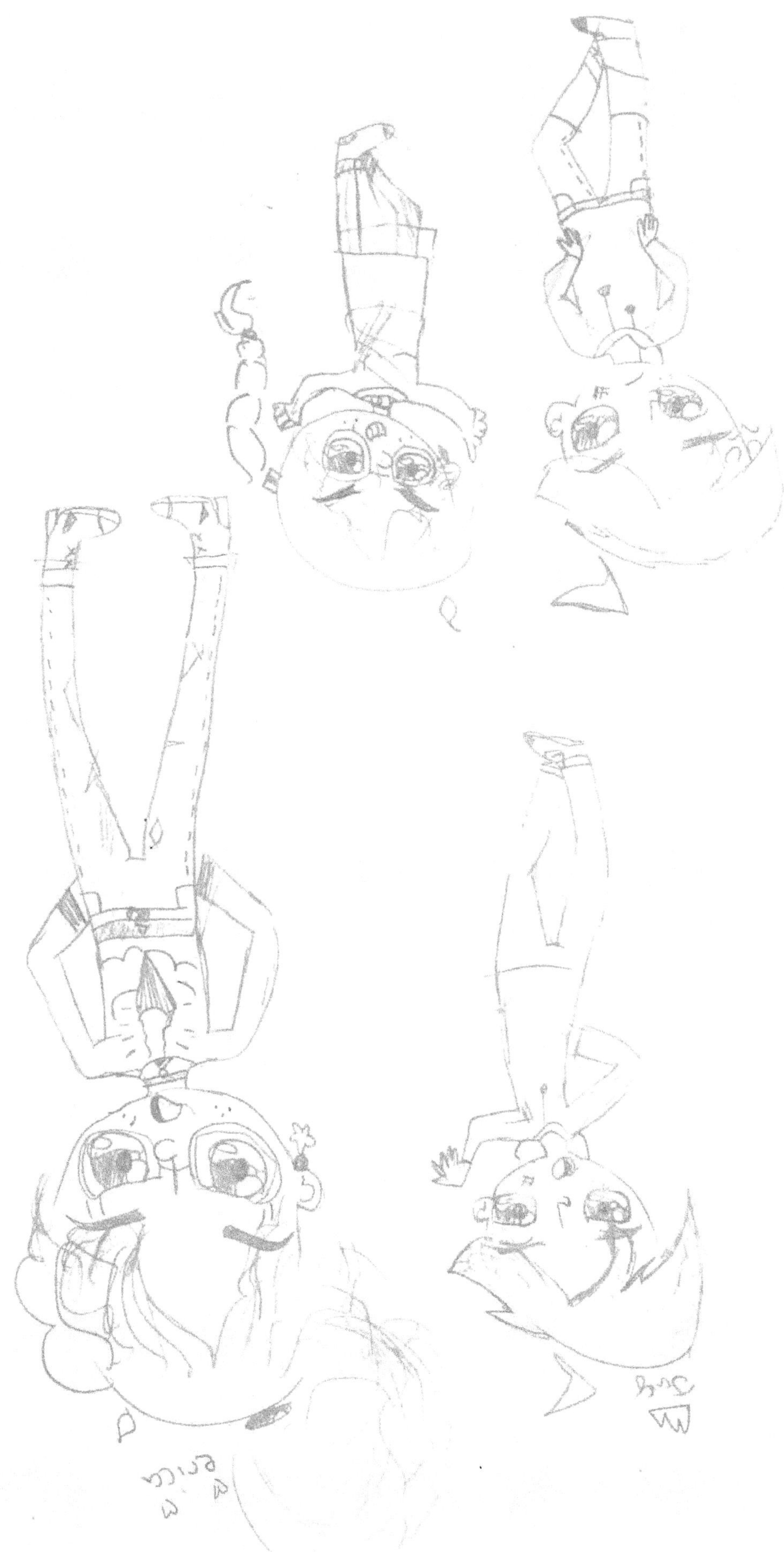

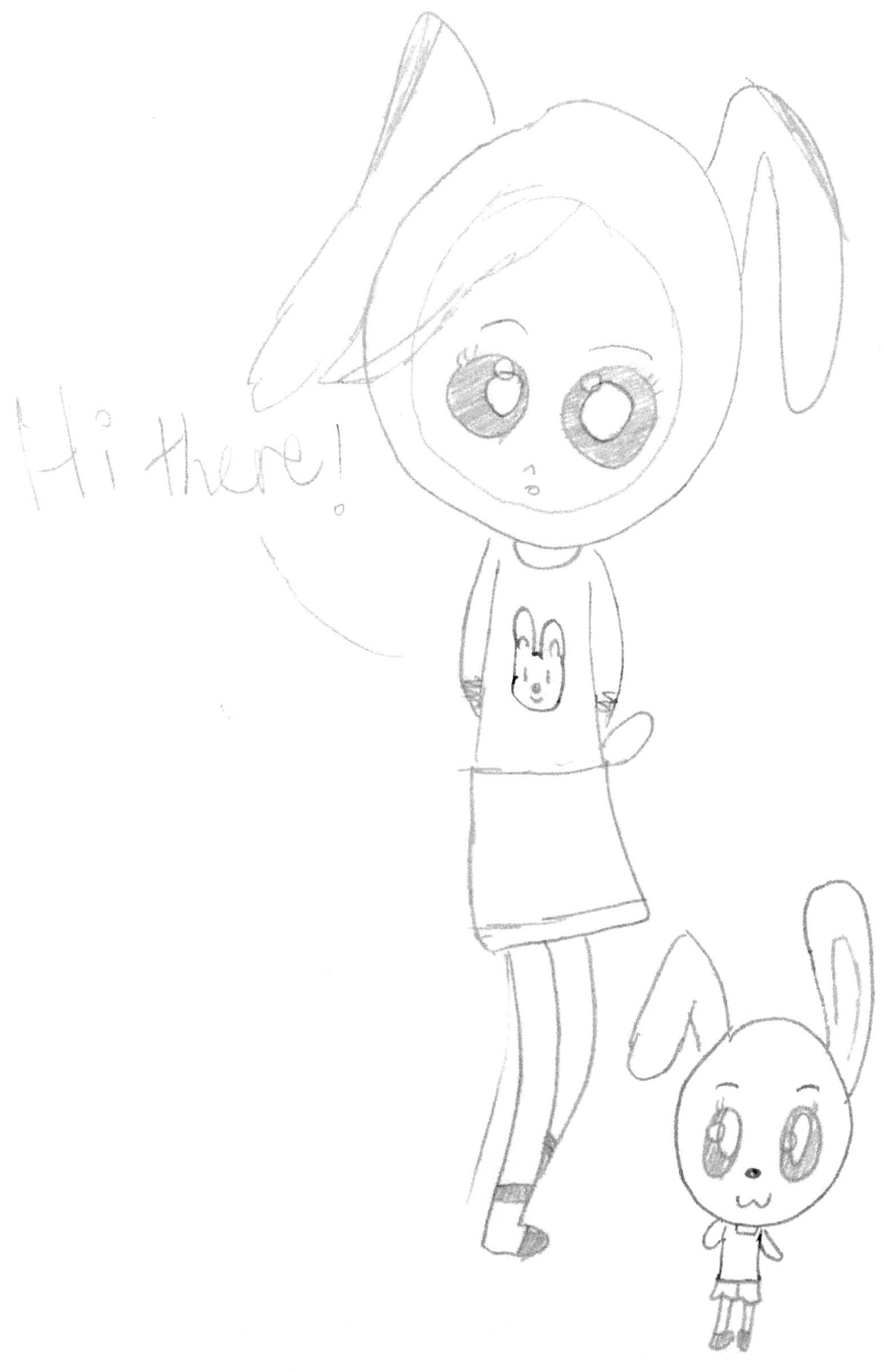
Bunni
Hi there!

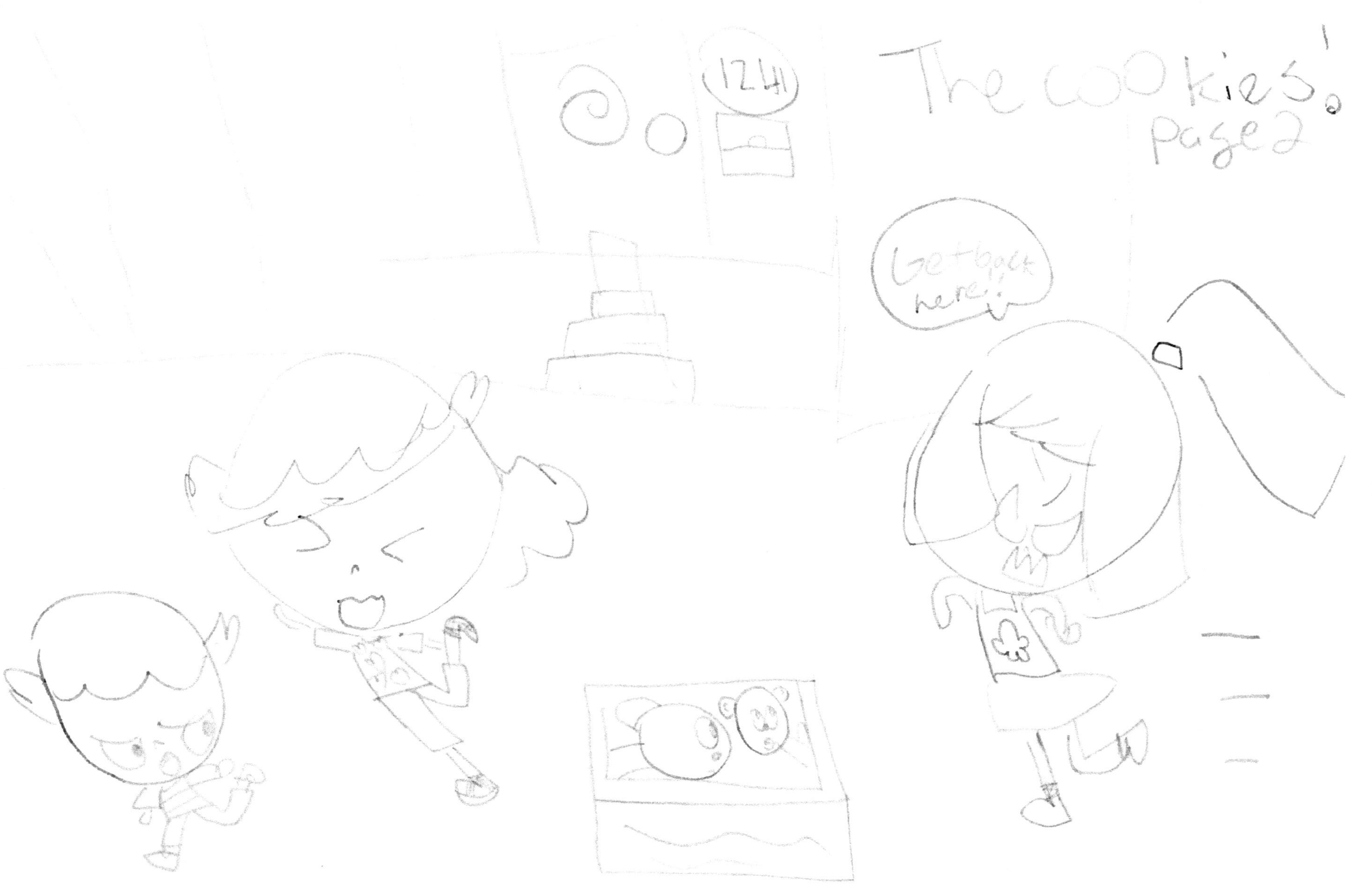
The cookies!
page 2
Get back here!

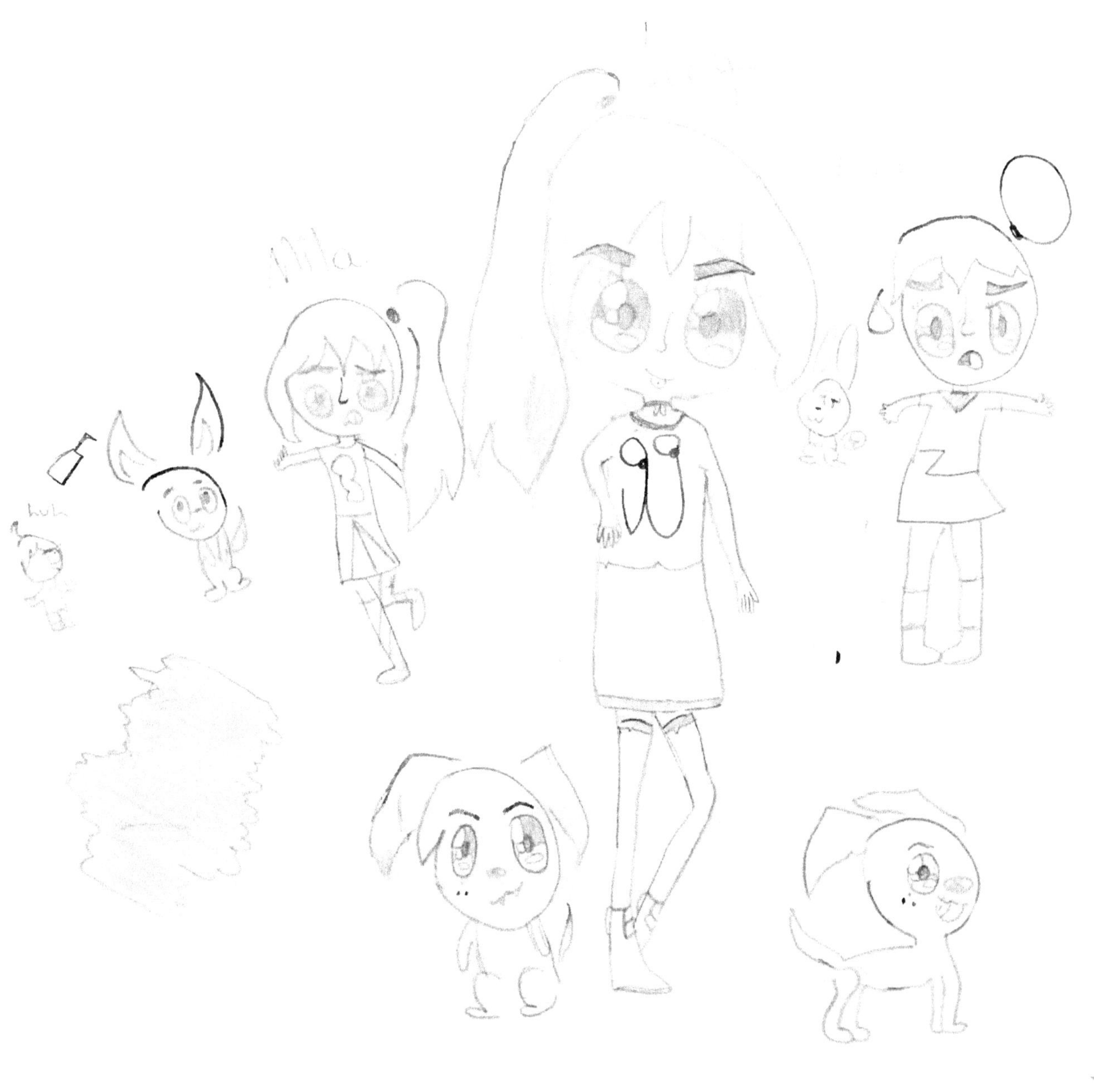
Mila

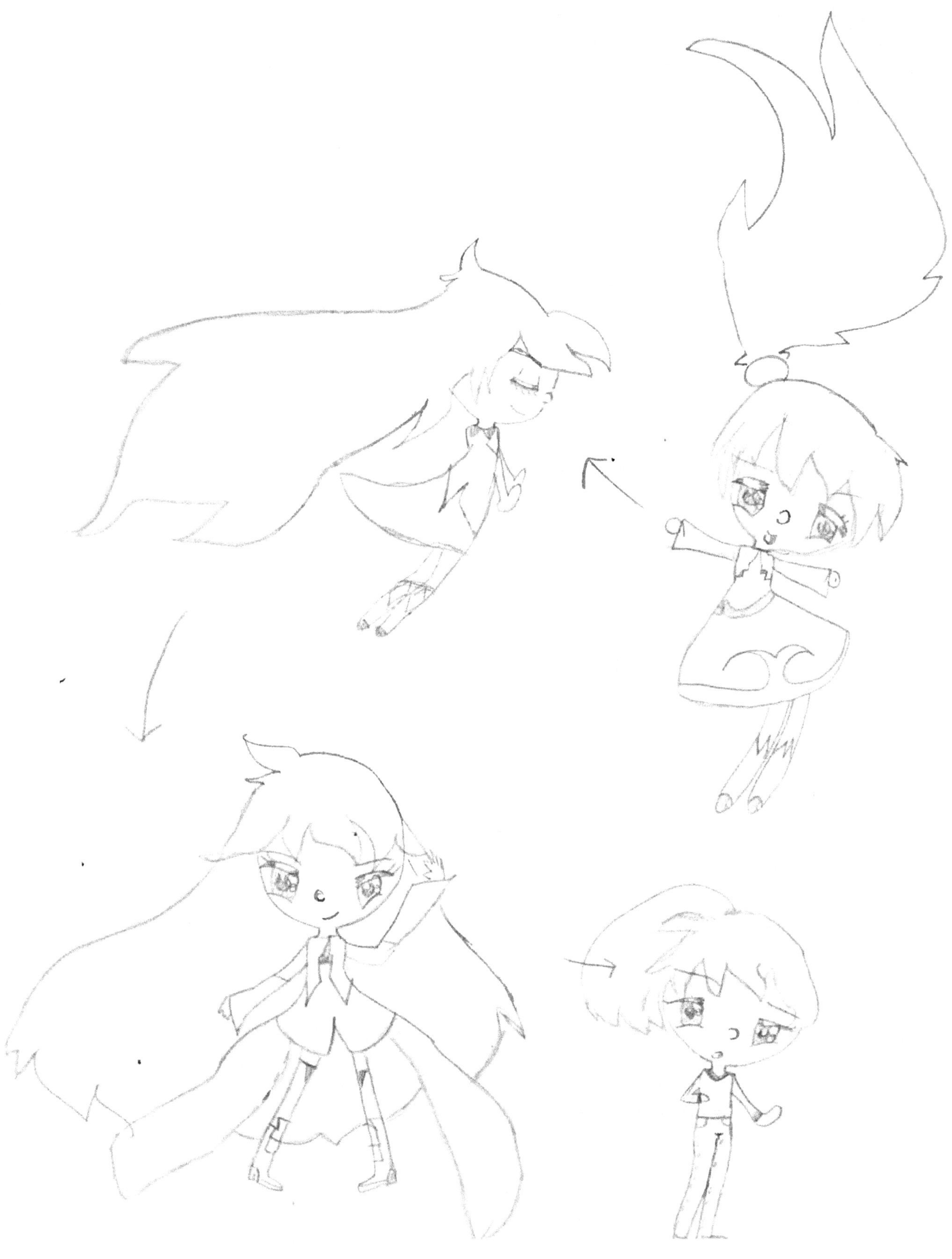

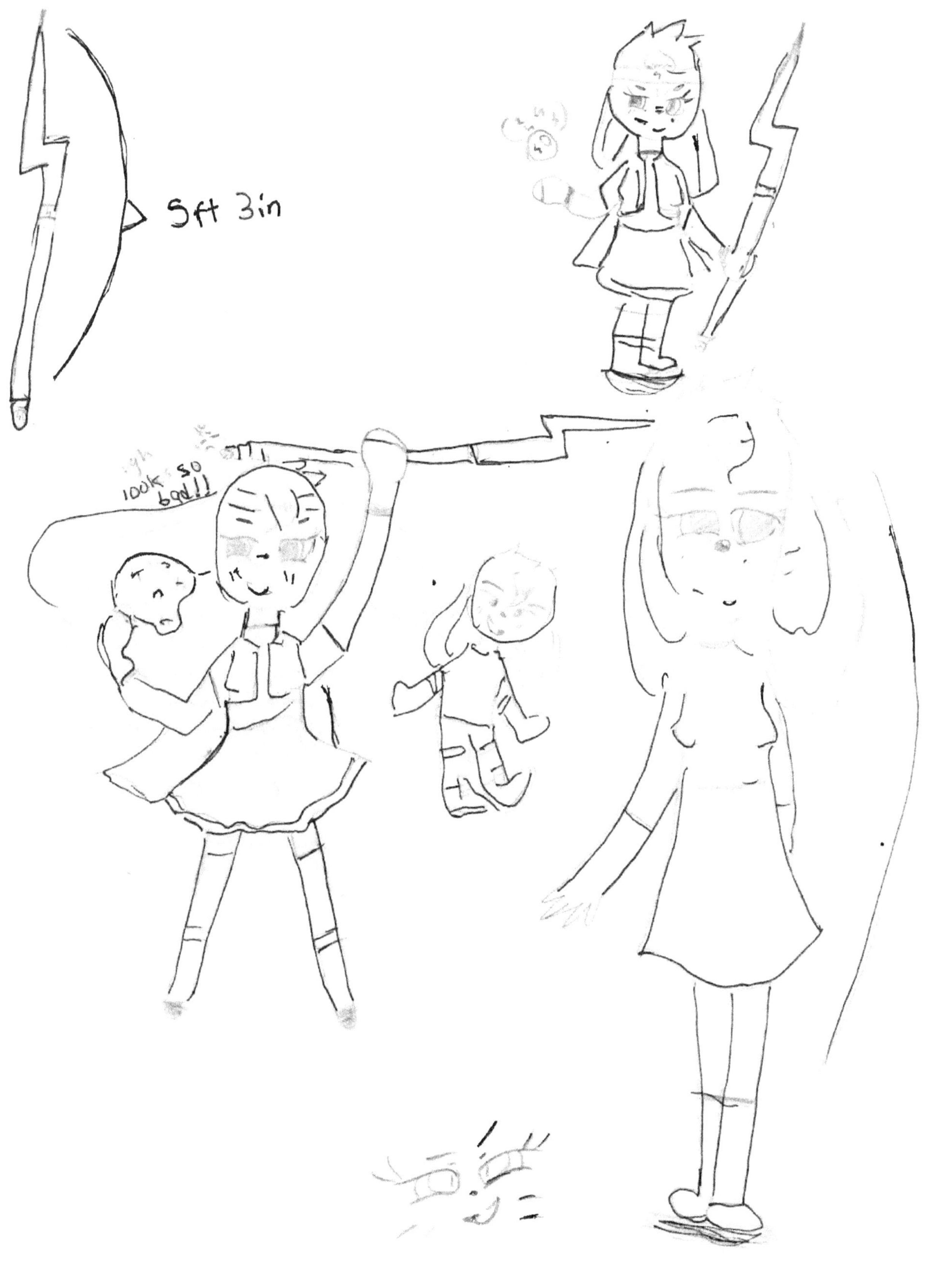
5ft 3in
looks so
bad!!

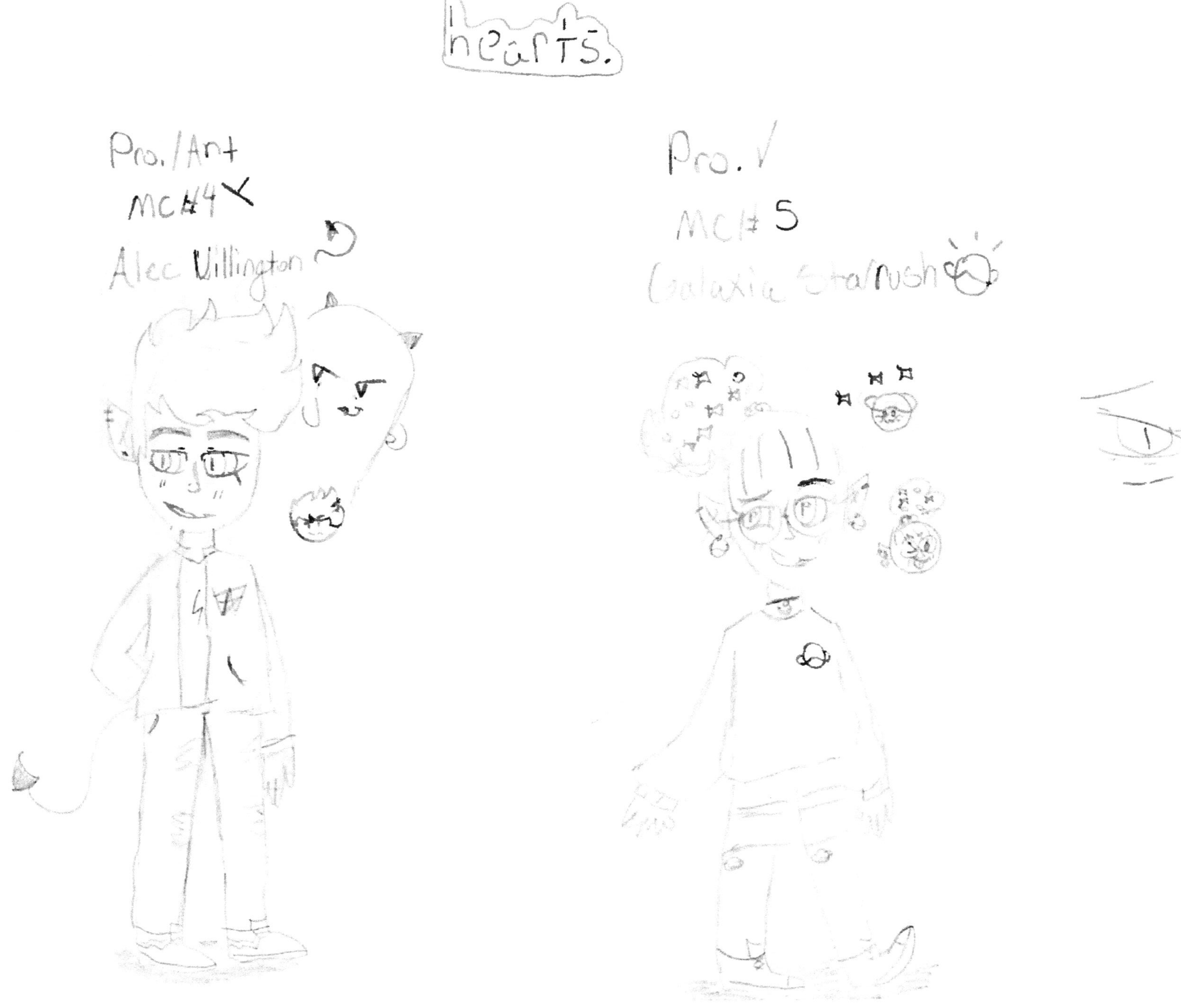
hearts.
Pro./Ant
MC#4
Alec Willington
Pro.
MC# 5
Galaxia Starrush

Kitties by ably

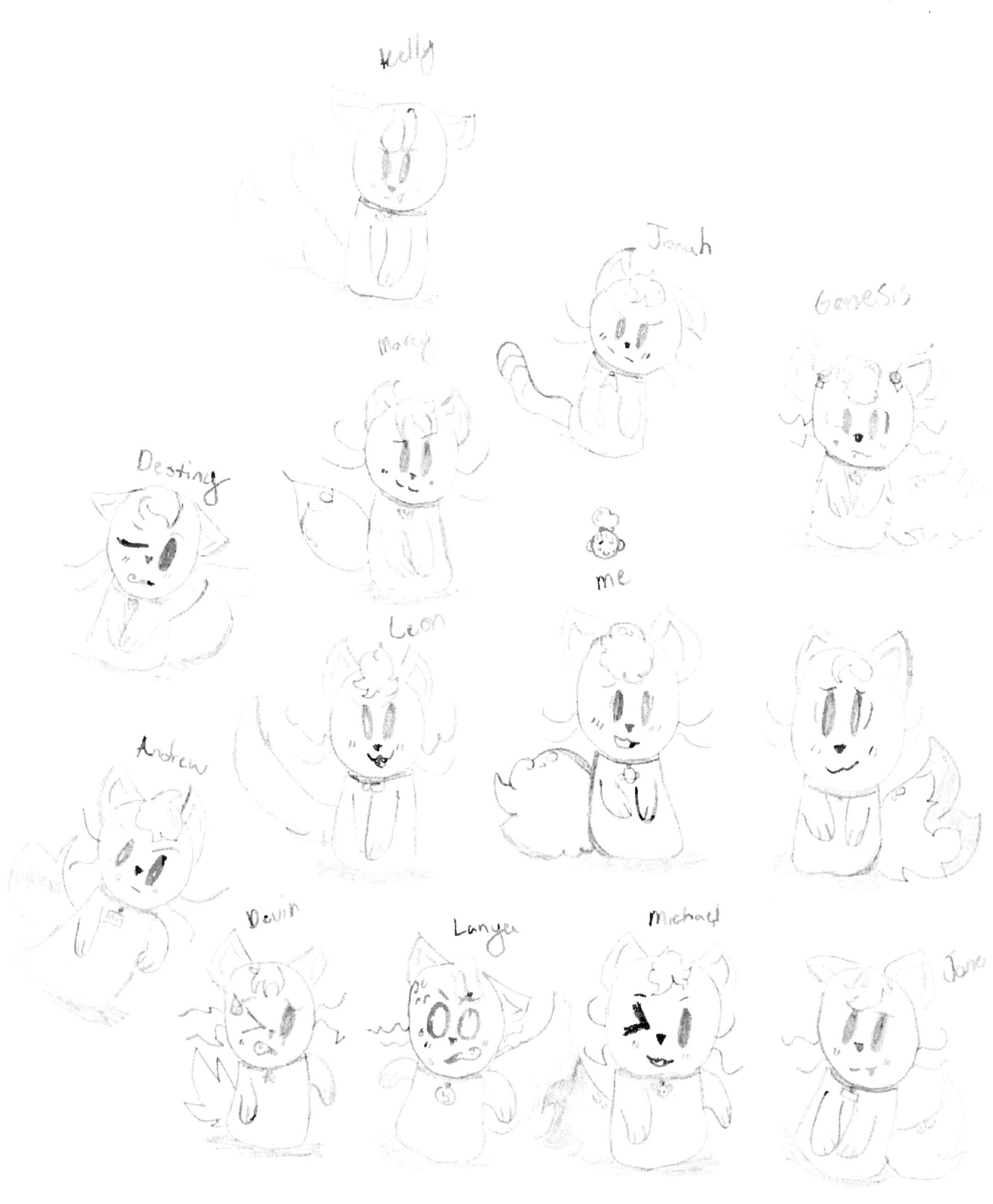

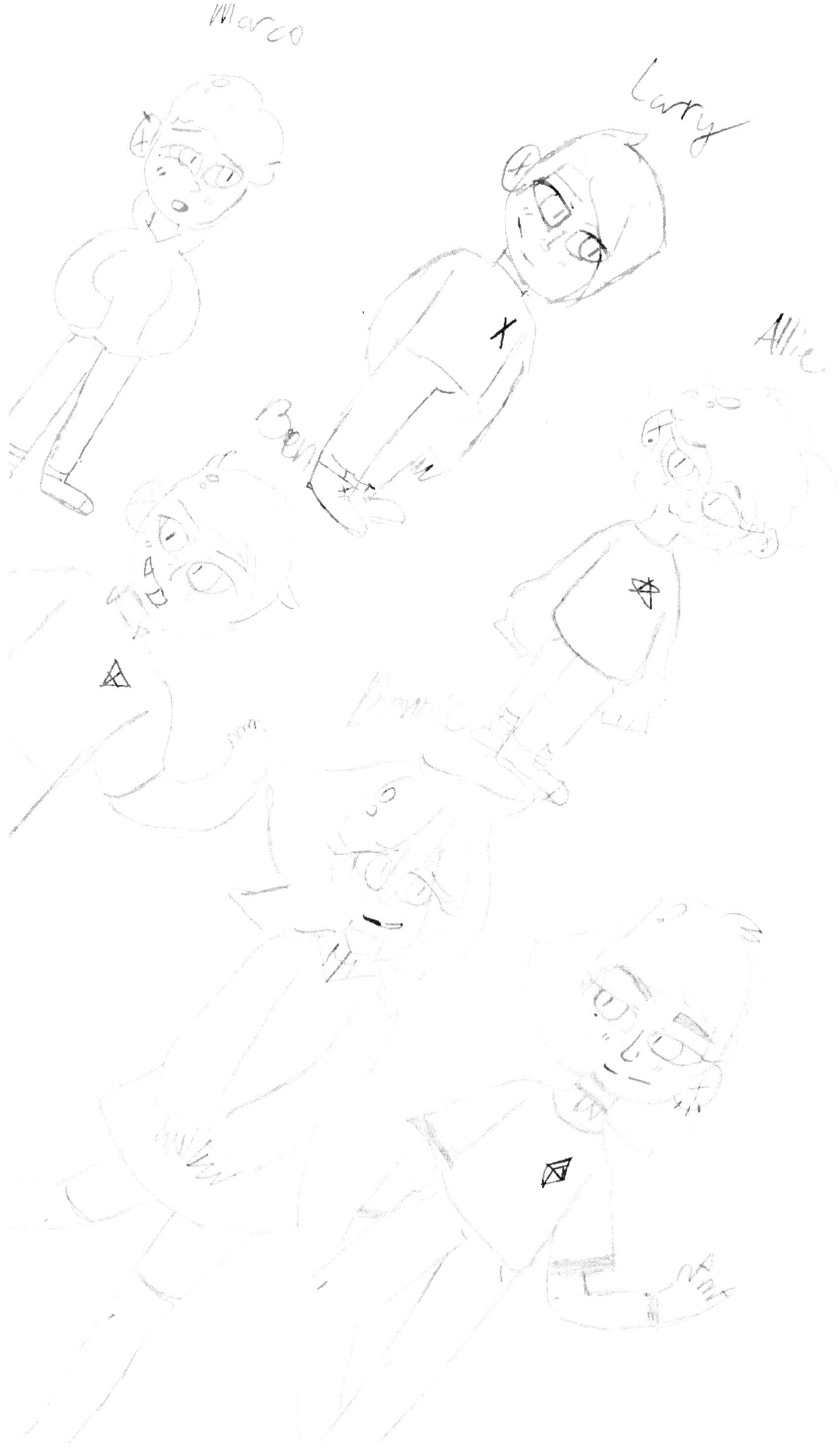
Marco
Larry
Allie

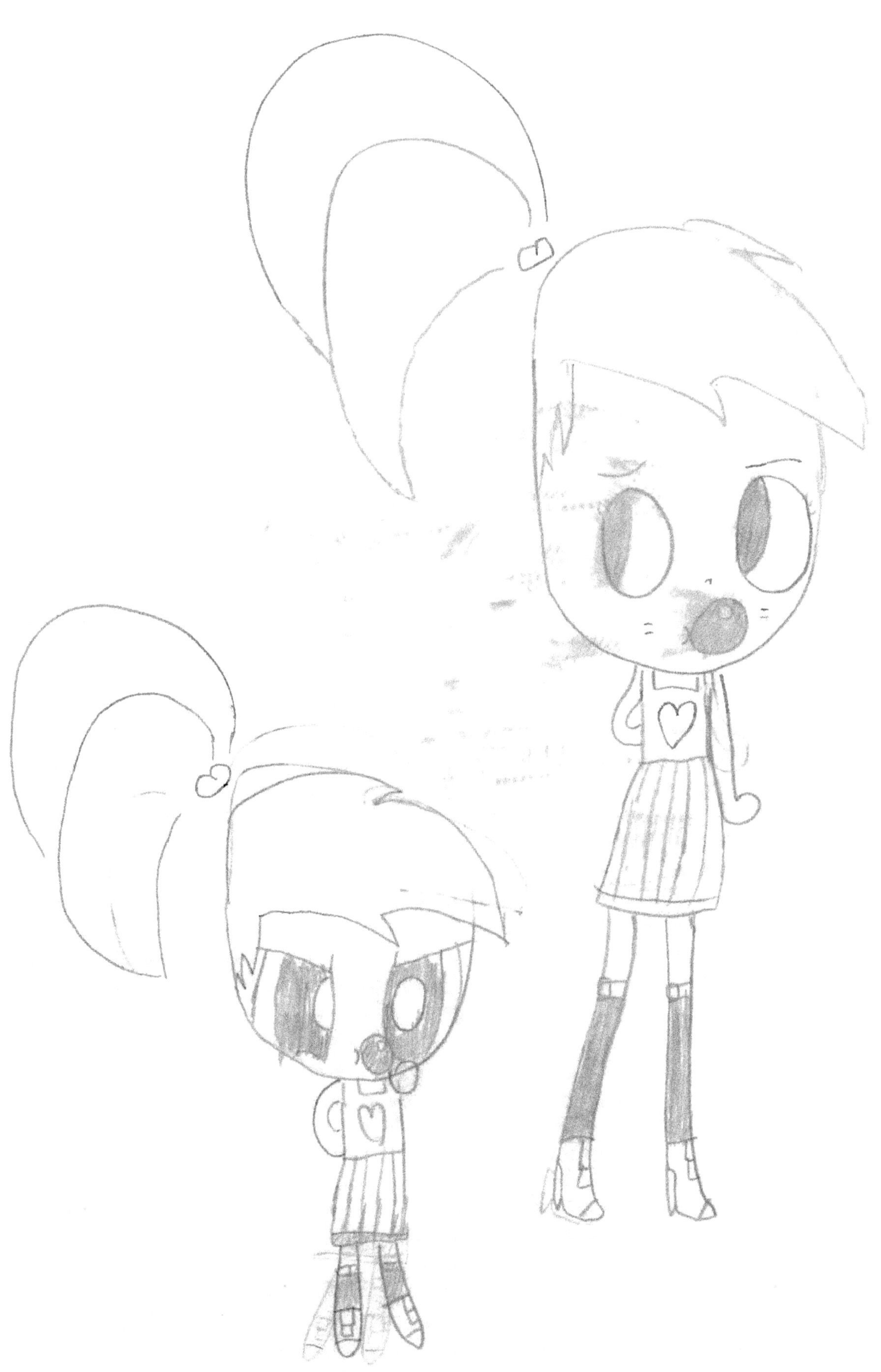

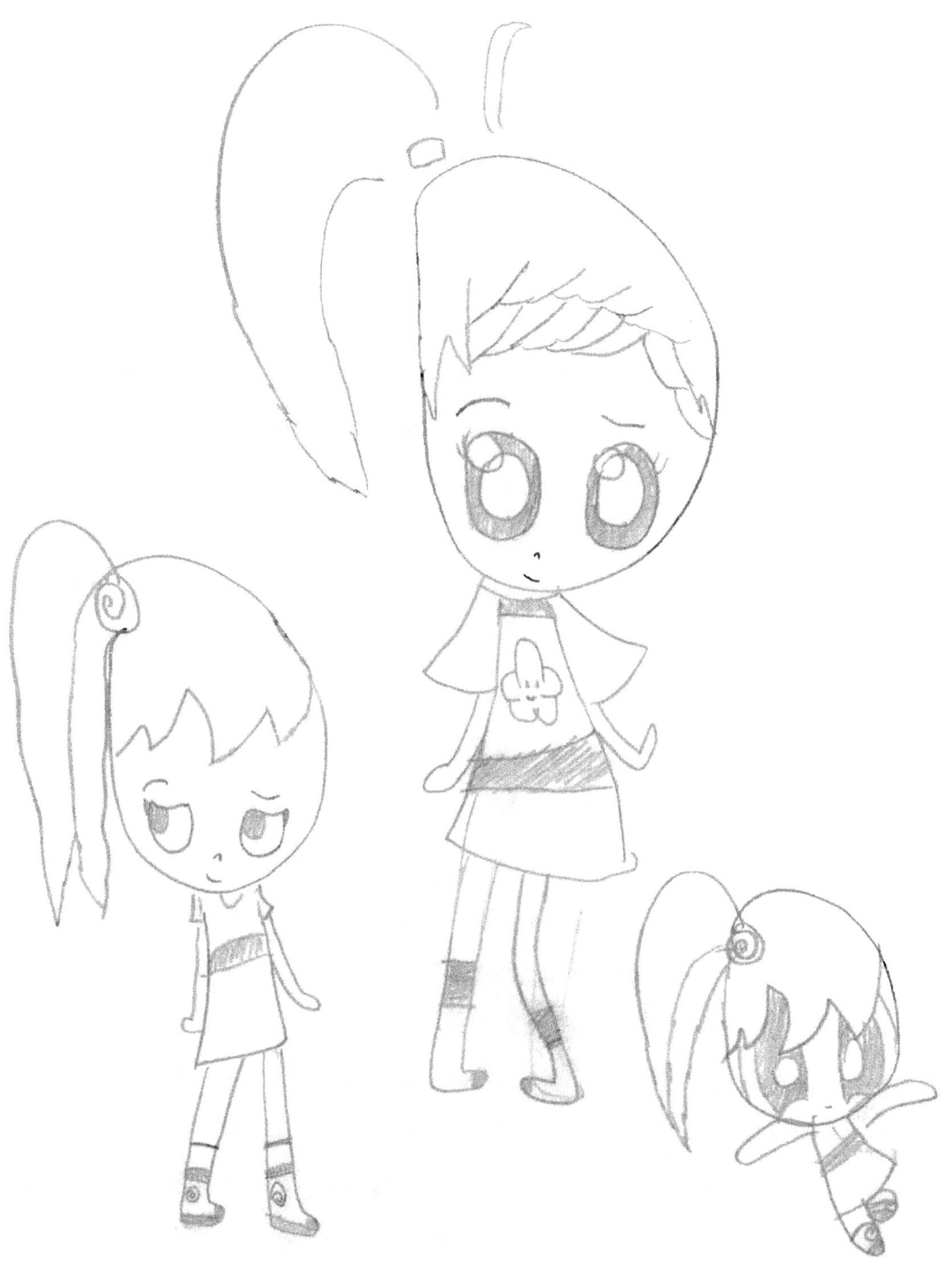

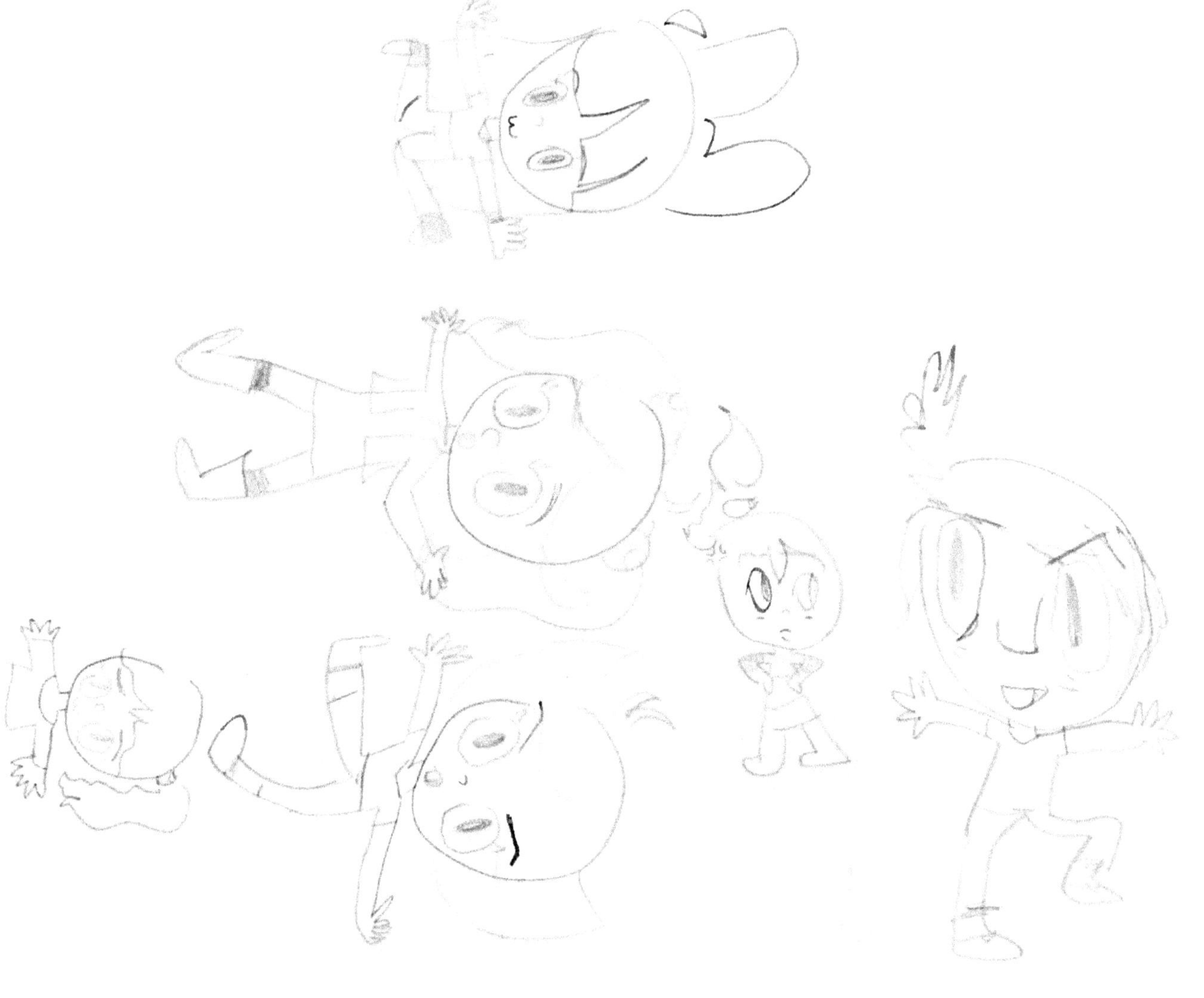

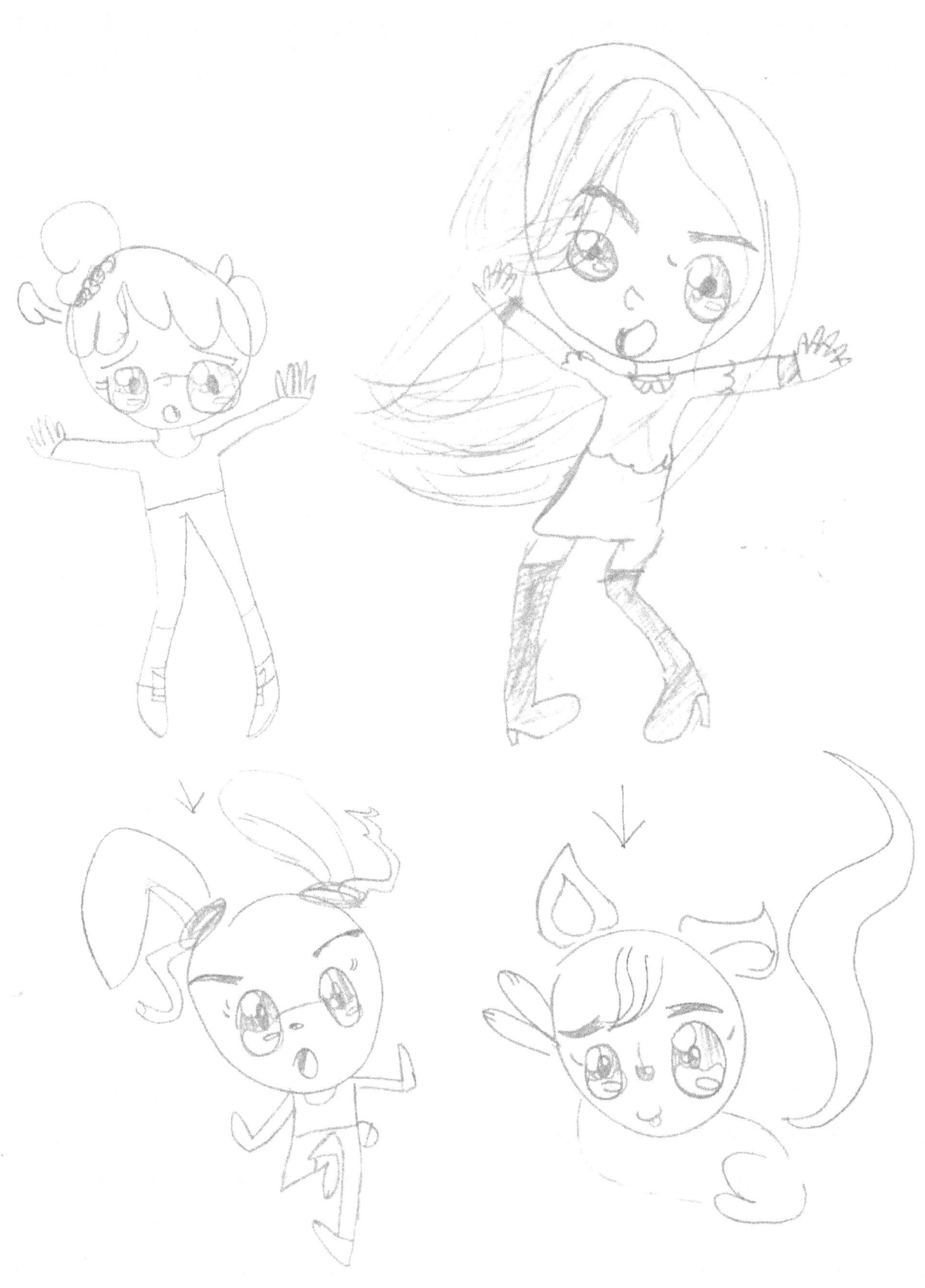

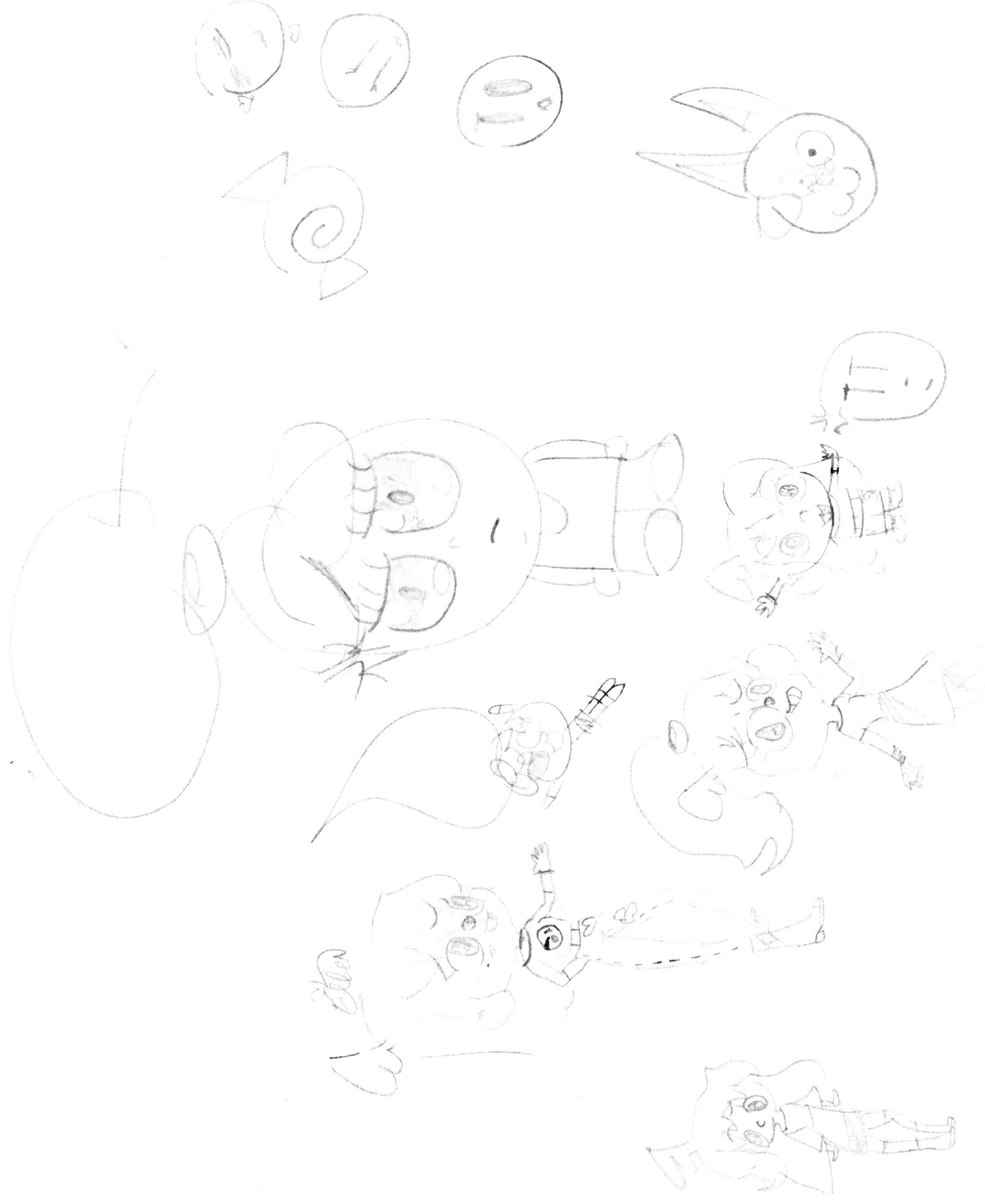

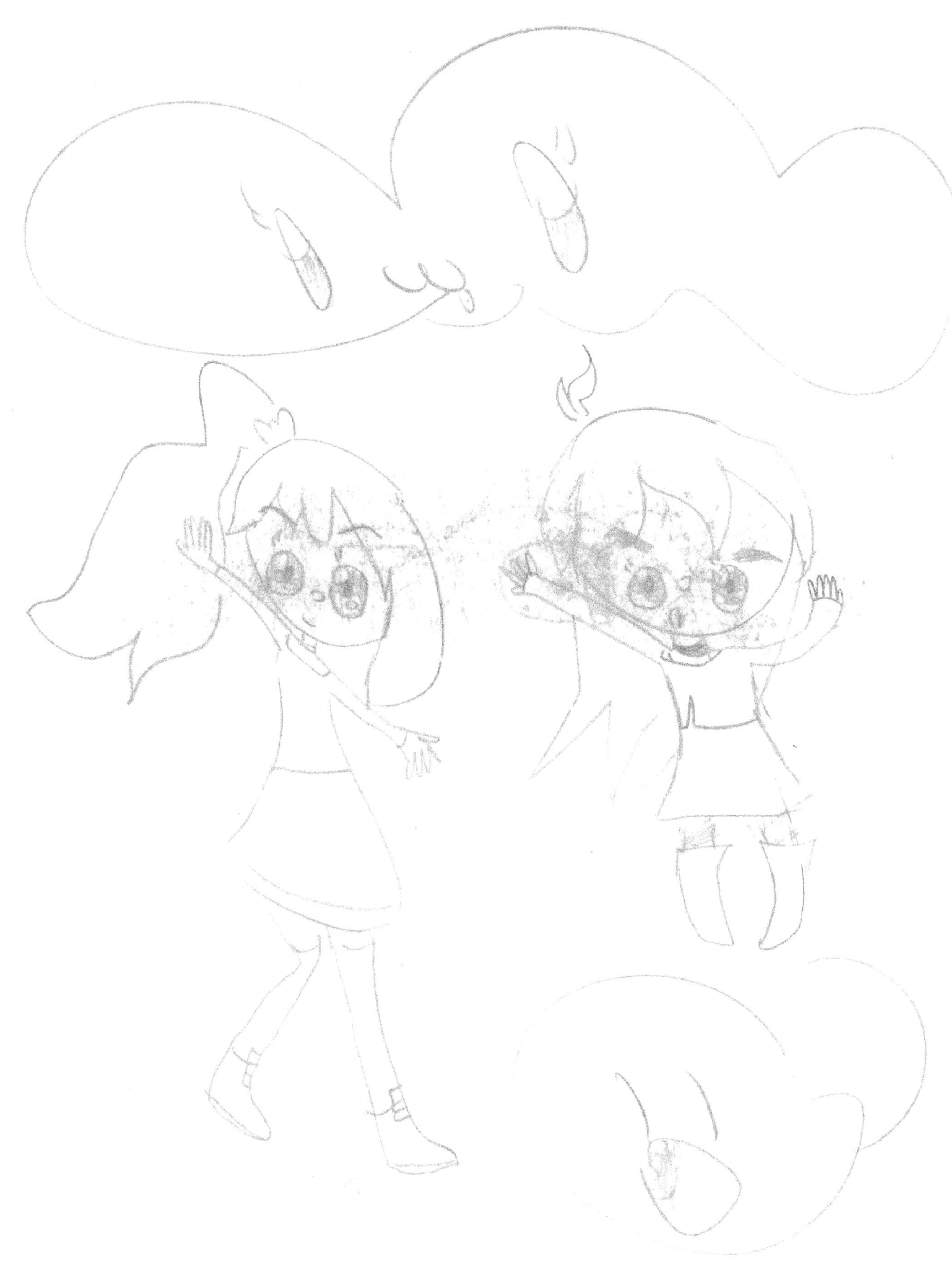

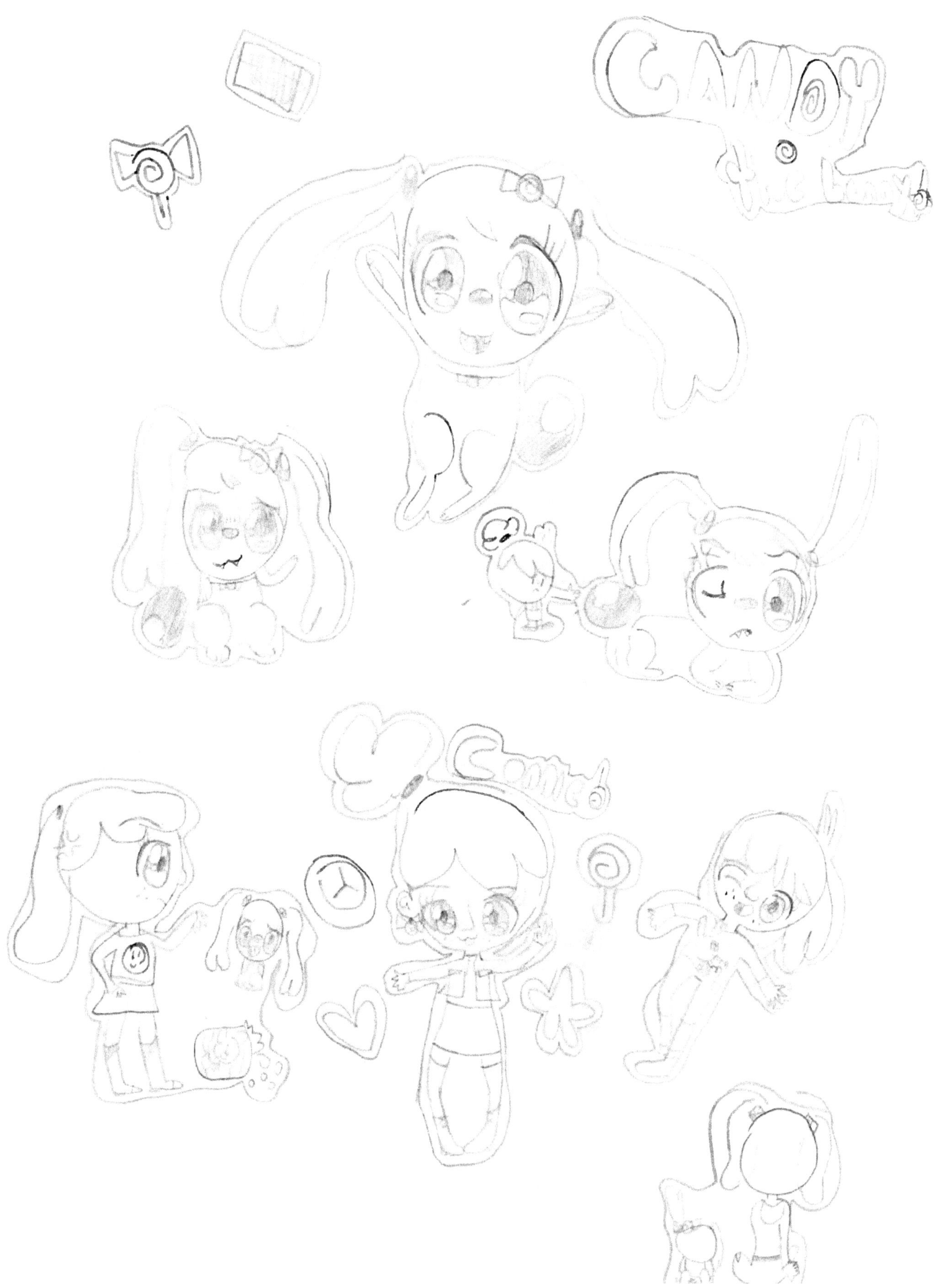
CANDY

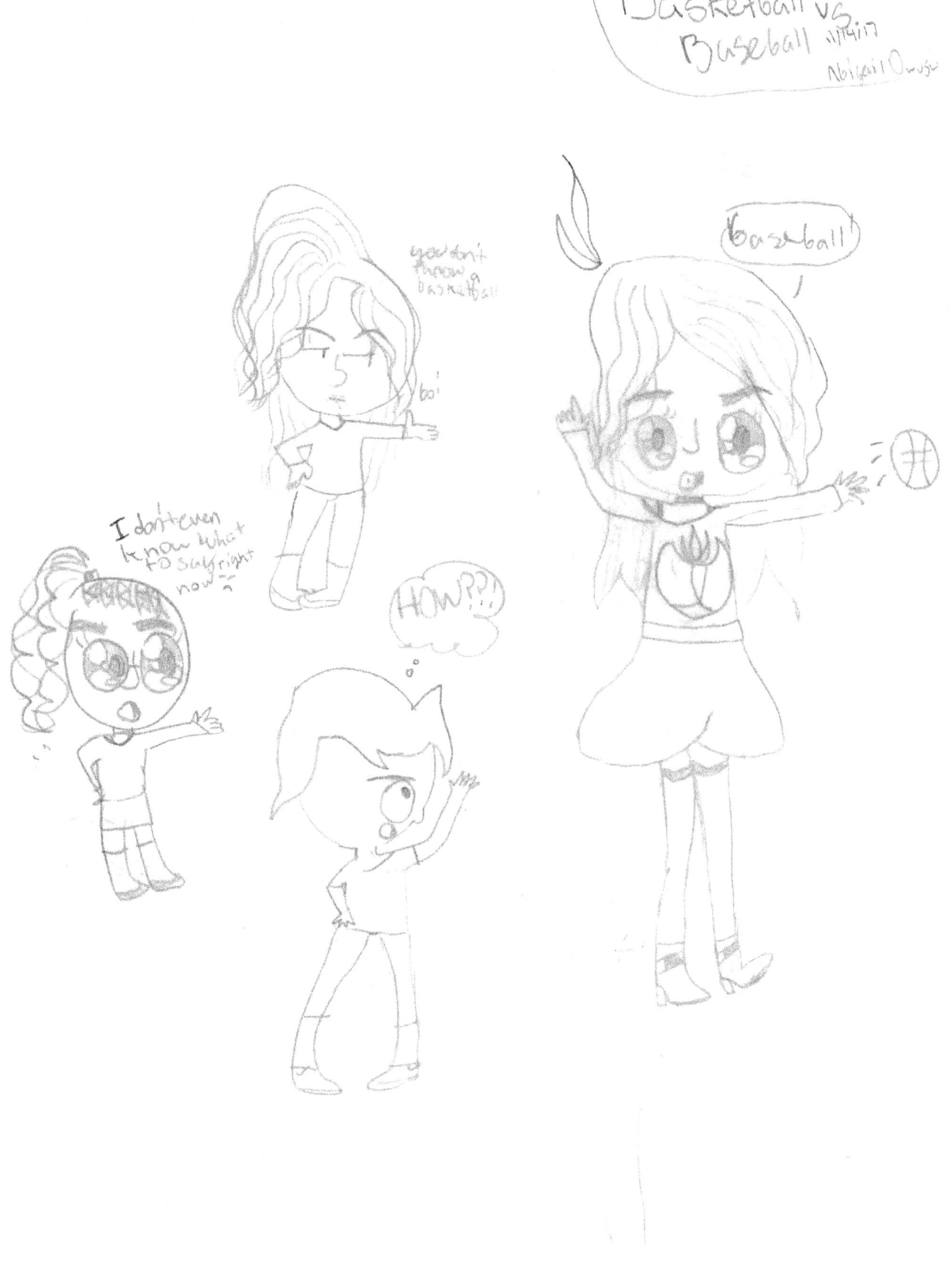
Basketball vs Baseball
Baseball!
you don't throw a basketball
HOW??!!
I don't even know what to say right now

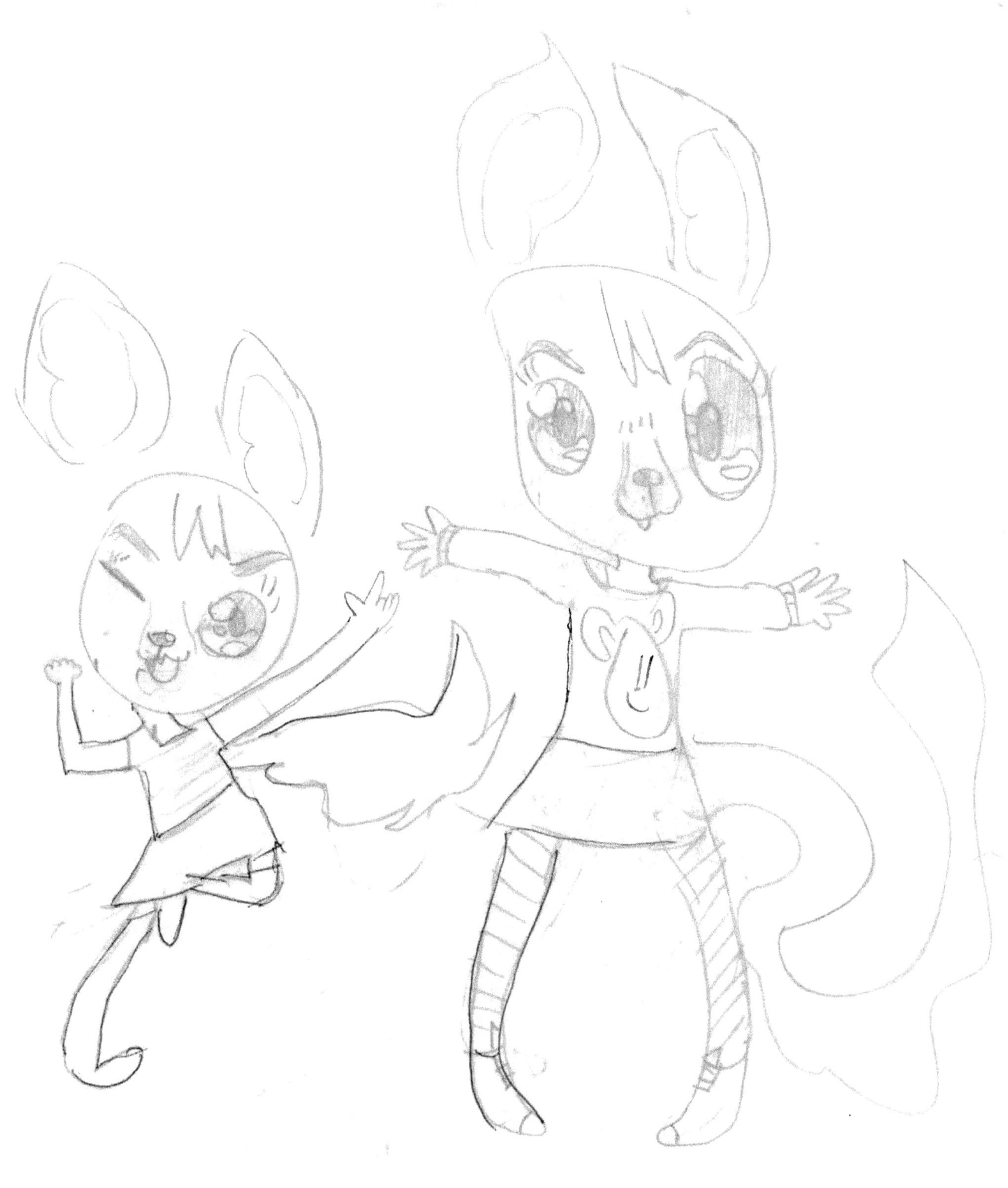

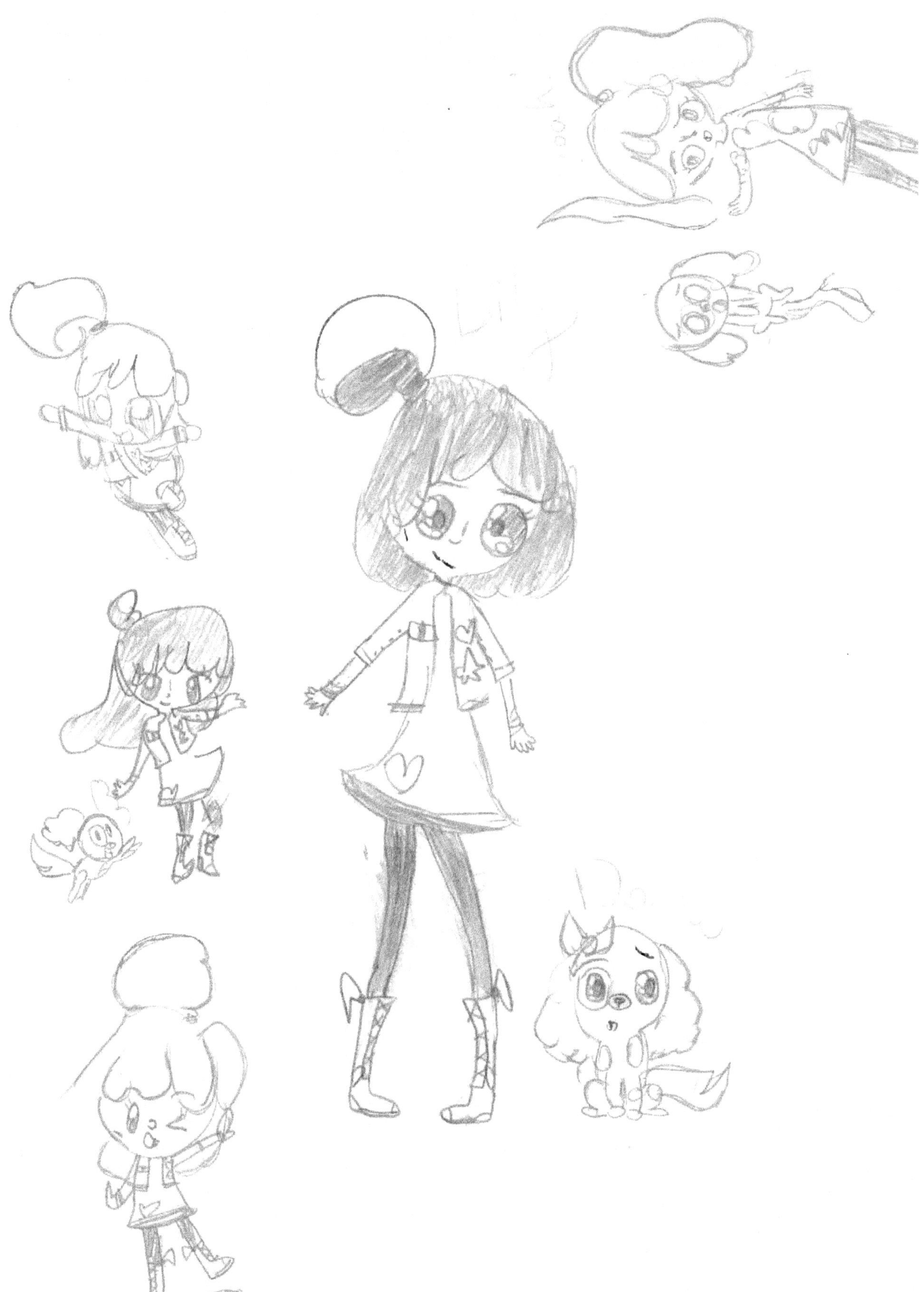

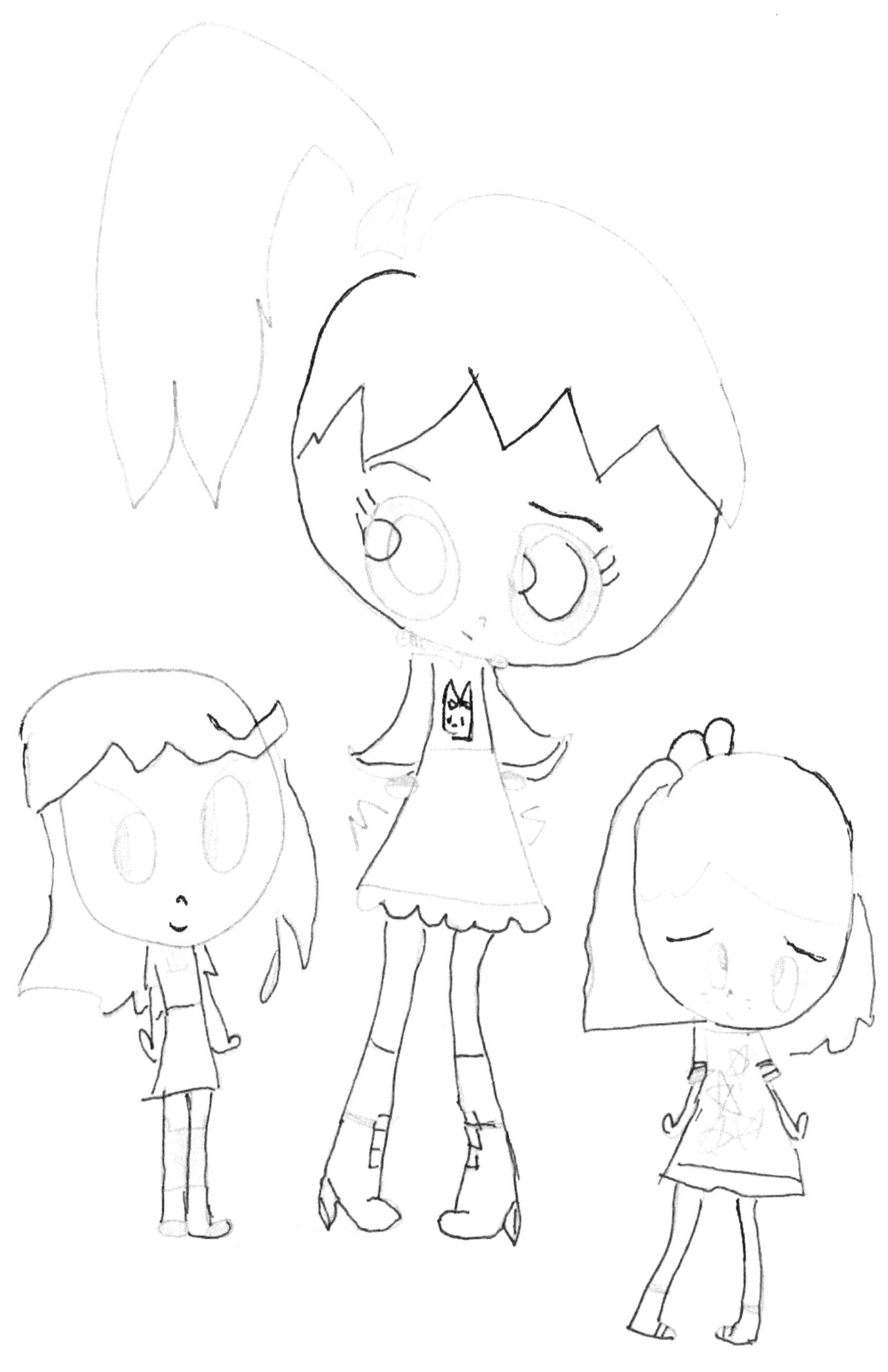

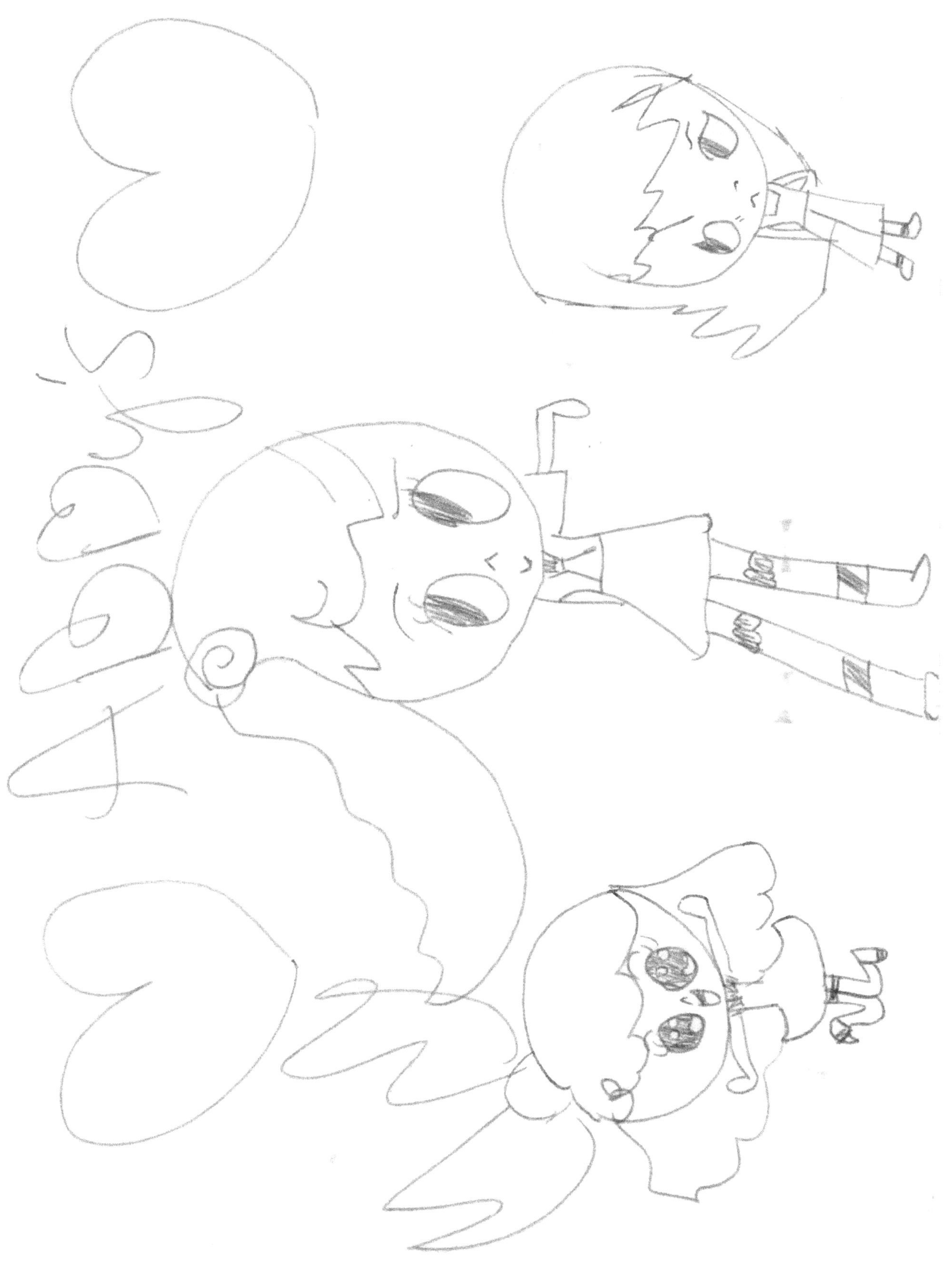
Abby's

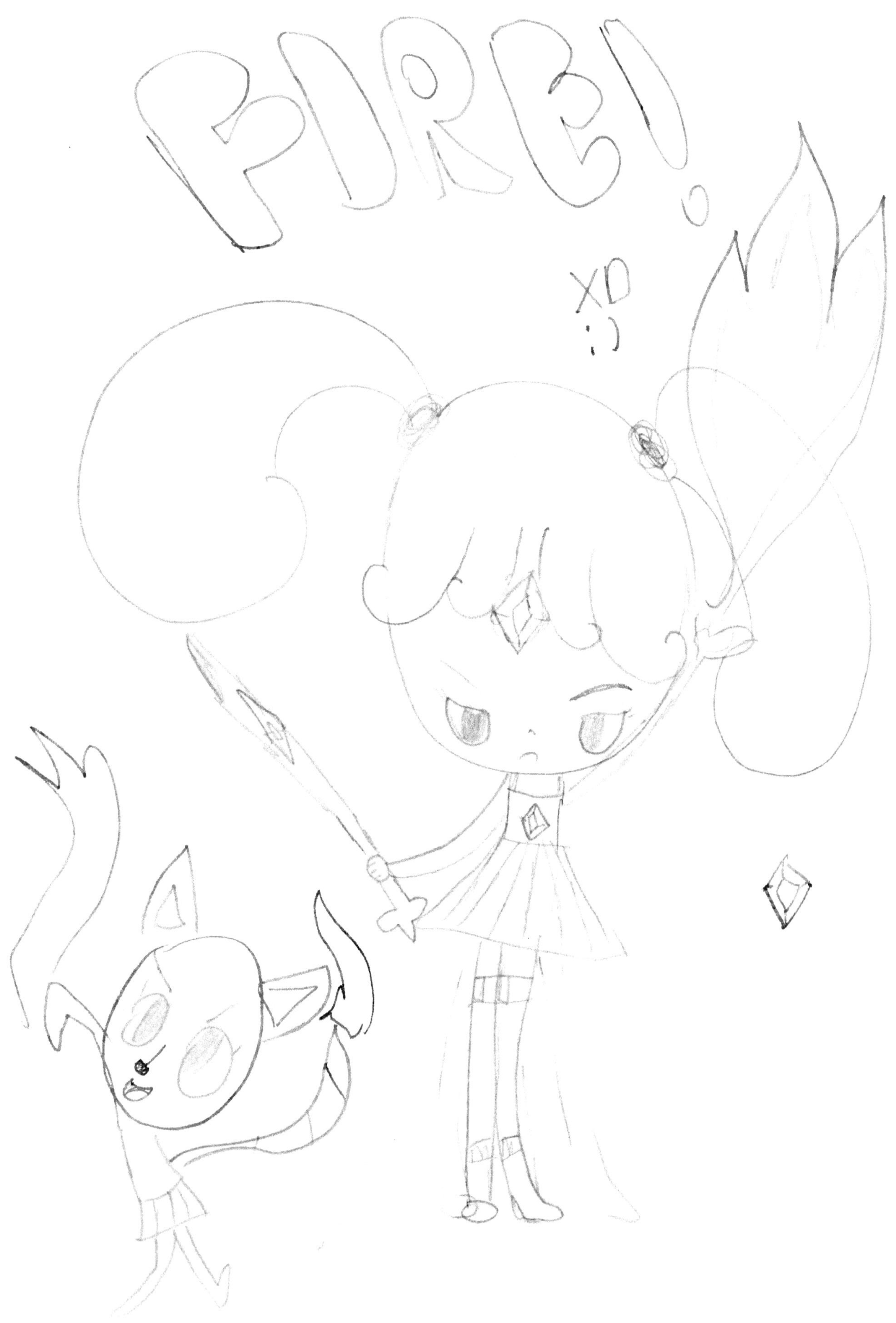
FIRE!
XD
;)

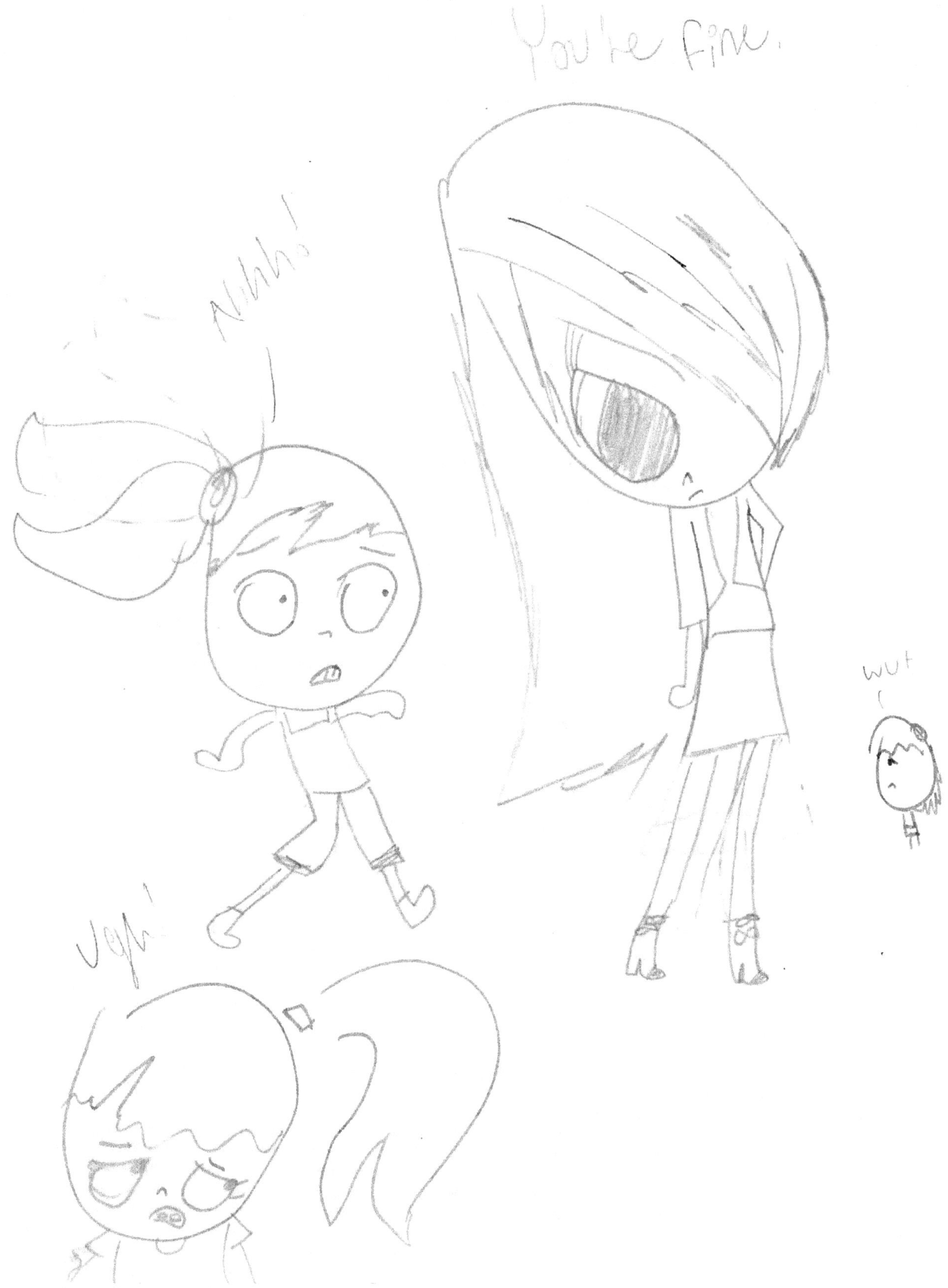
You're fine.
wut

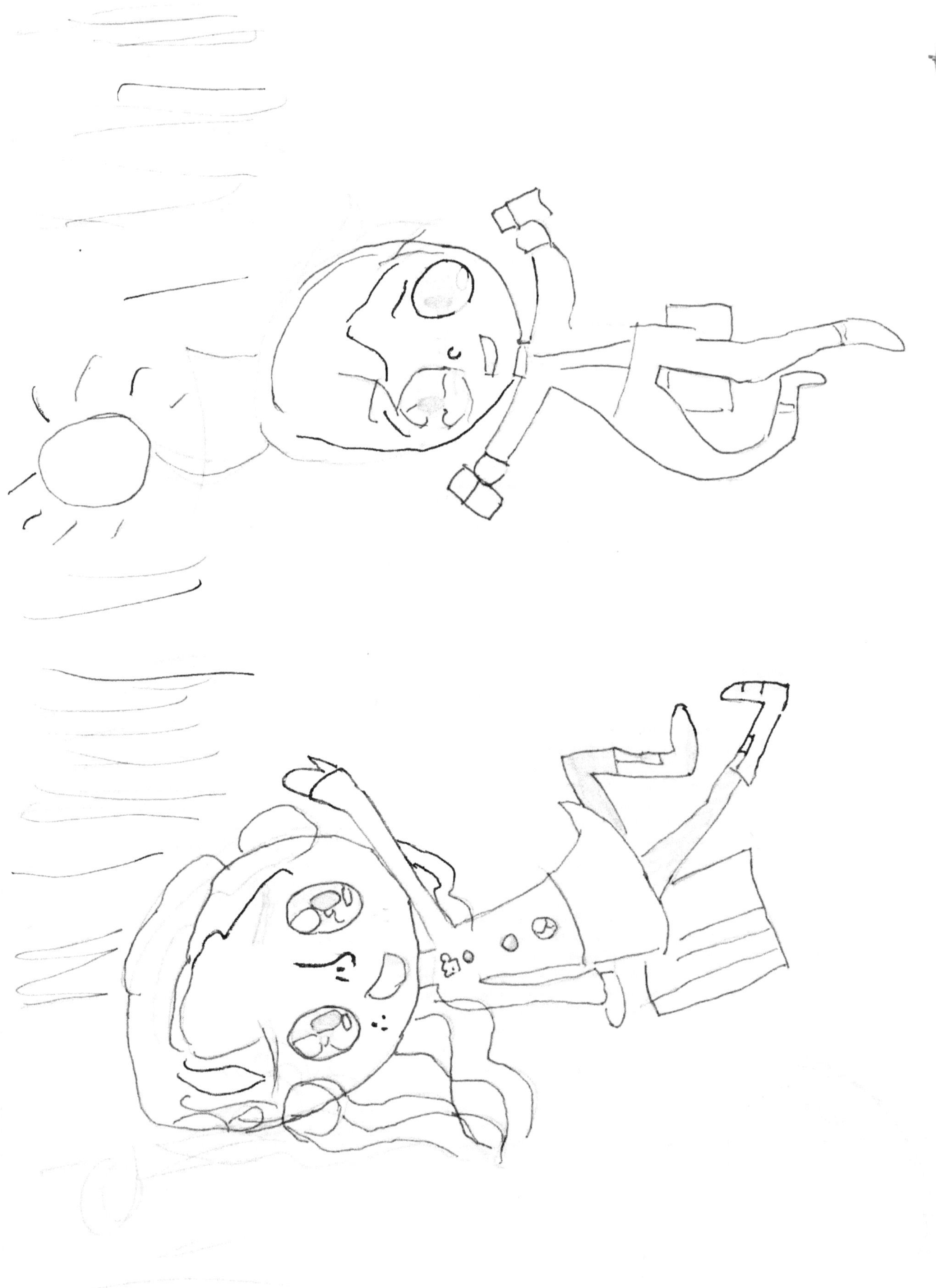

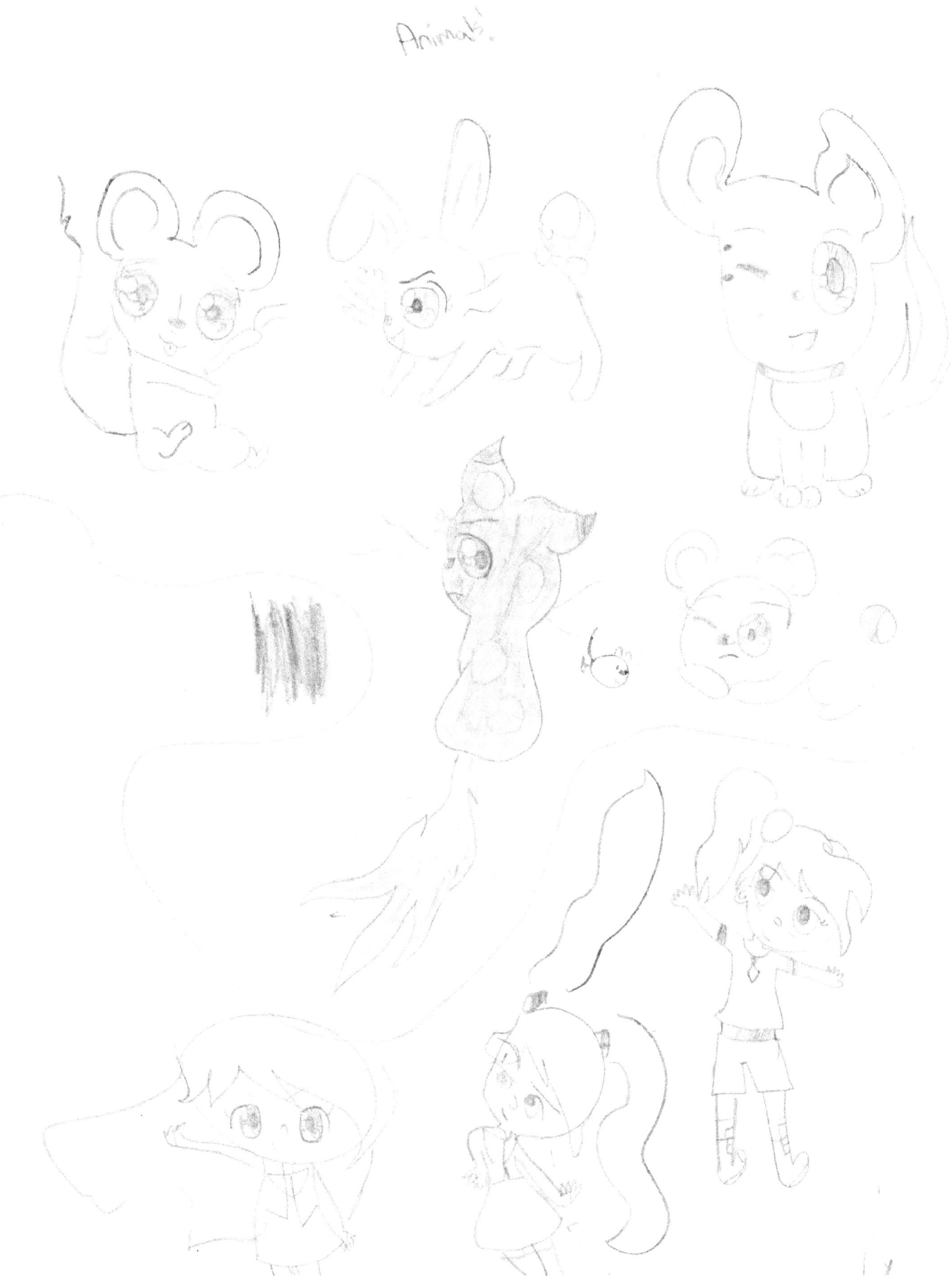
Animals!

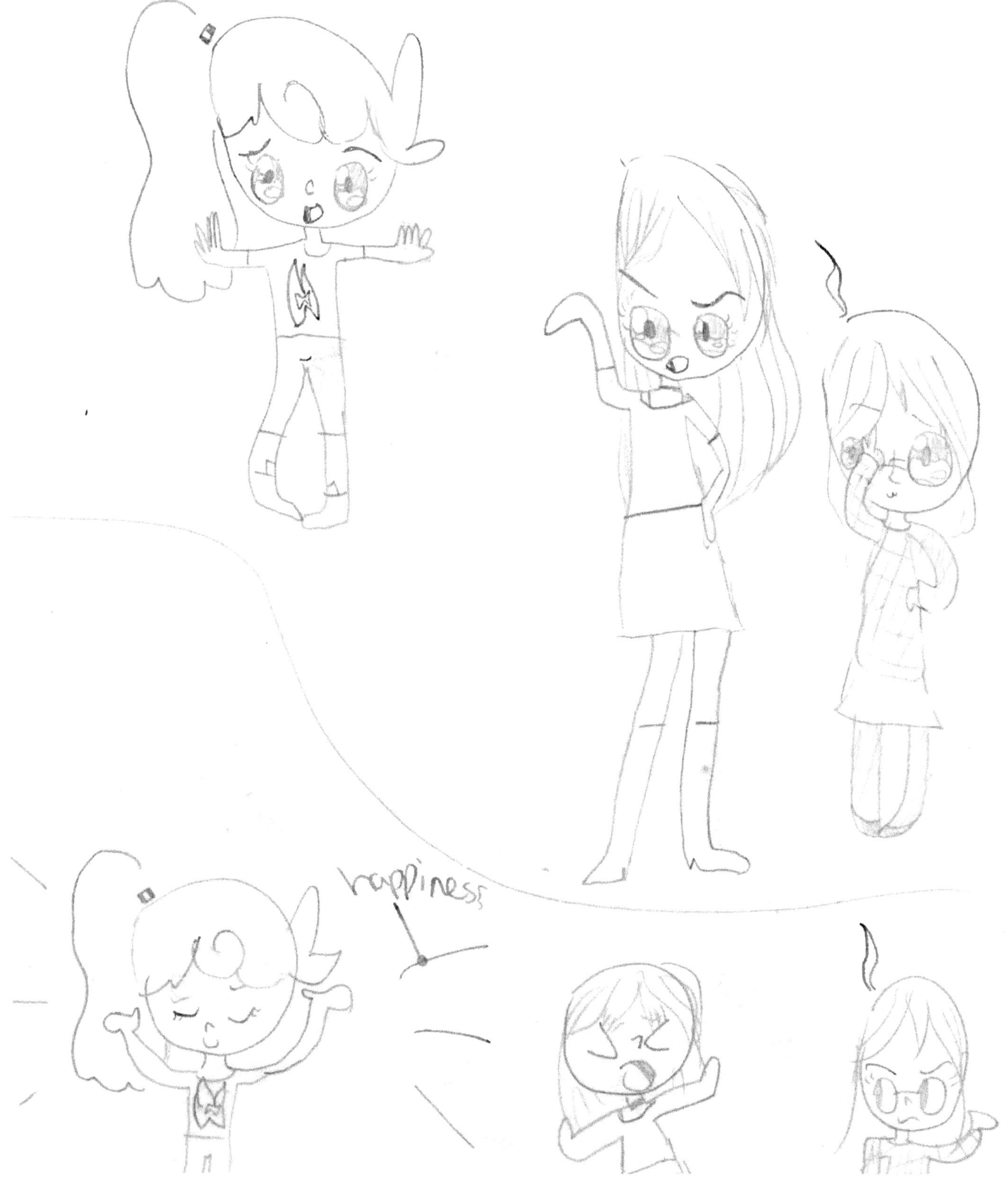
happiness

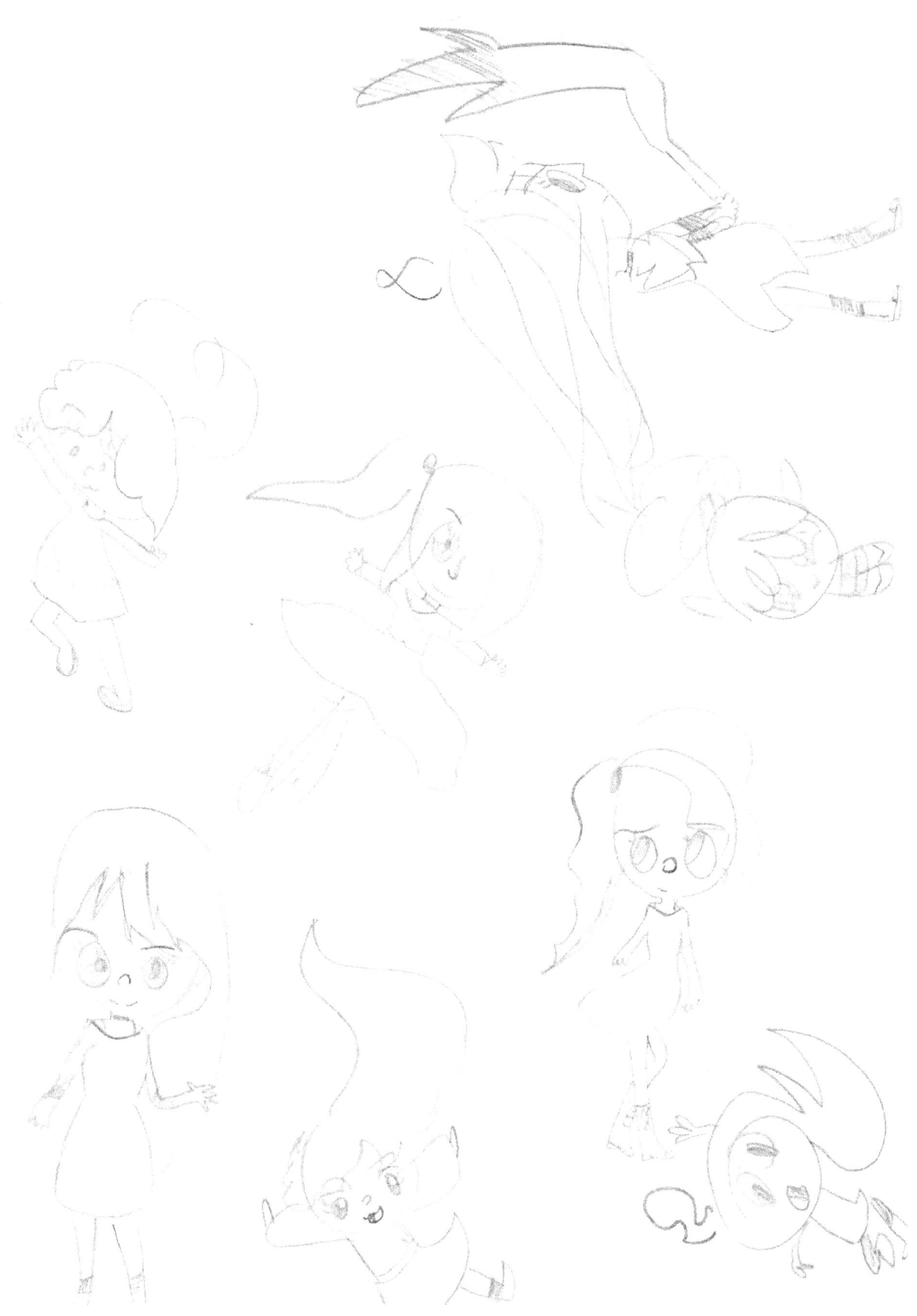

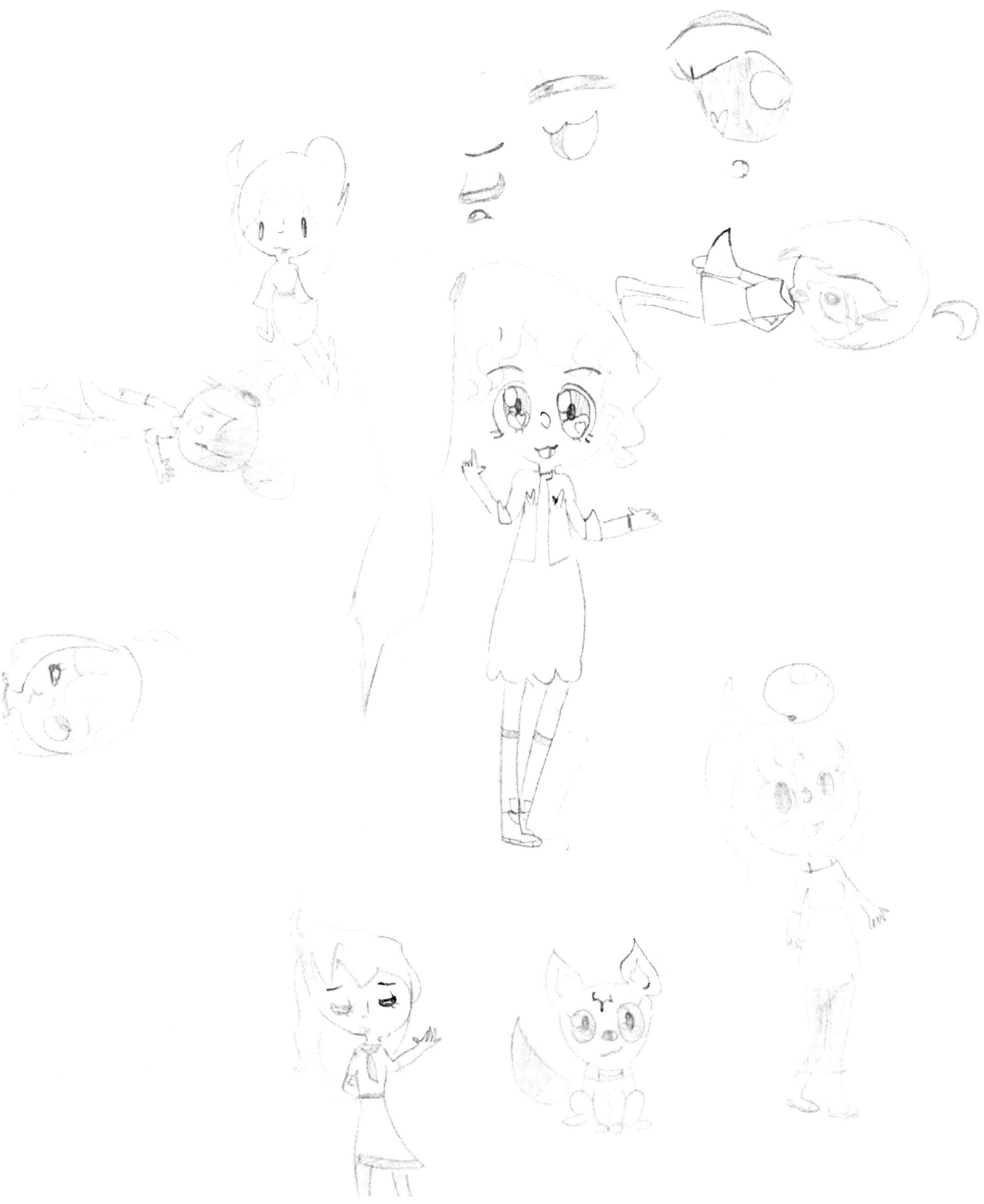

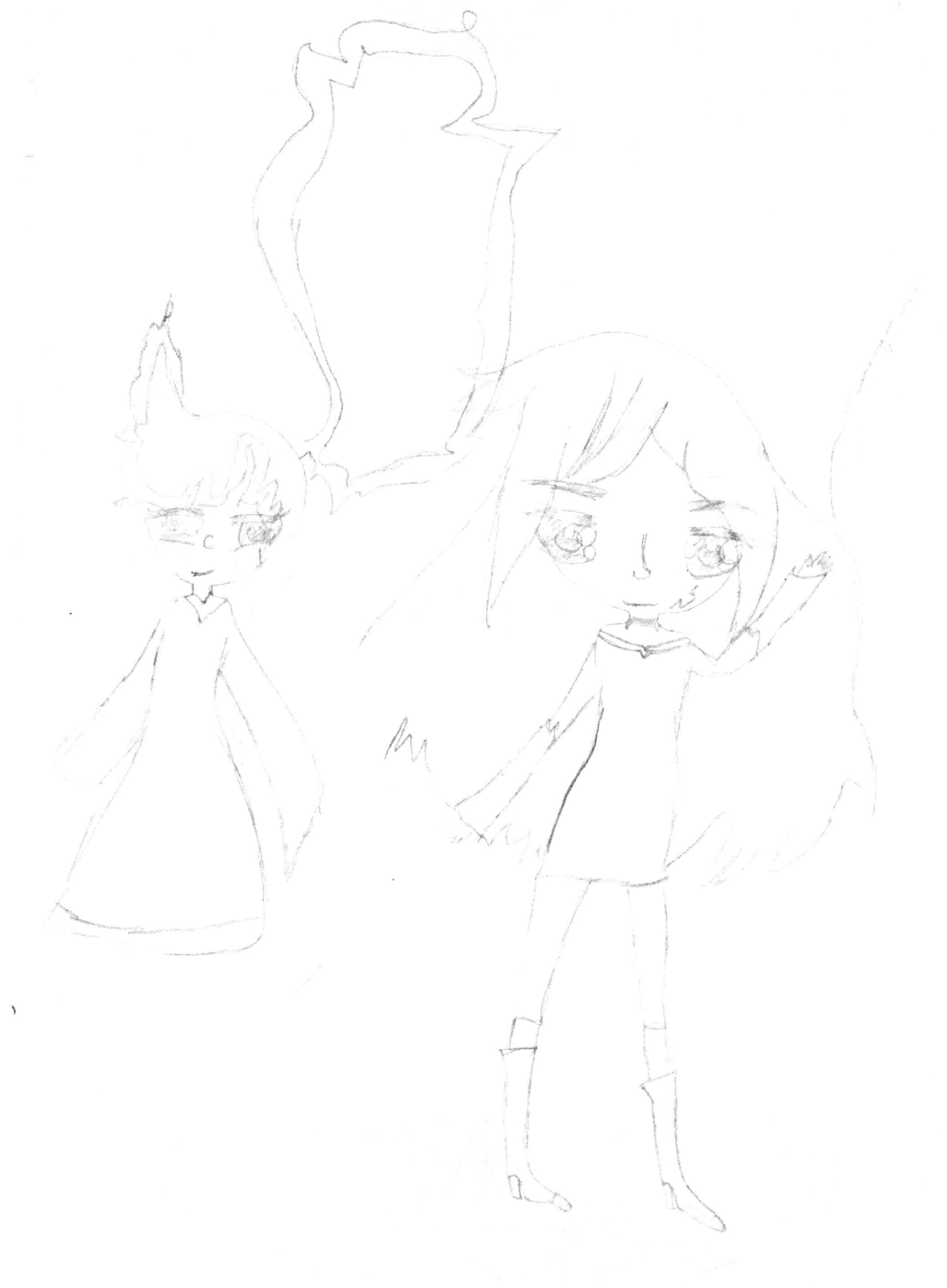

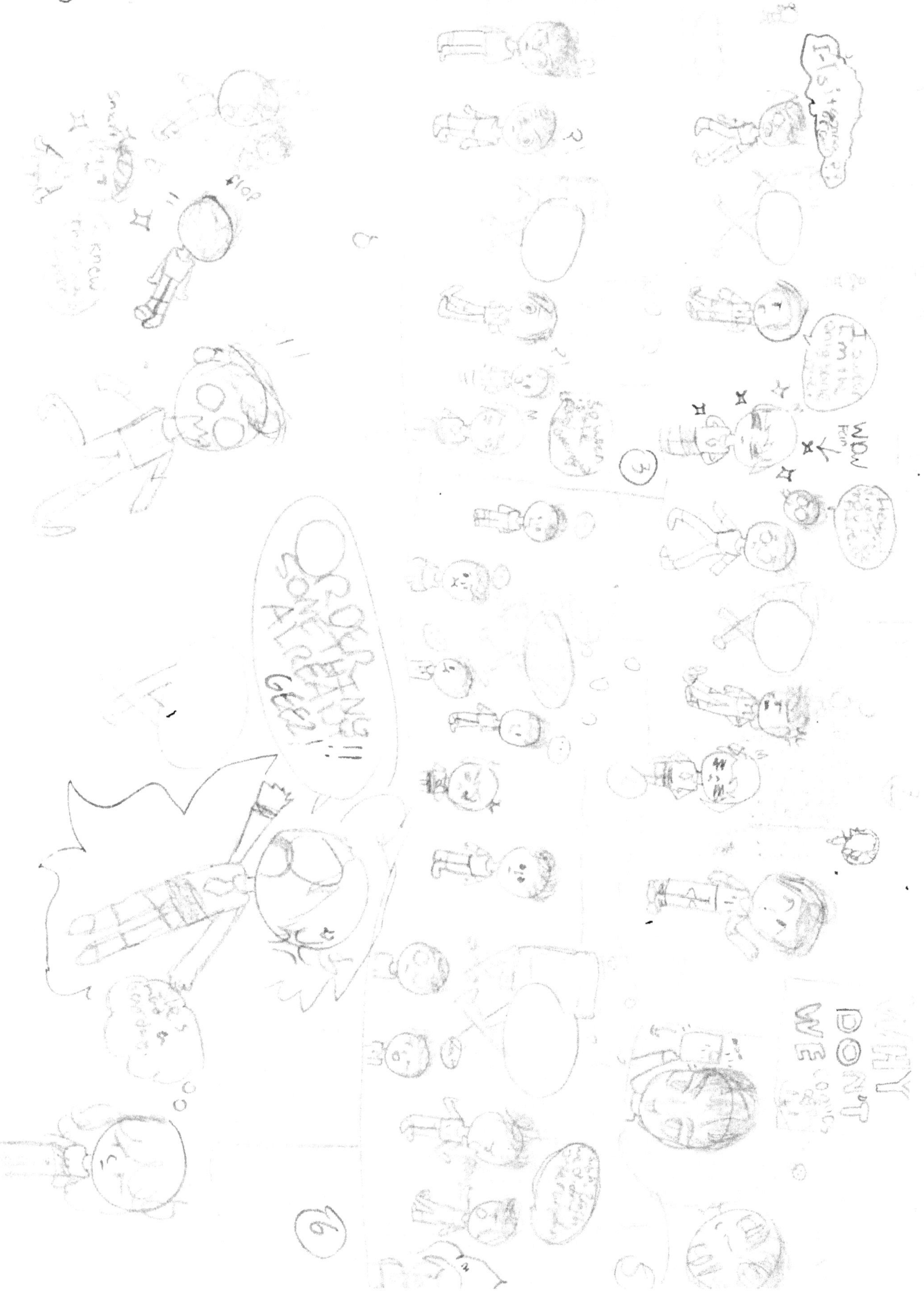
WHY DON'T WE
SOMETHING ALREADY GEEZ!!
WOW

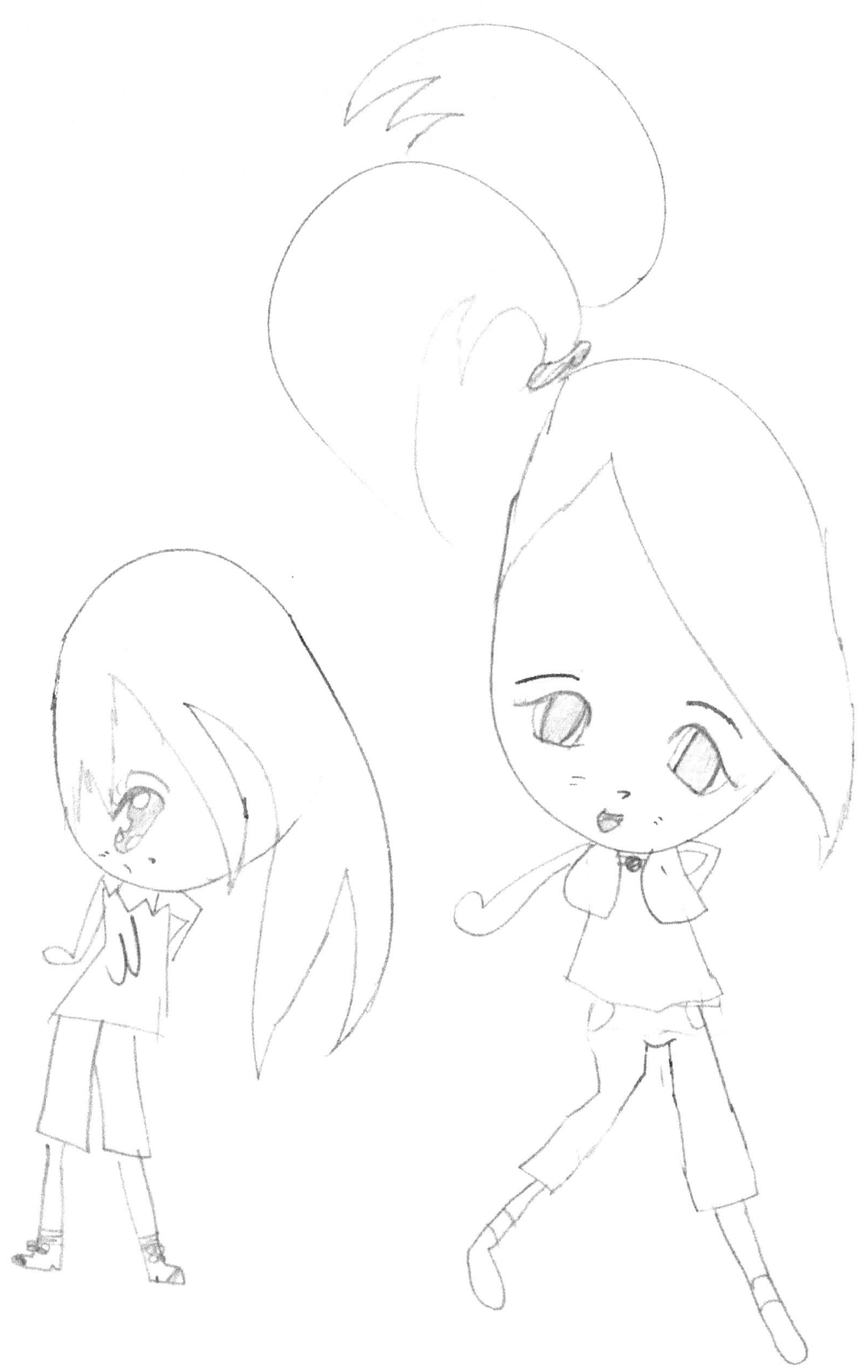

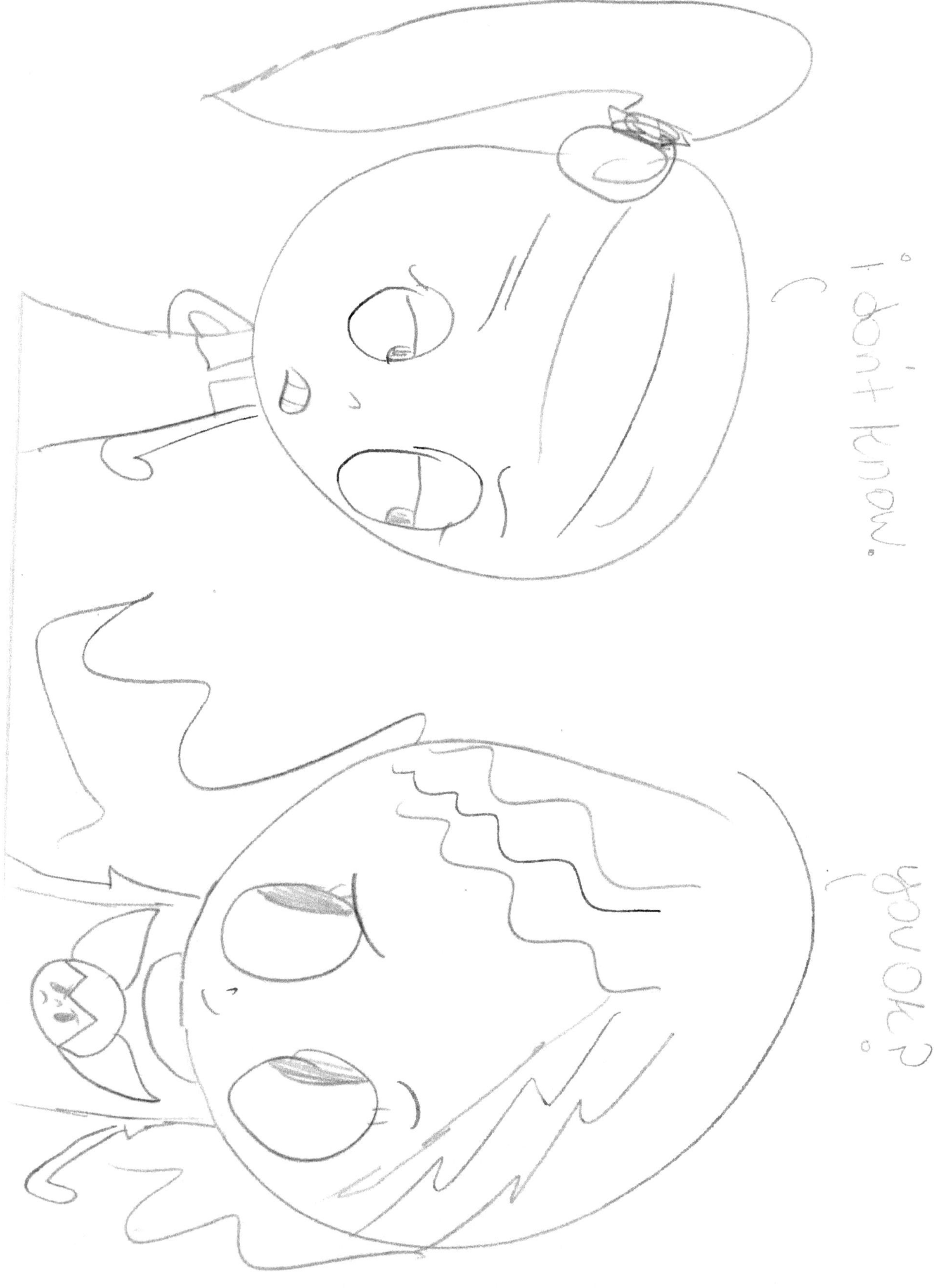
i don't know.
you ok?

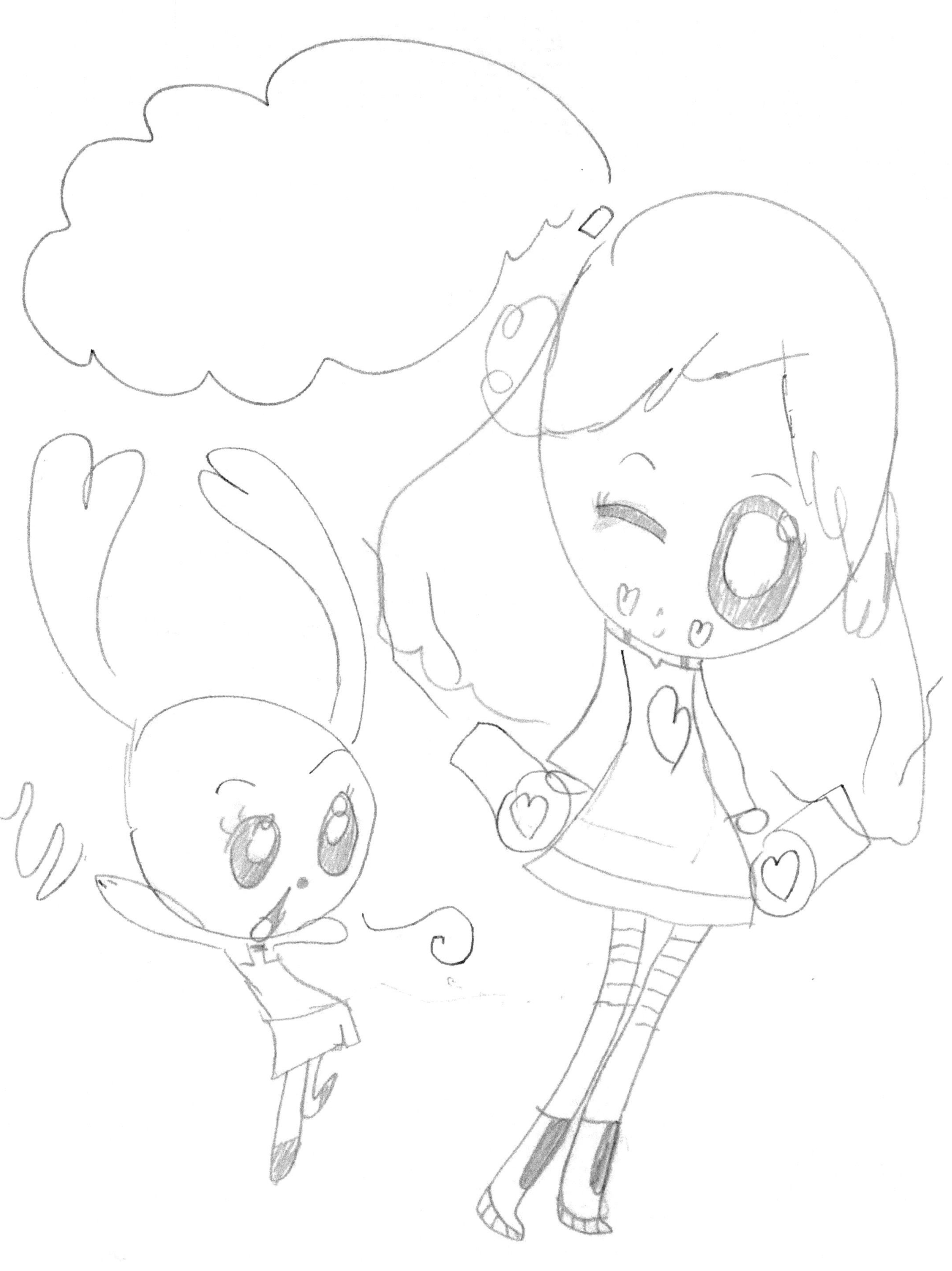

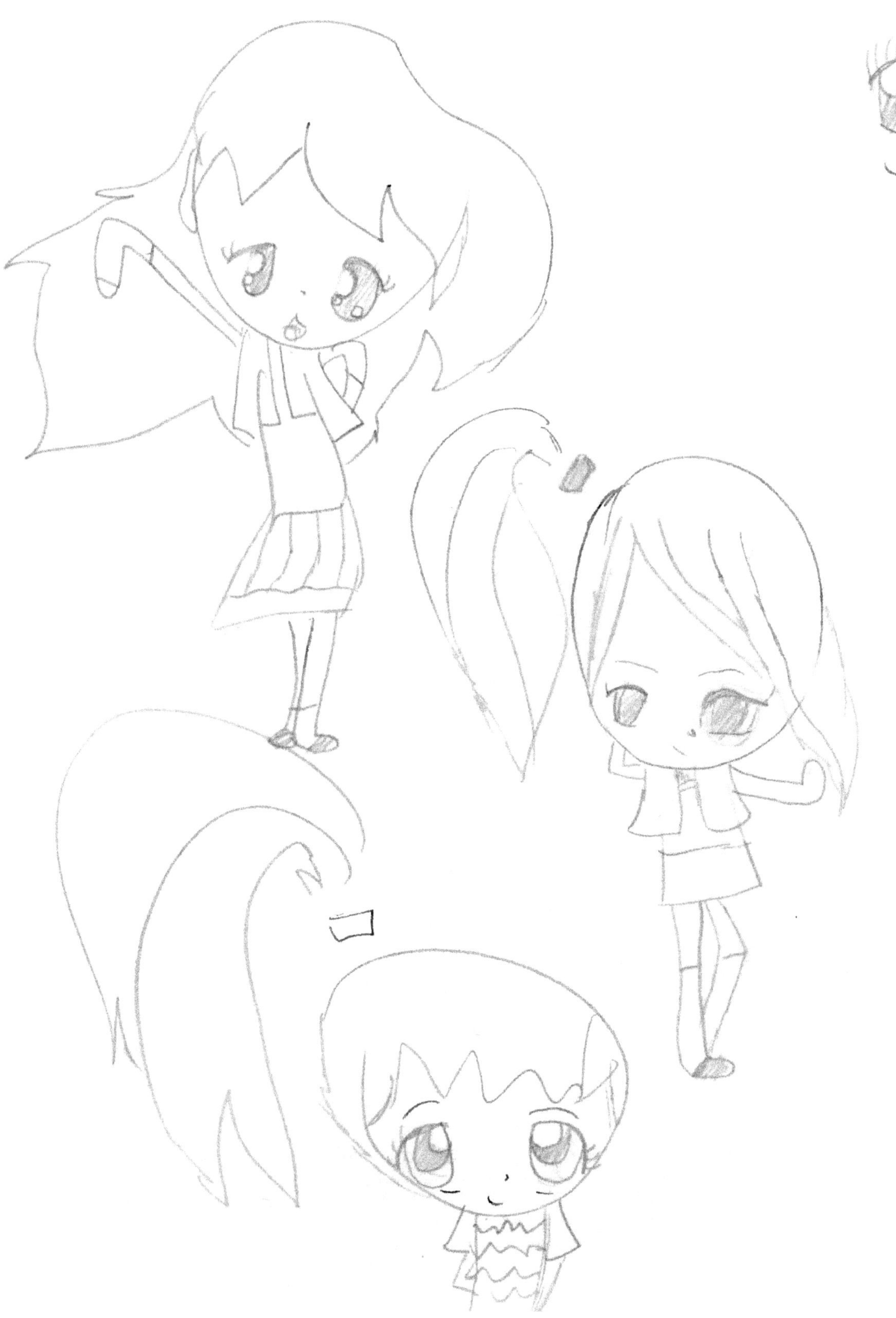

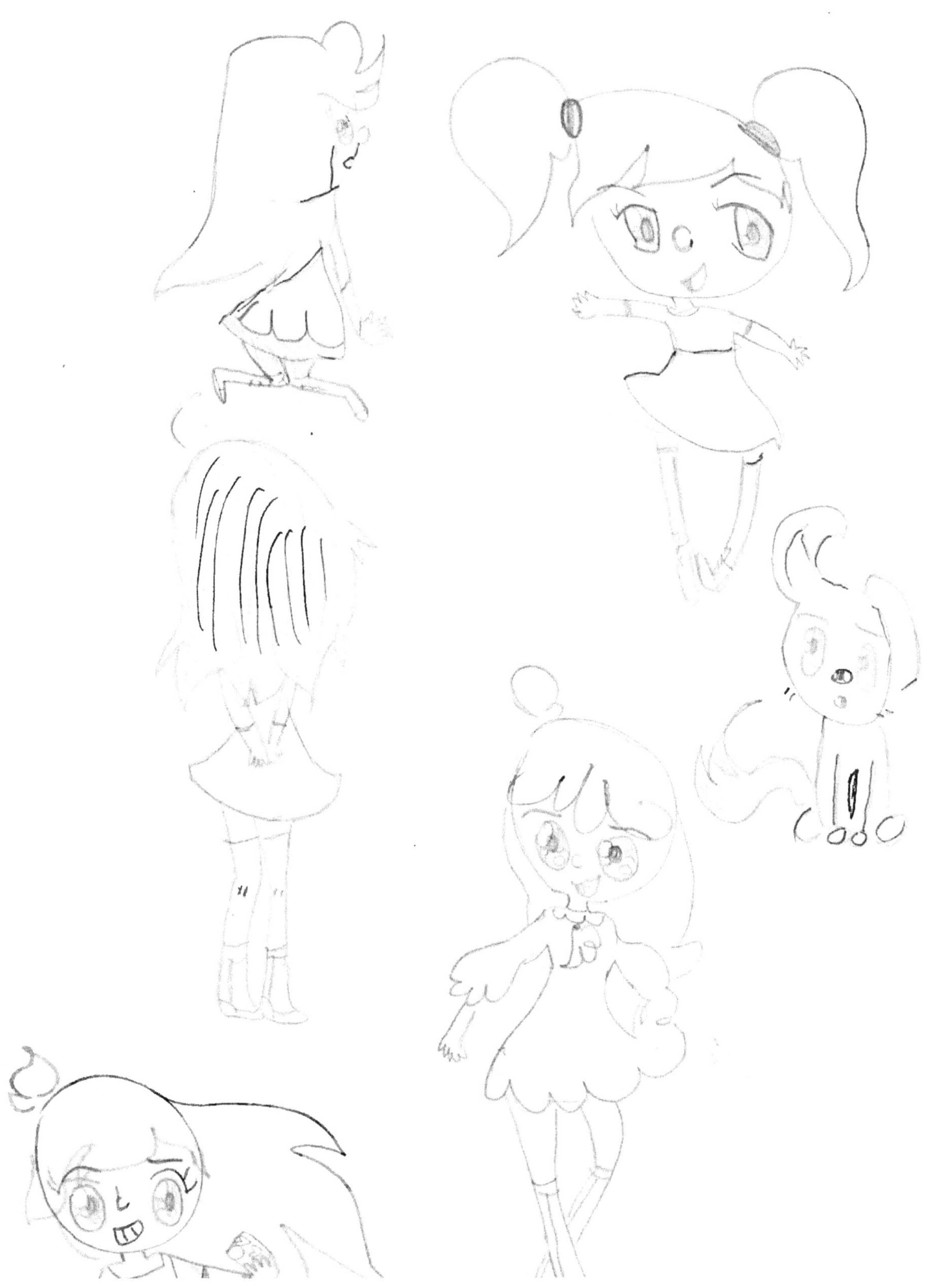

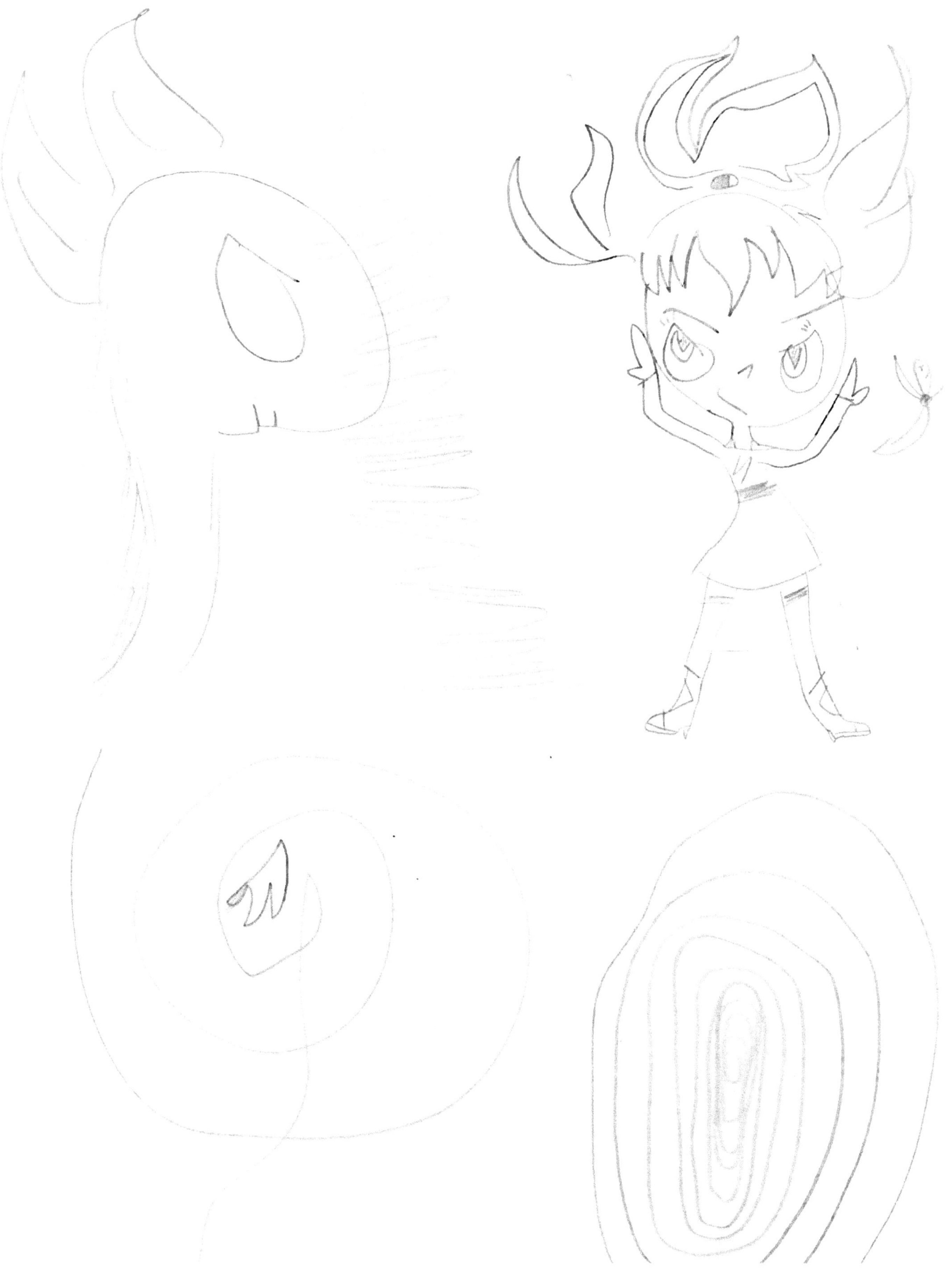

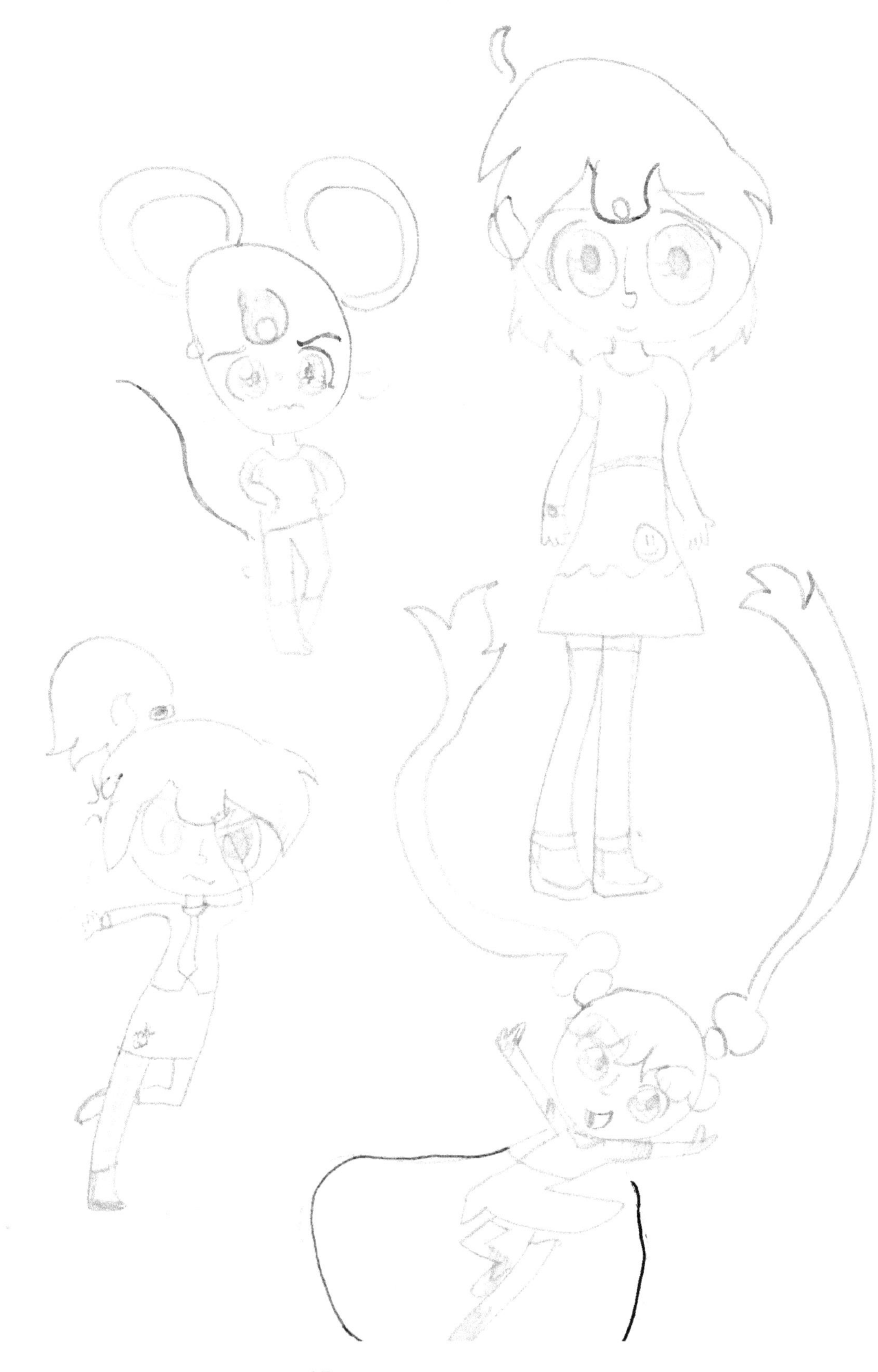

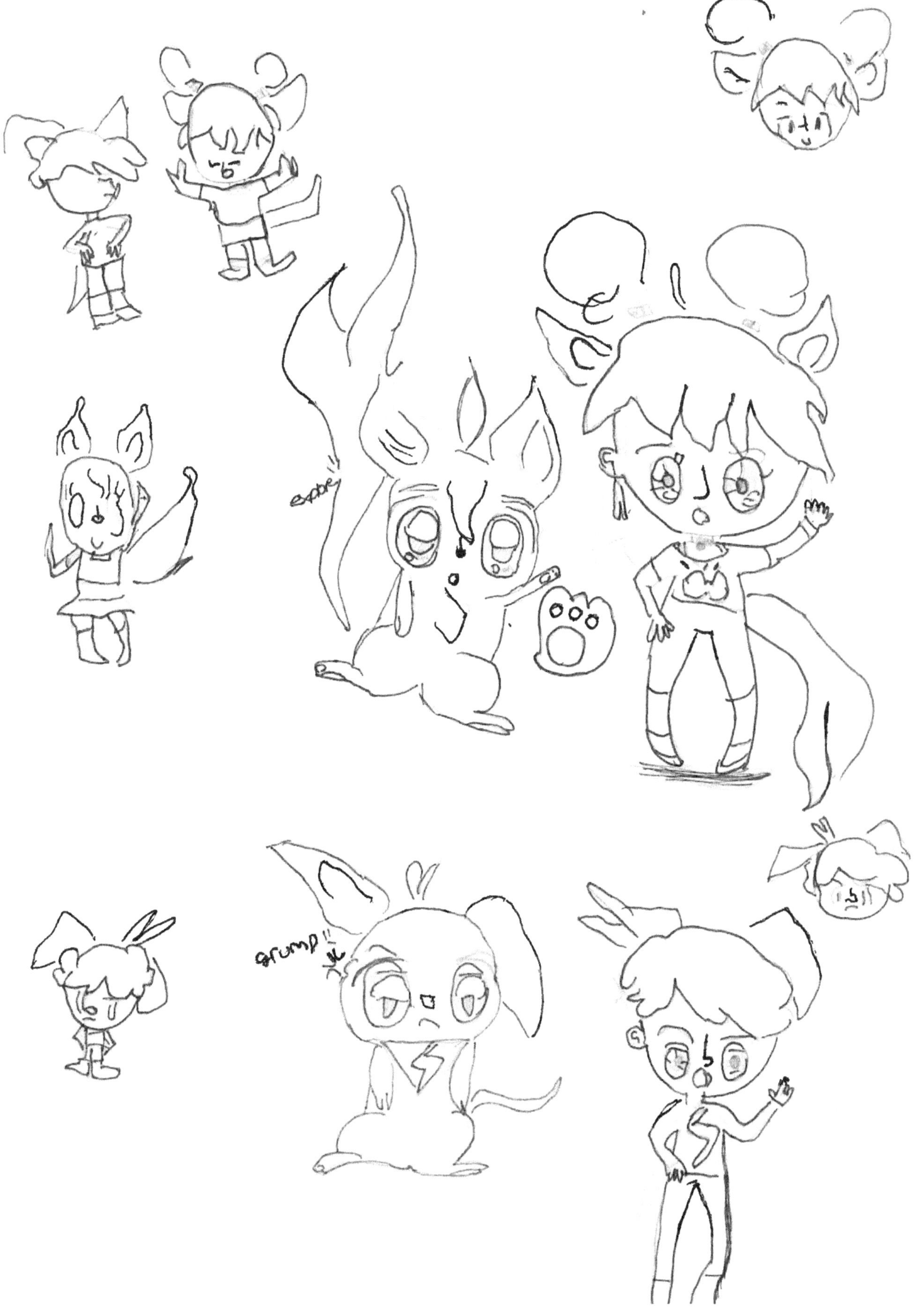
grump!!

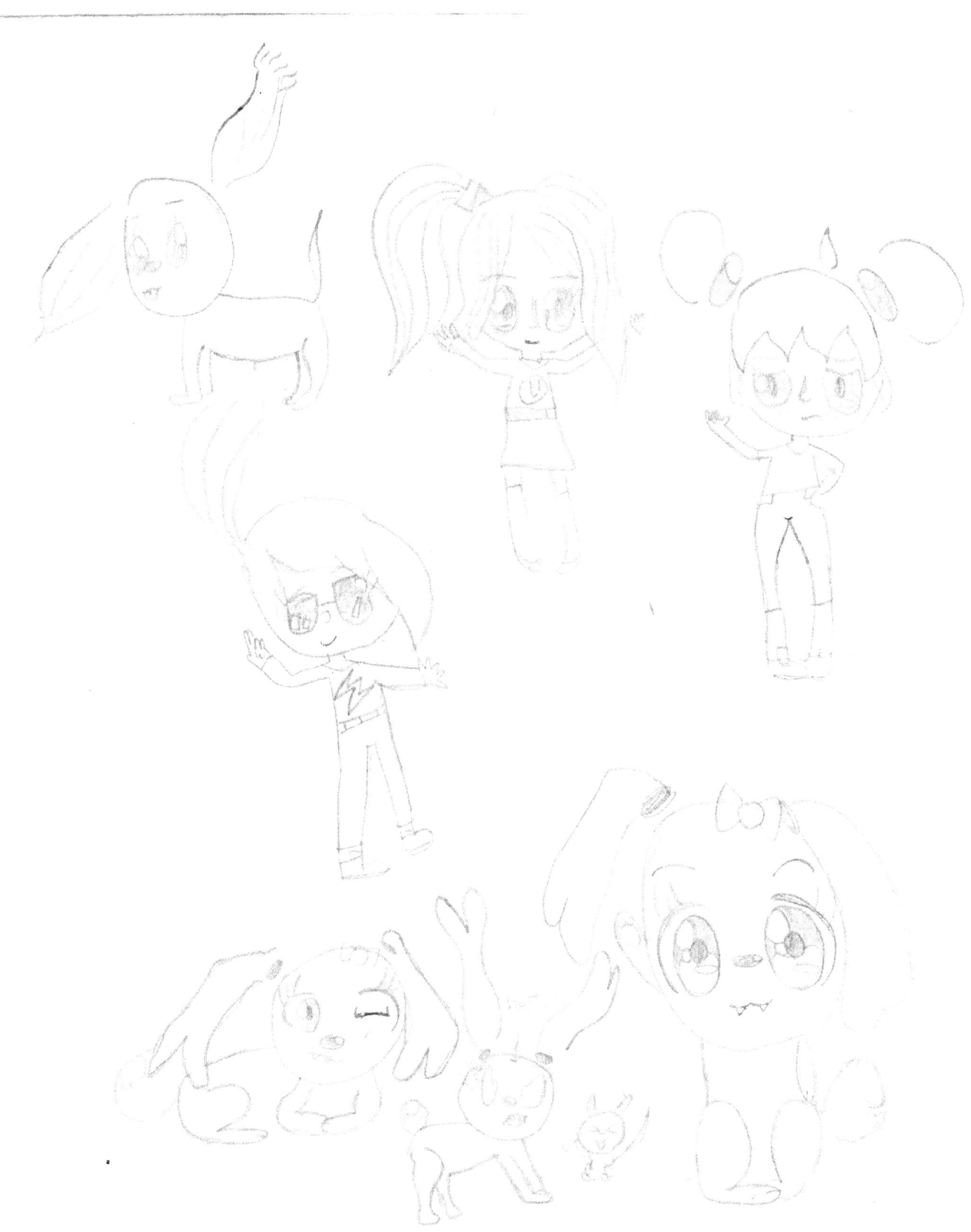

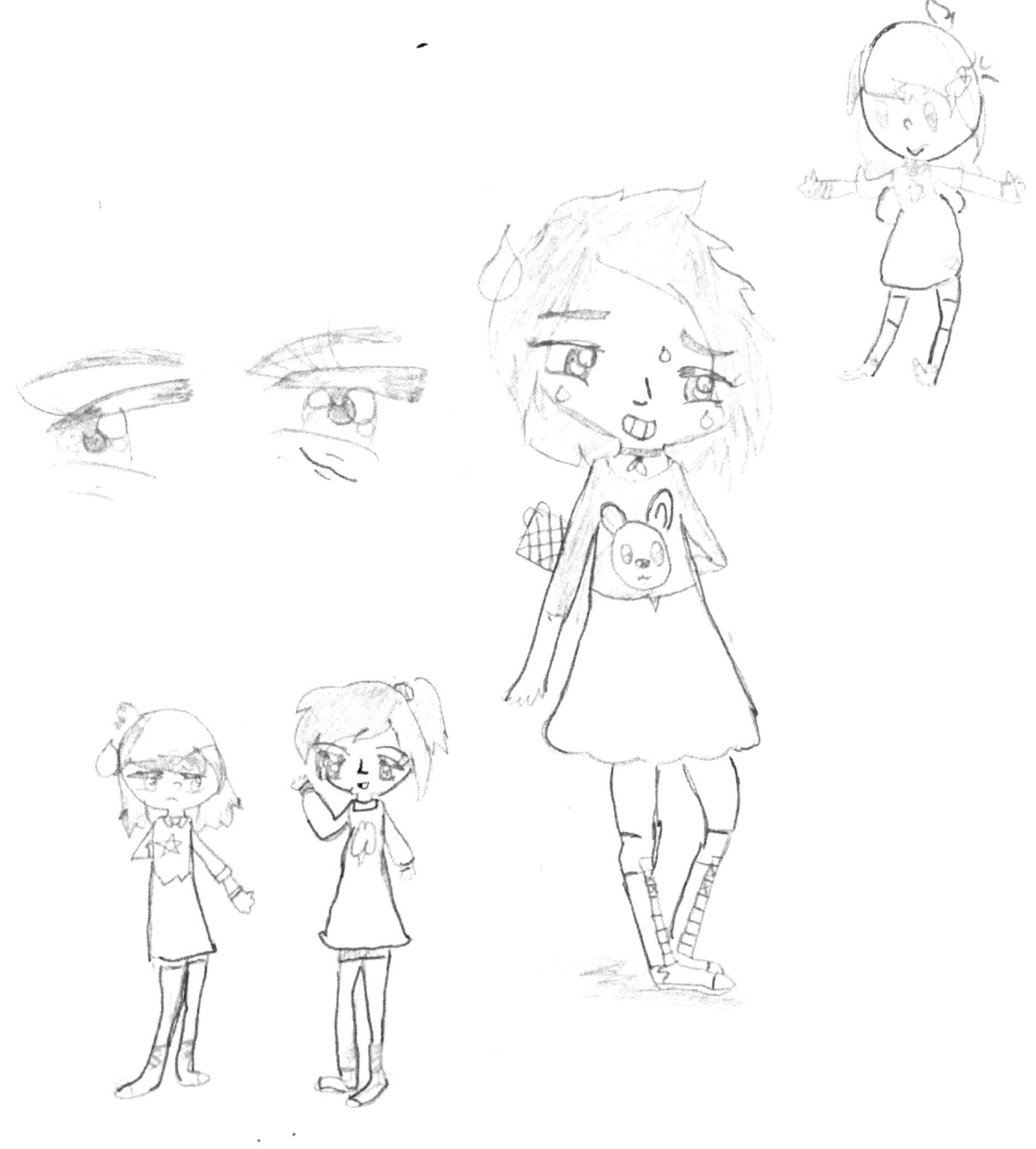

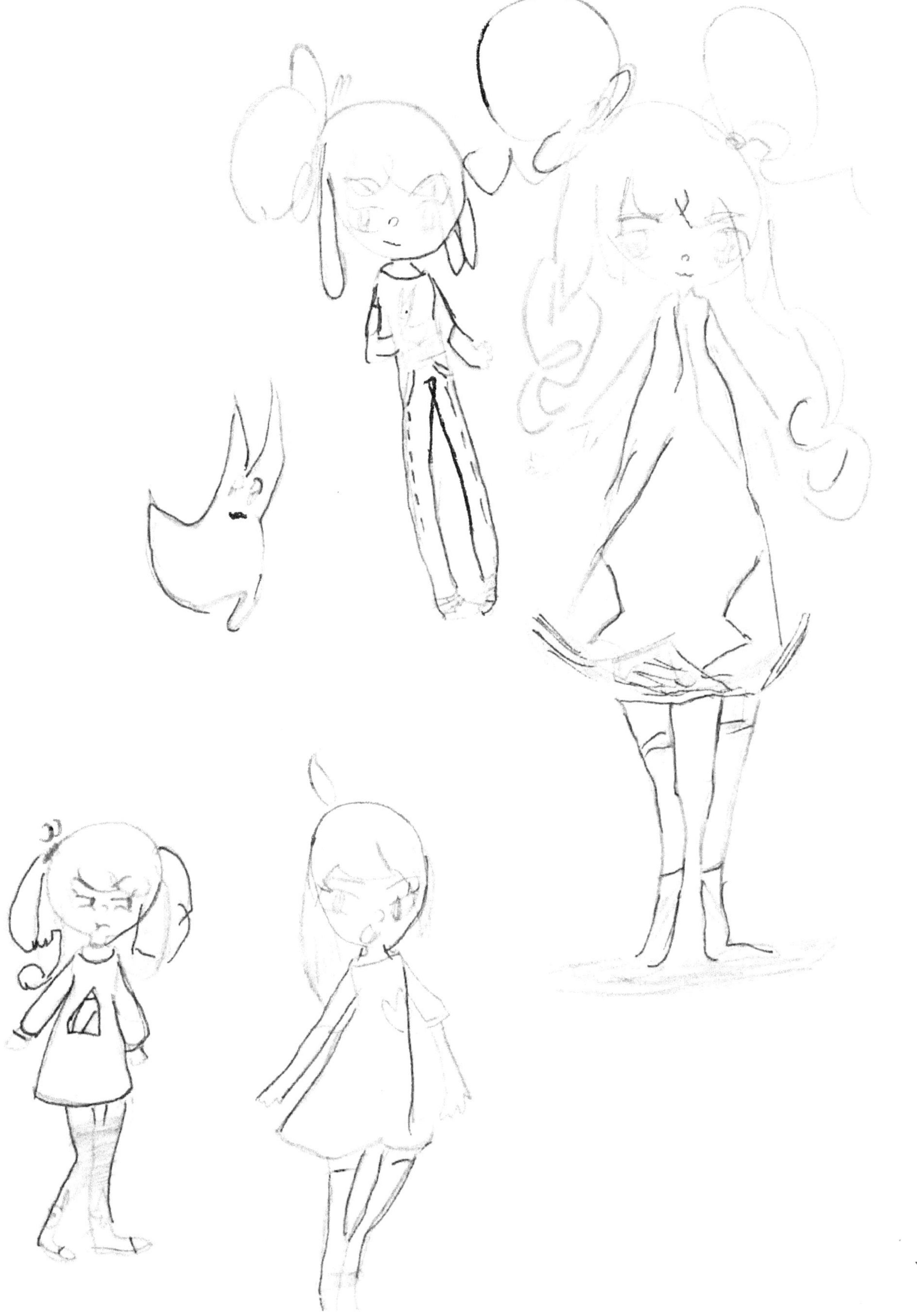

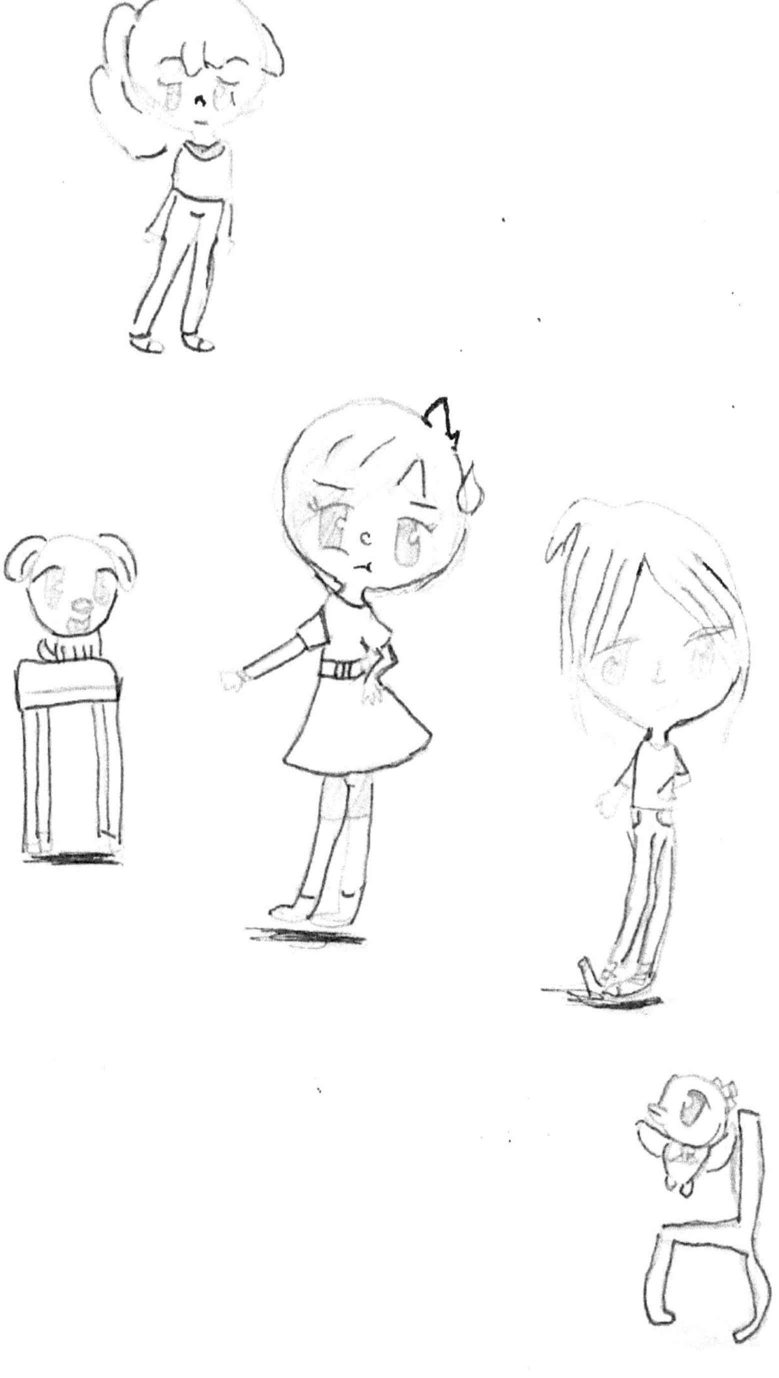

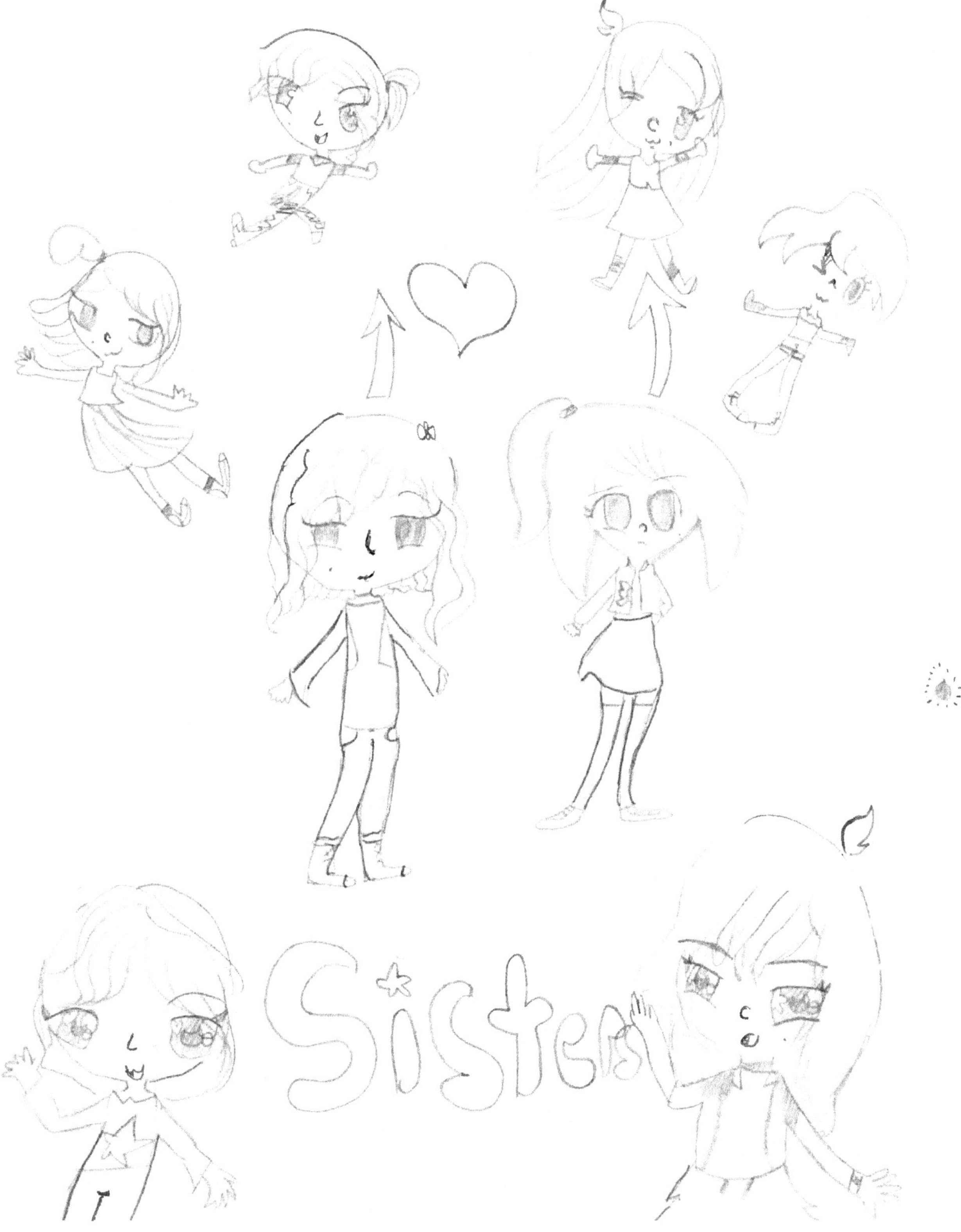
Sisters

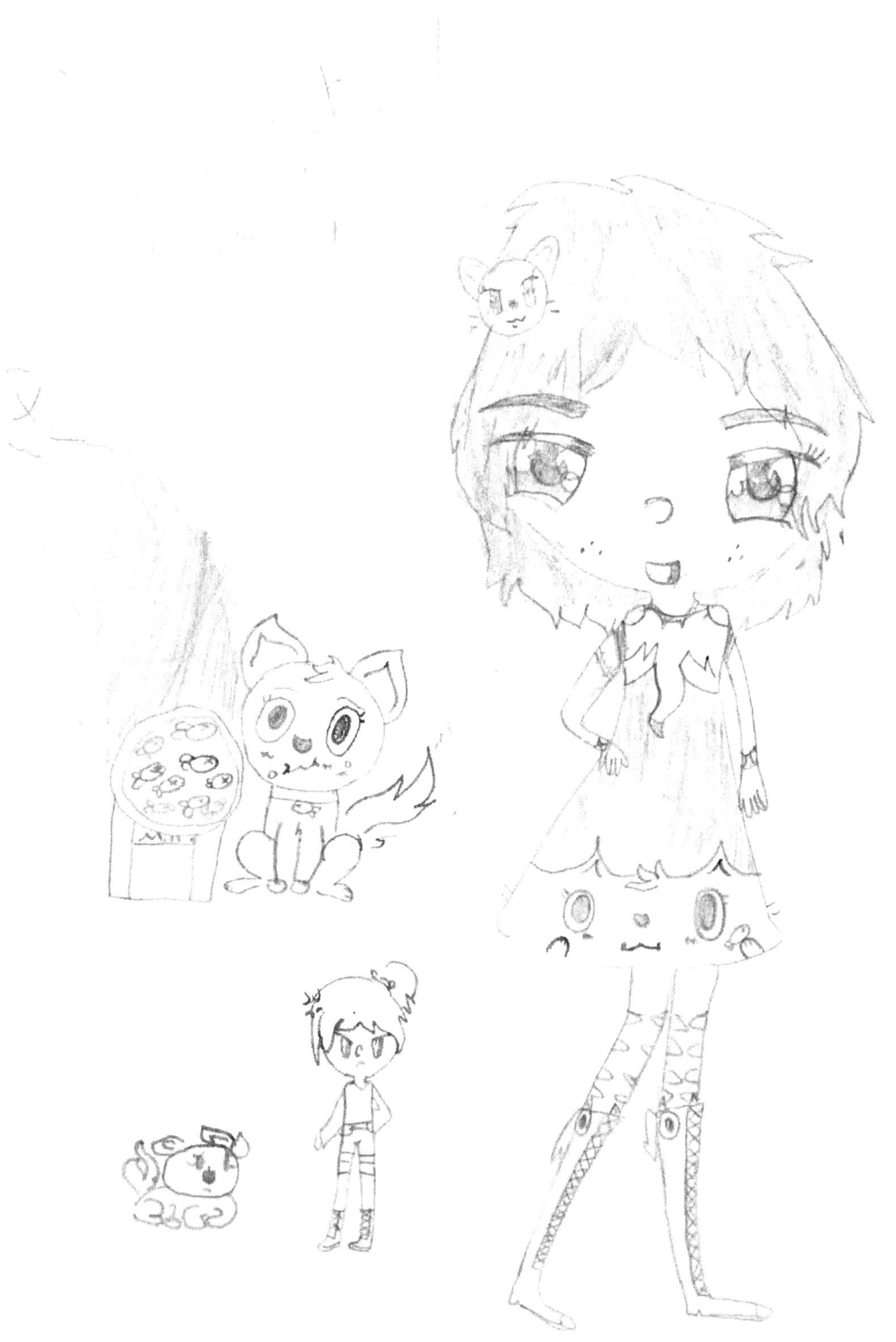

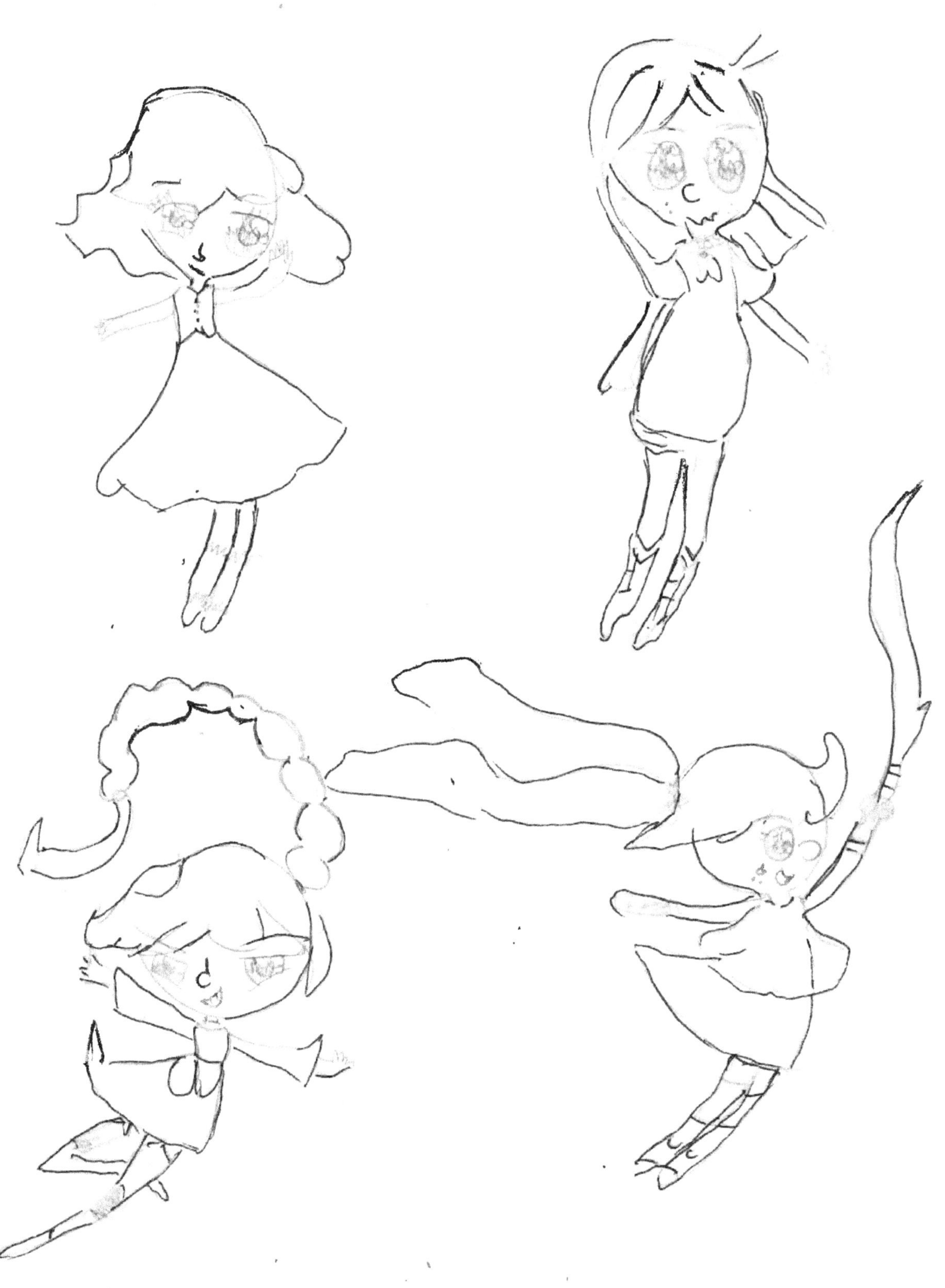

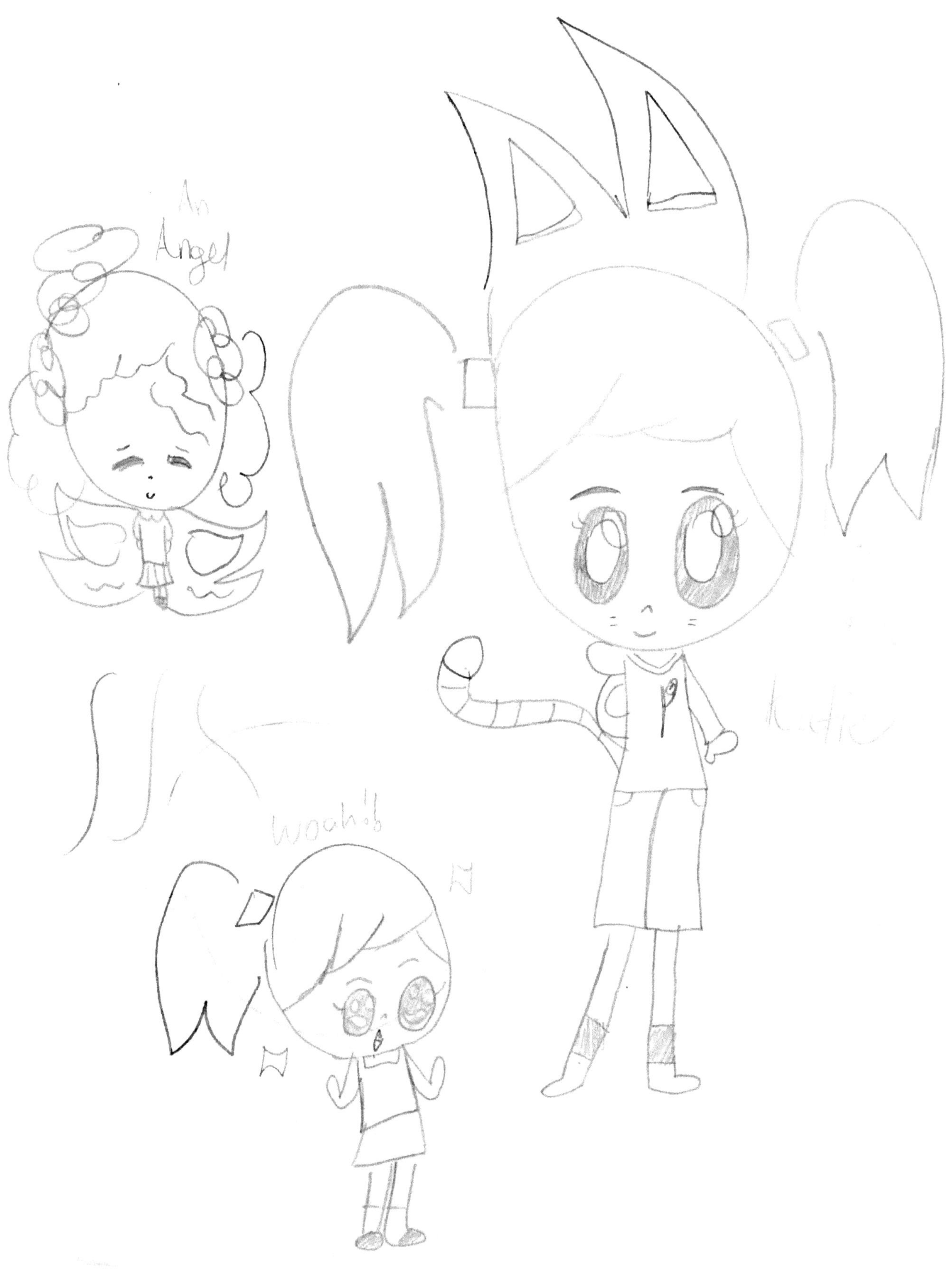
An Angel
Woah!!

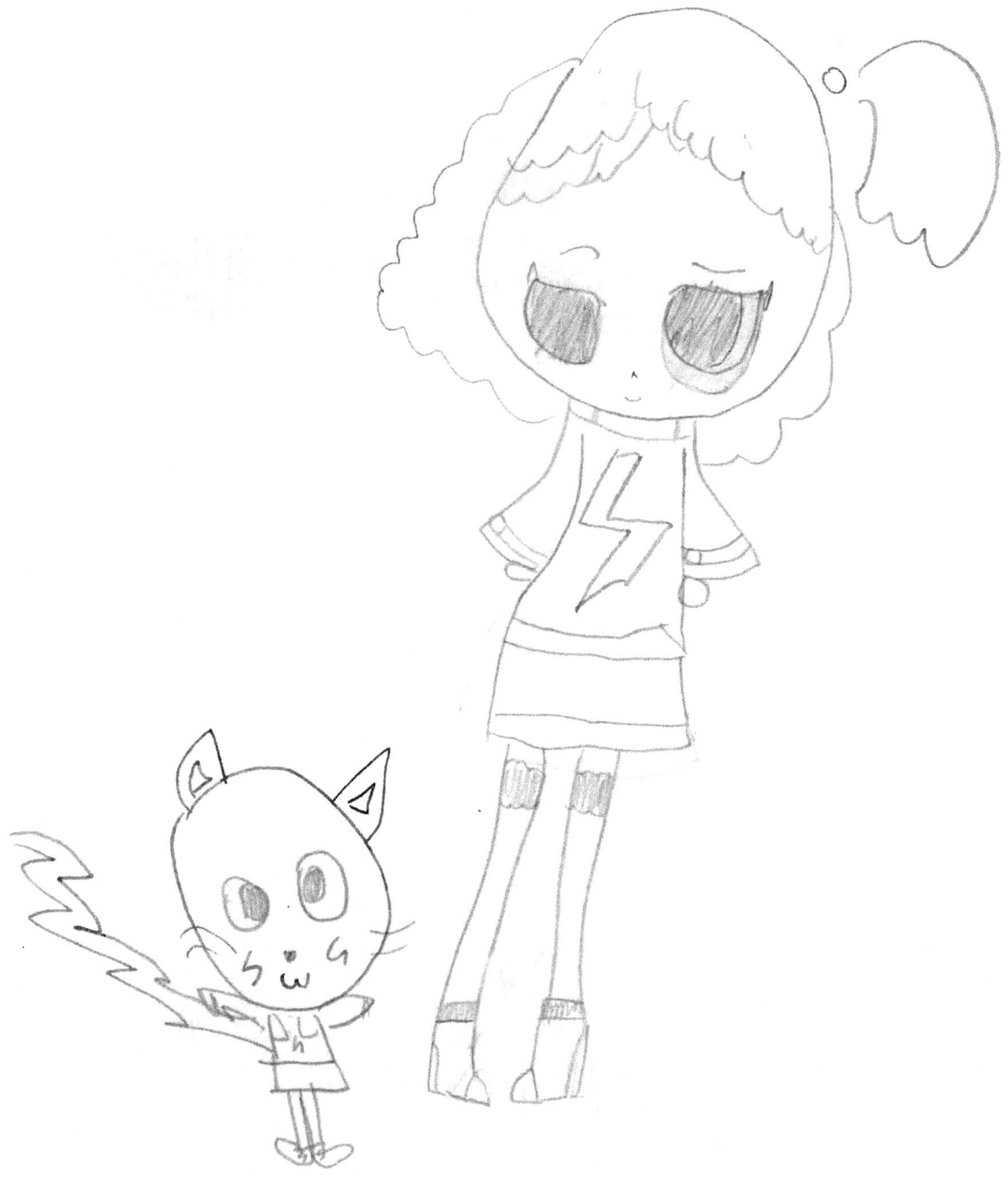

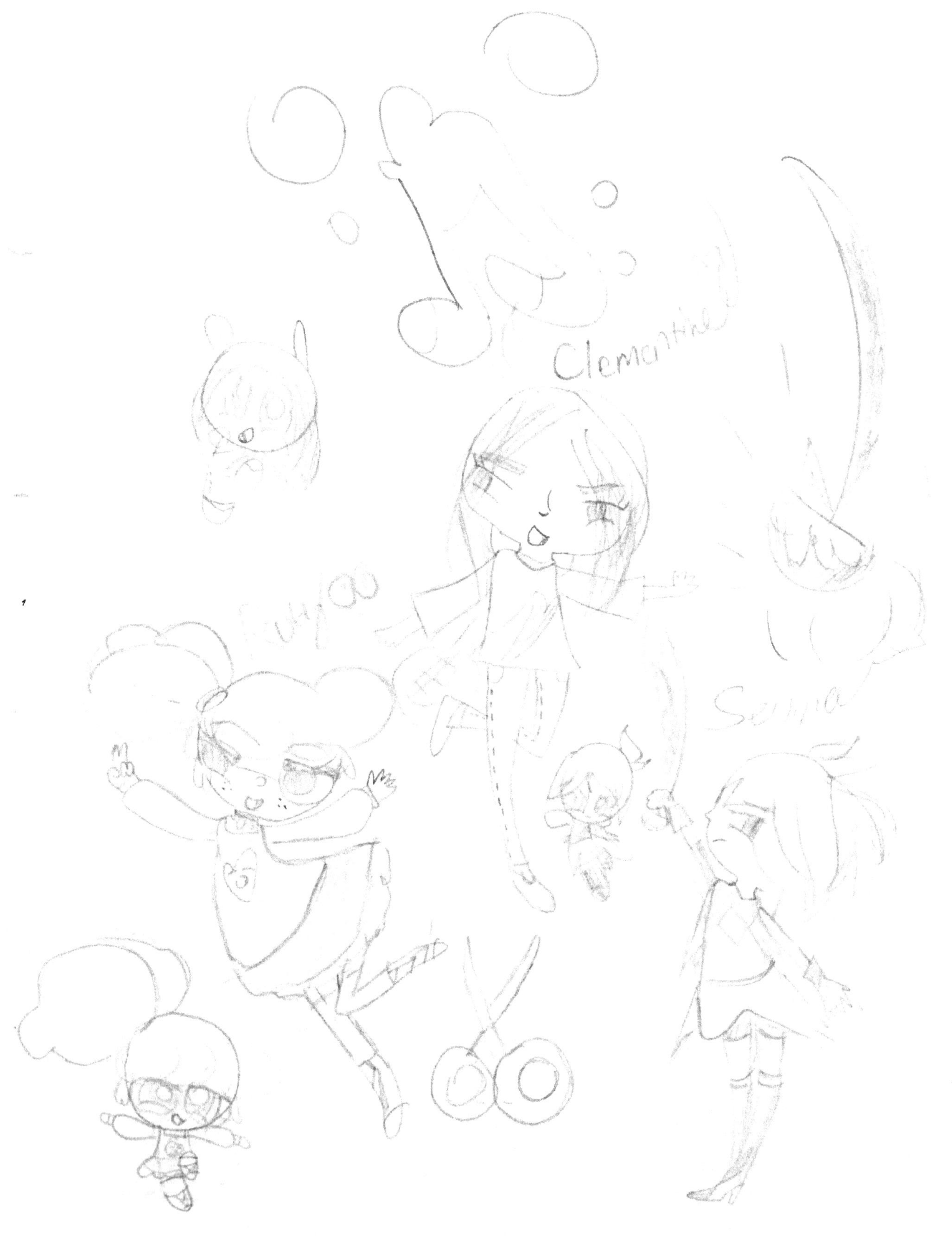
Clemantine

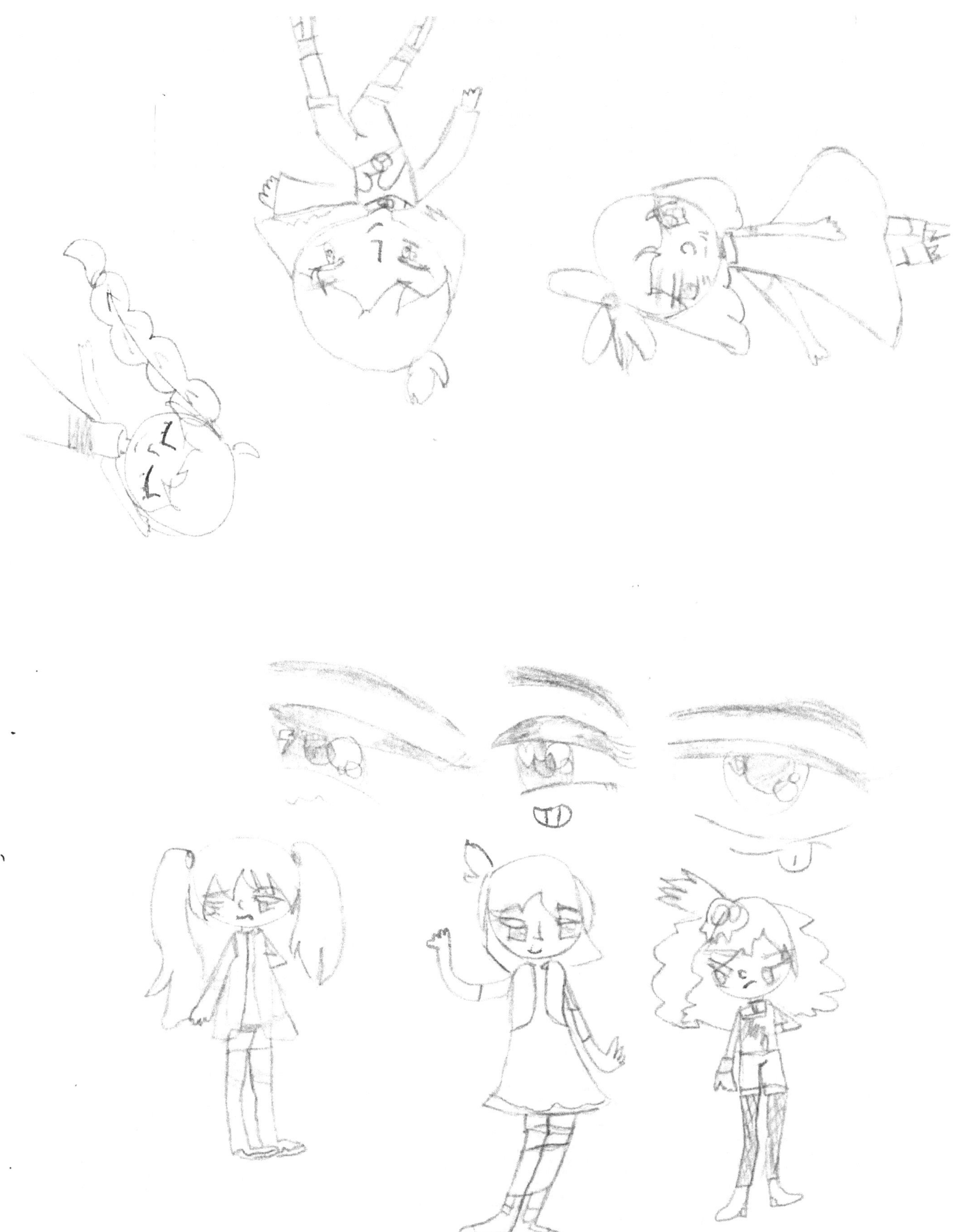

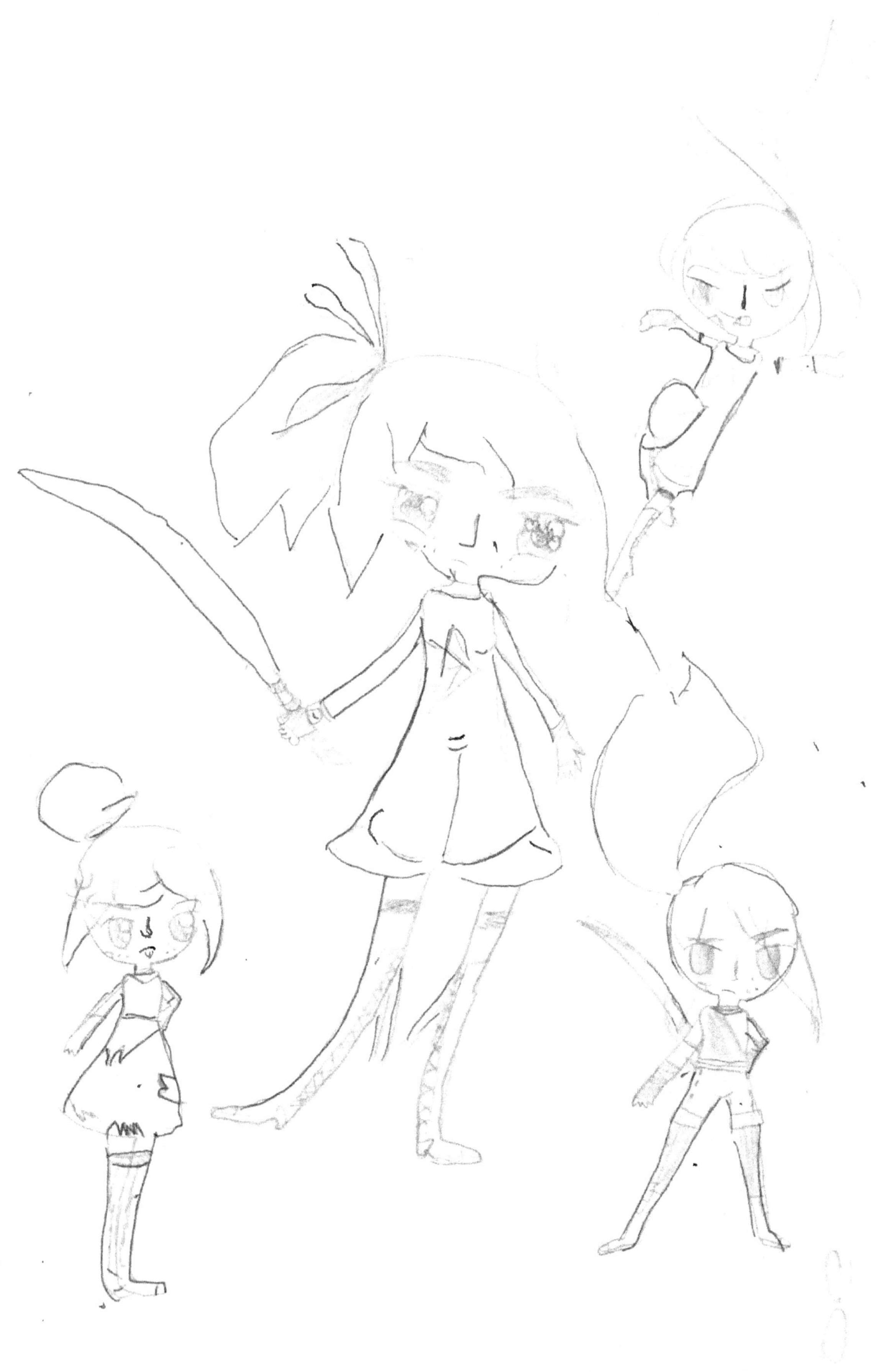

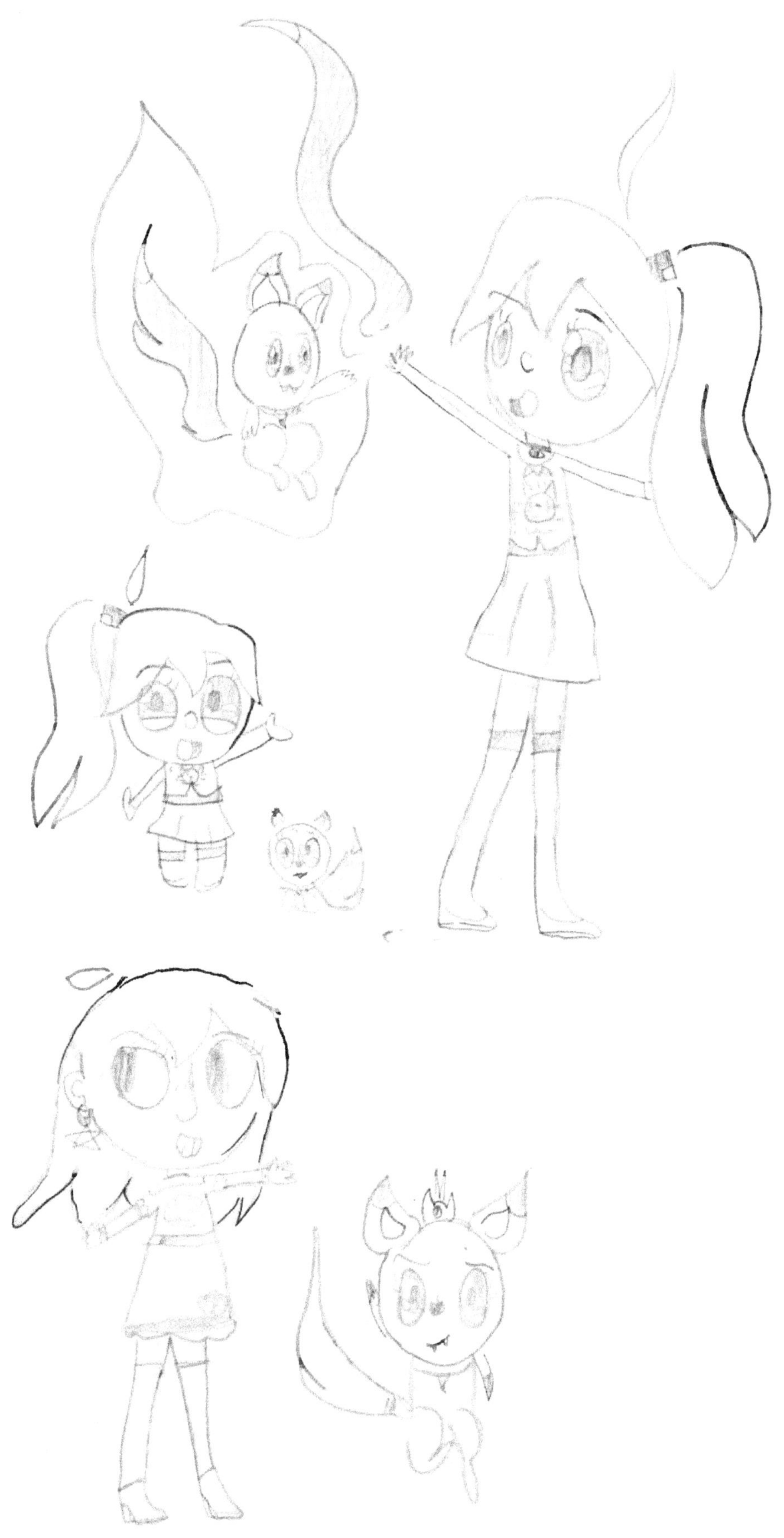

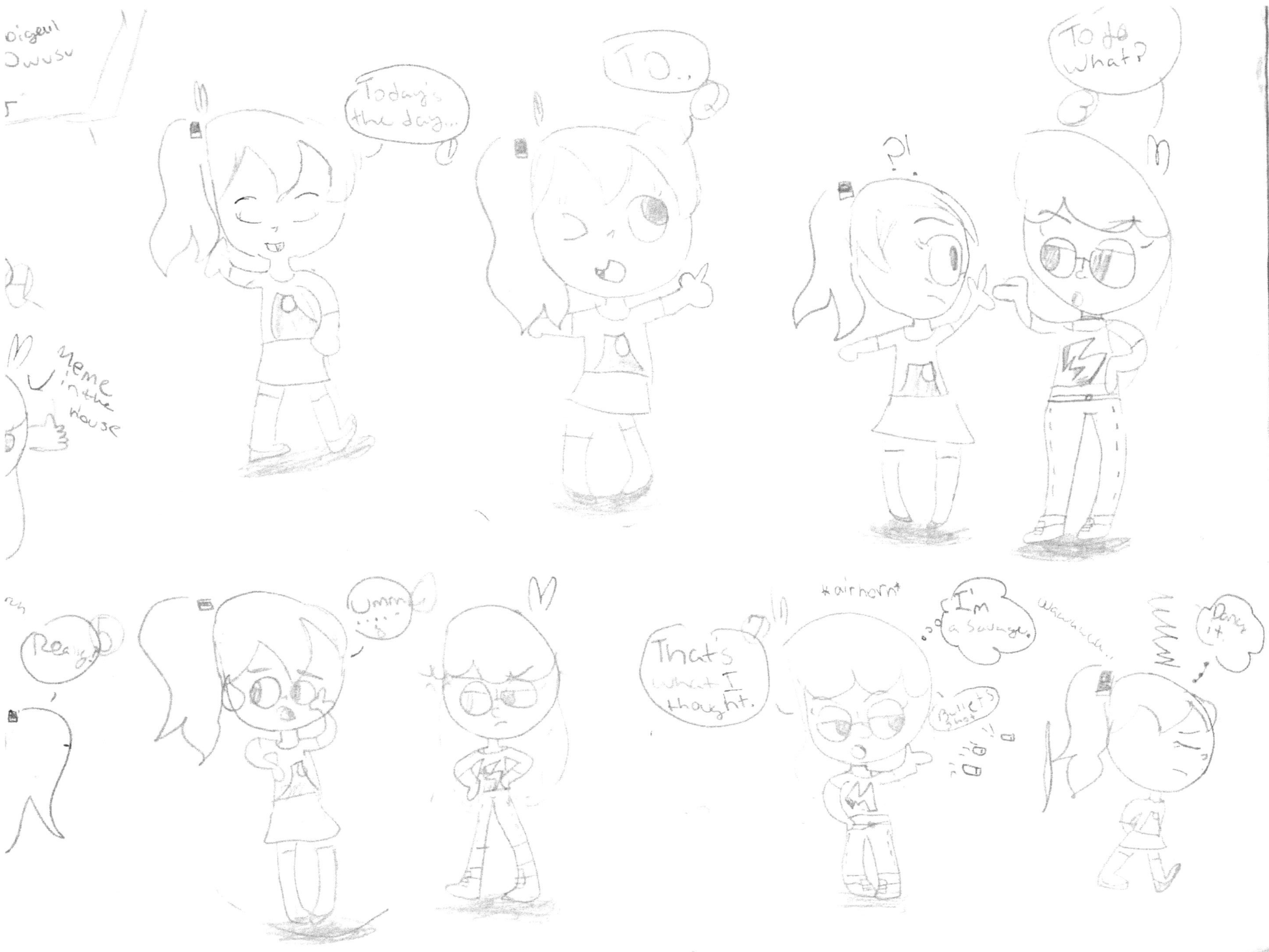
Today's the day...
TO..
To do what?
?!
Meme in the house
Really?
Umm...
That's what I thought.
airhorn
I'm a Savage.
Bullets shot
Waaaa...
Done it.

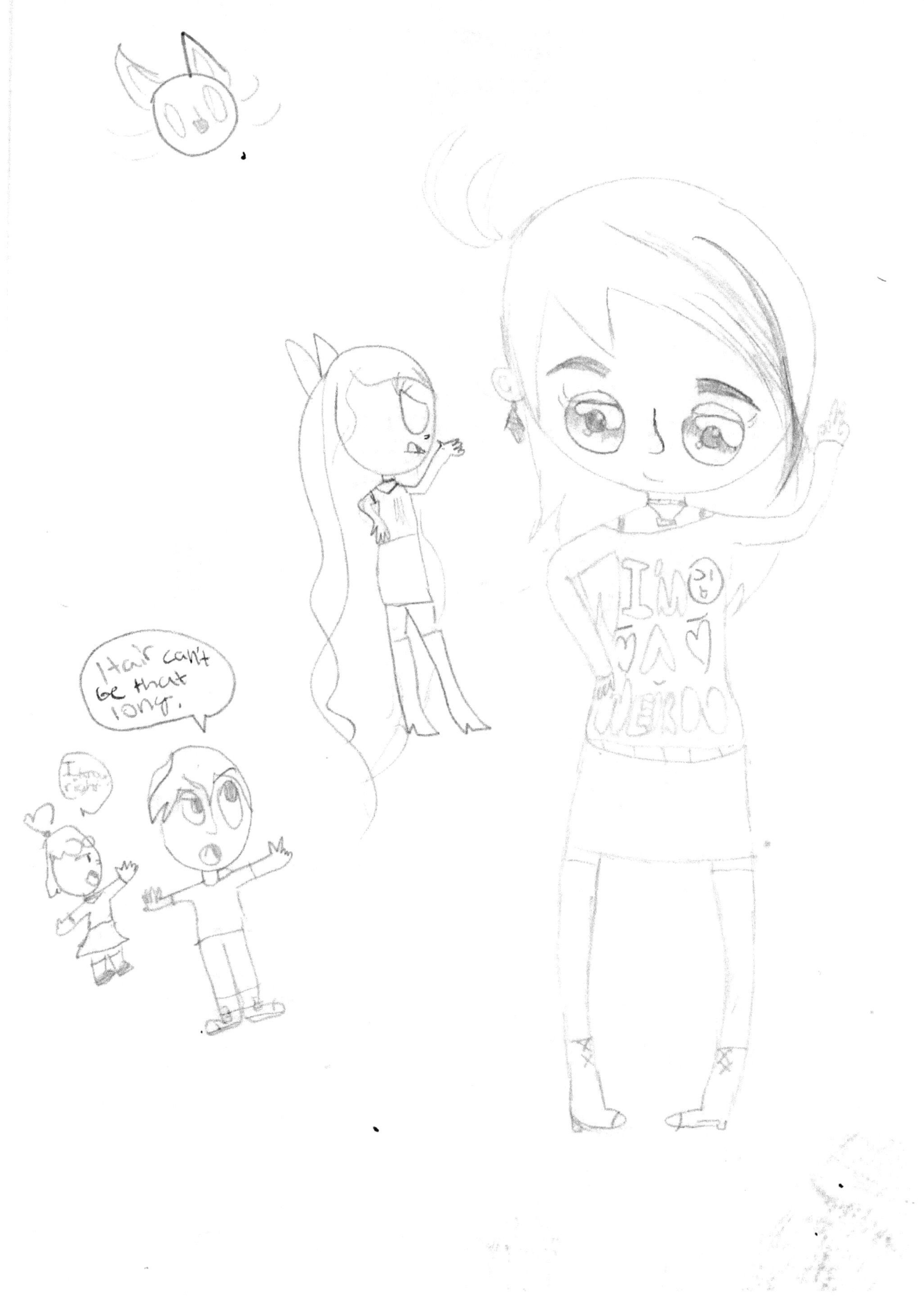
Hair can't be that long.

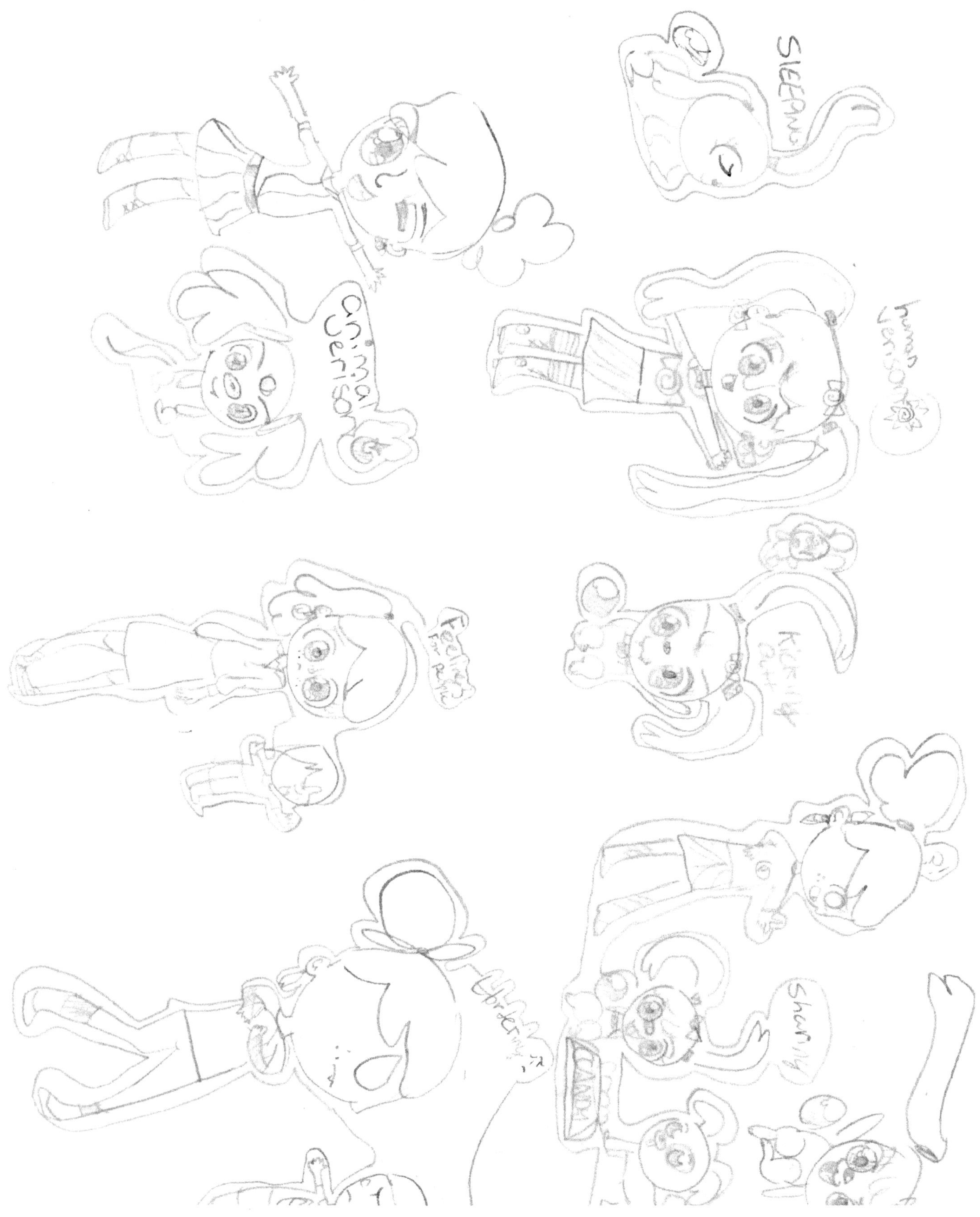
animal verison
human verison
Sharing
CANDY

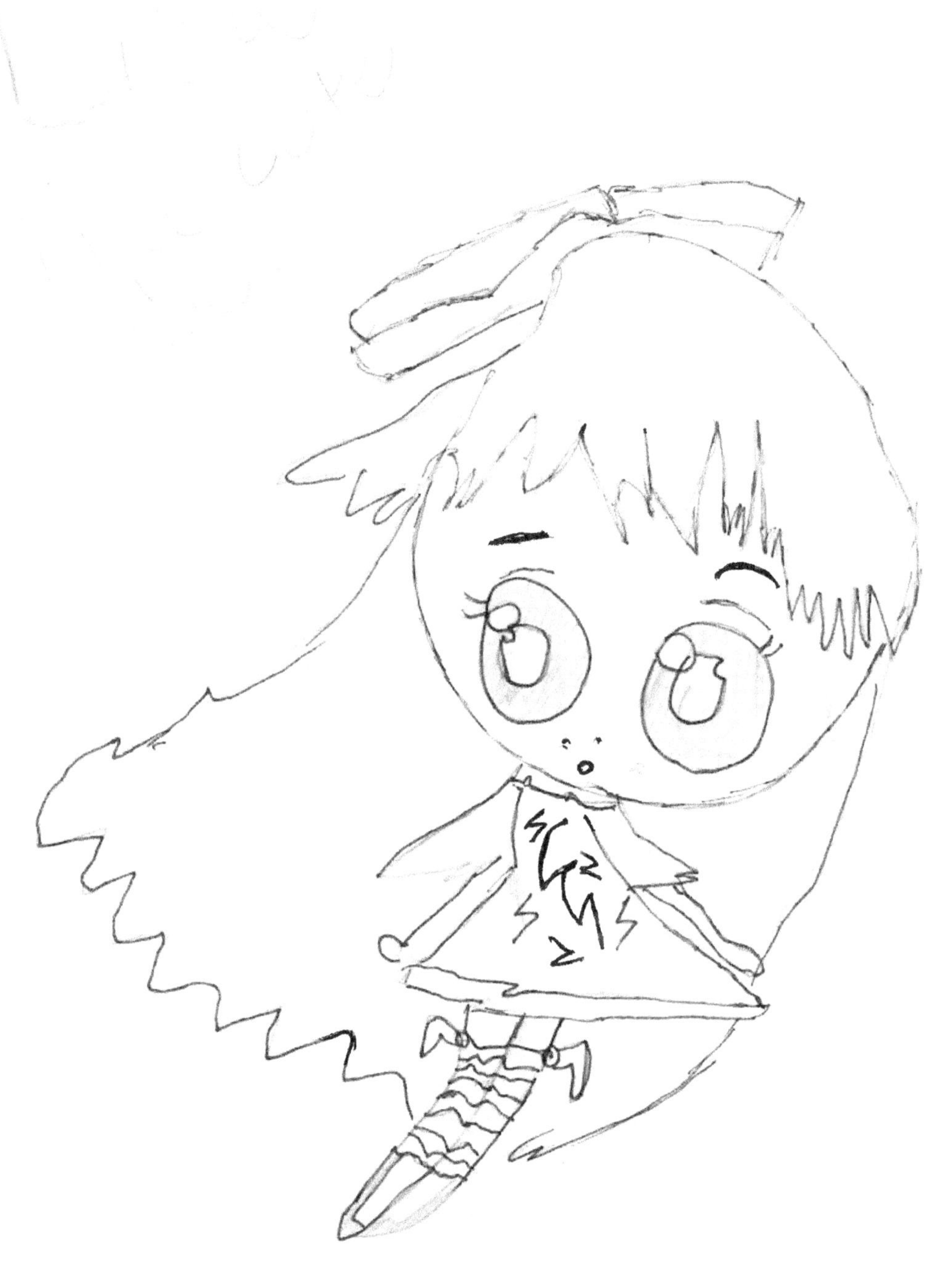

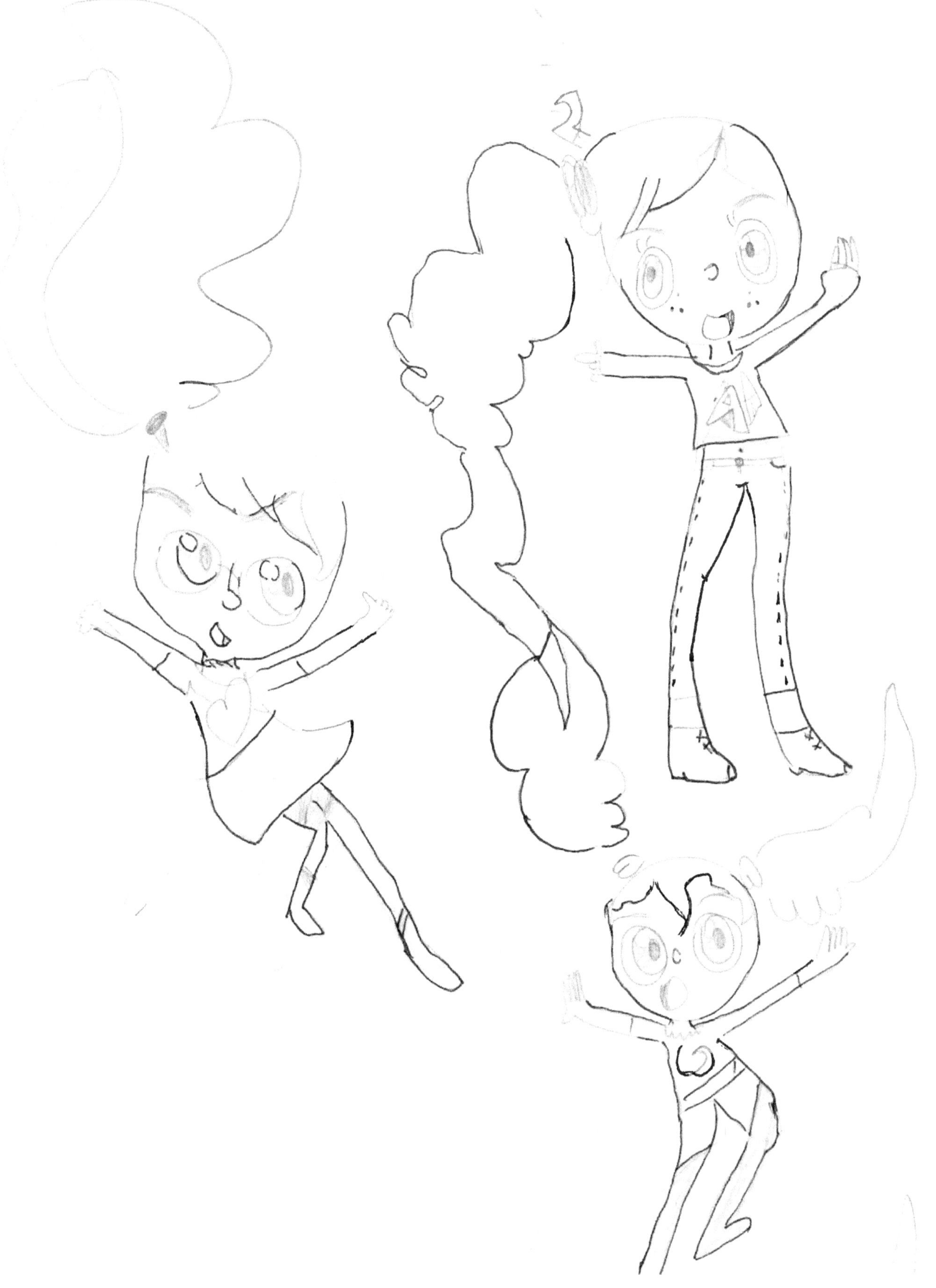

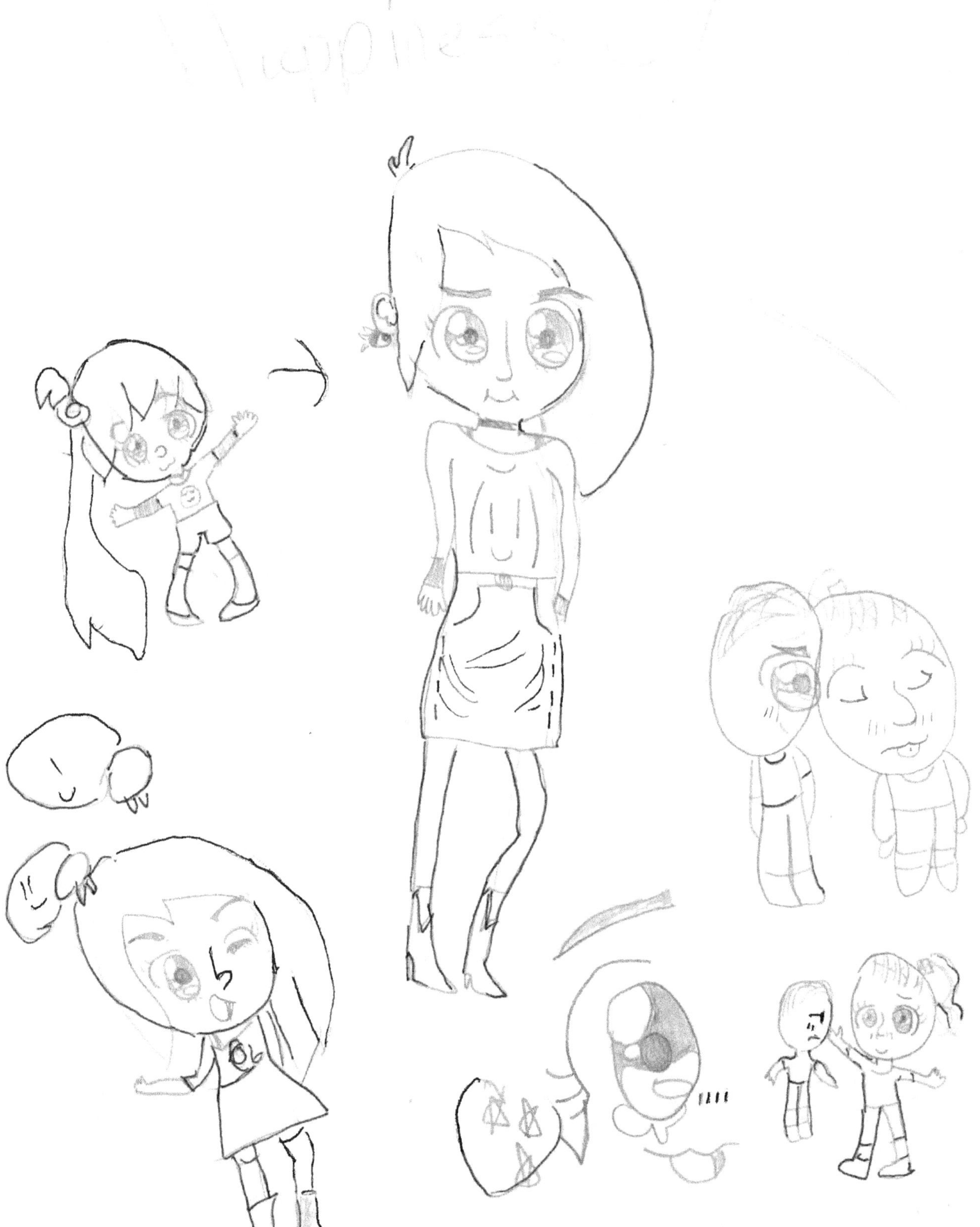

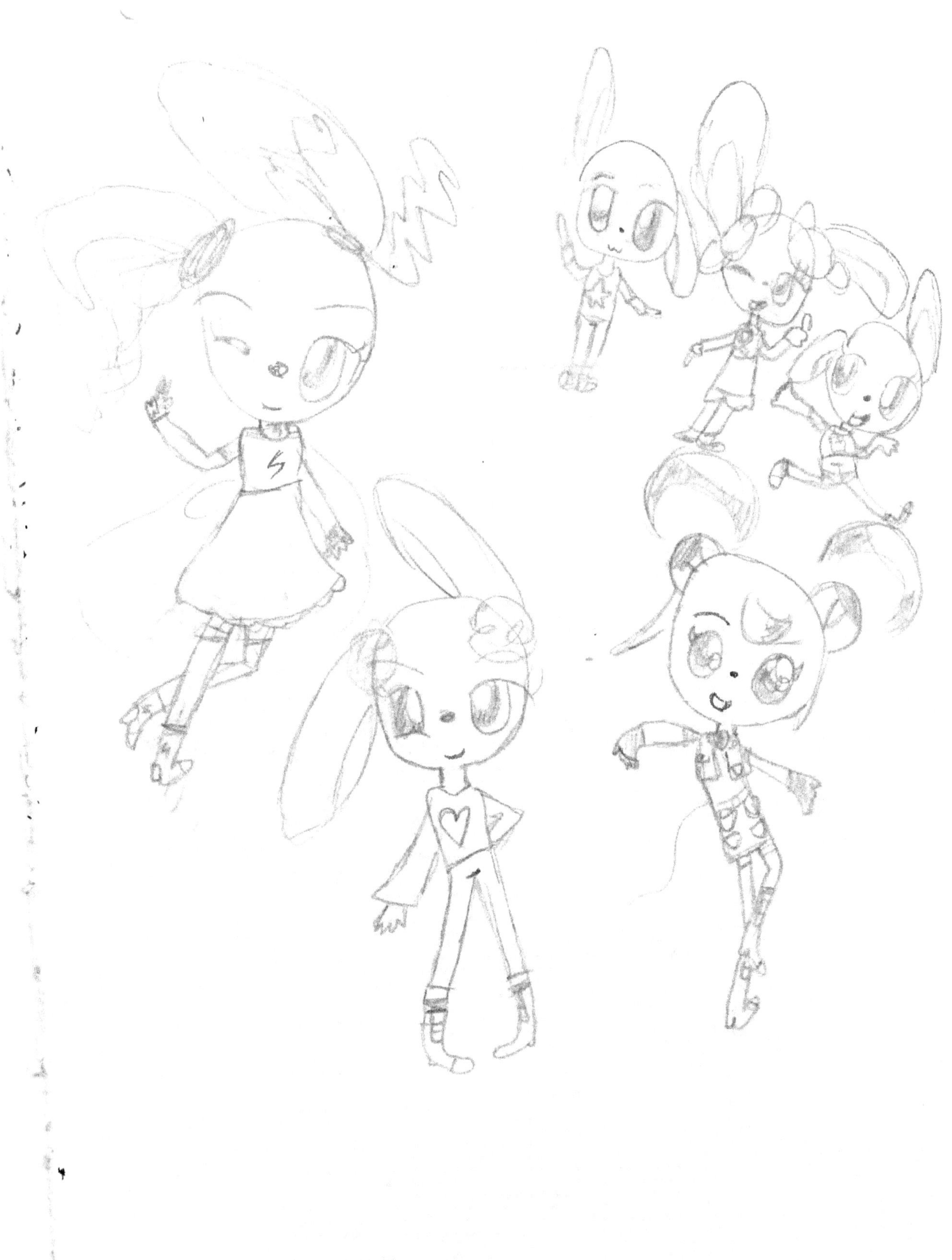

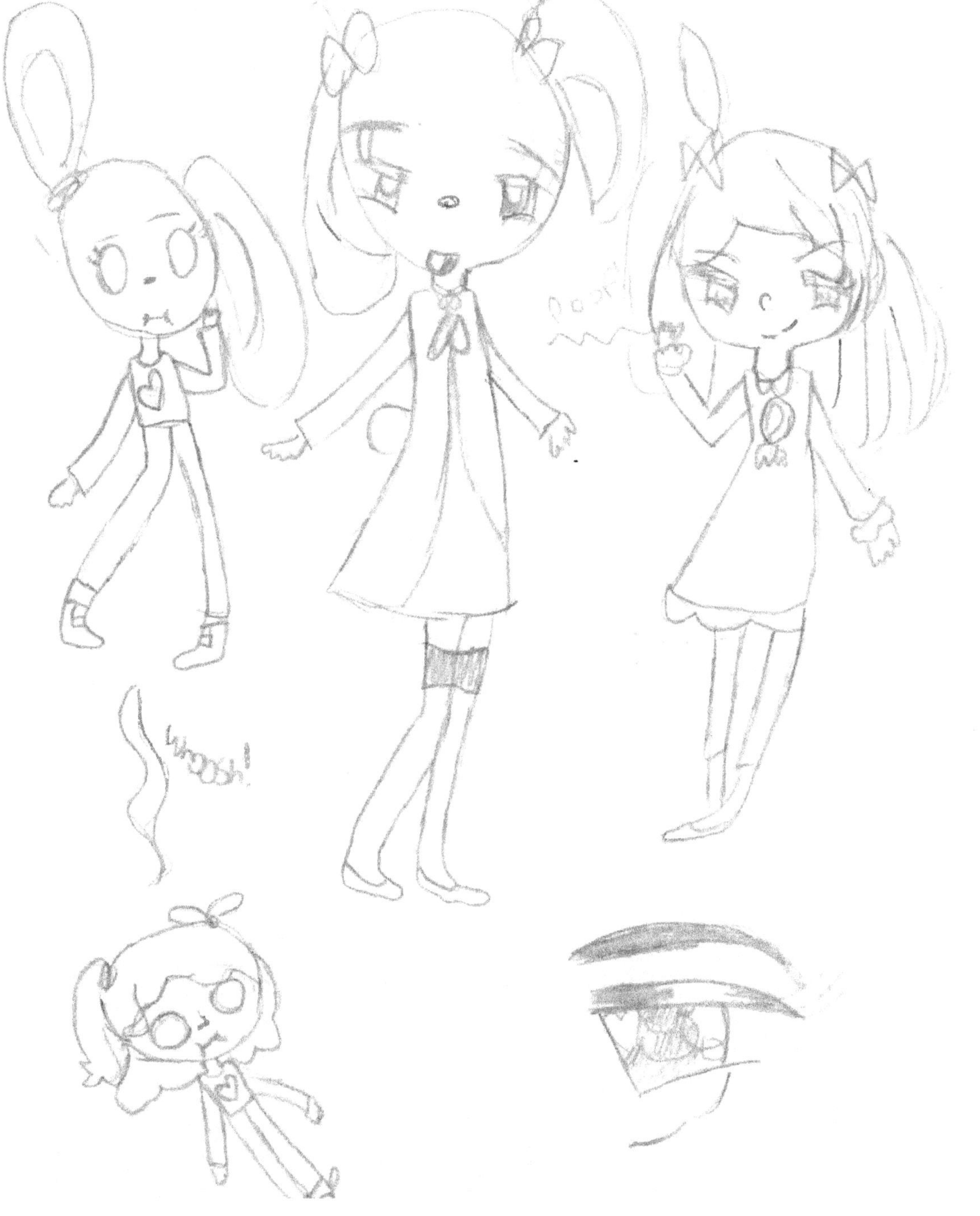
Whoosh!

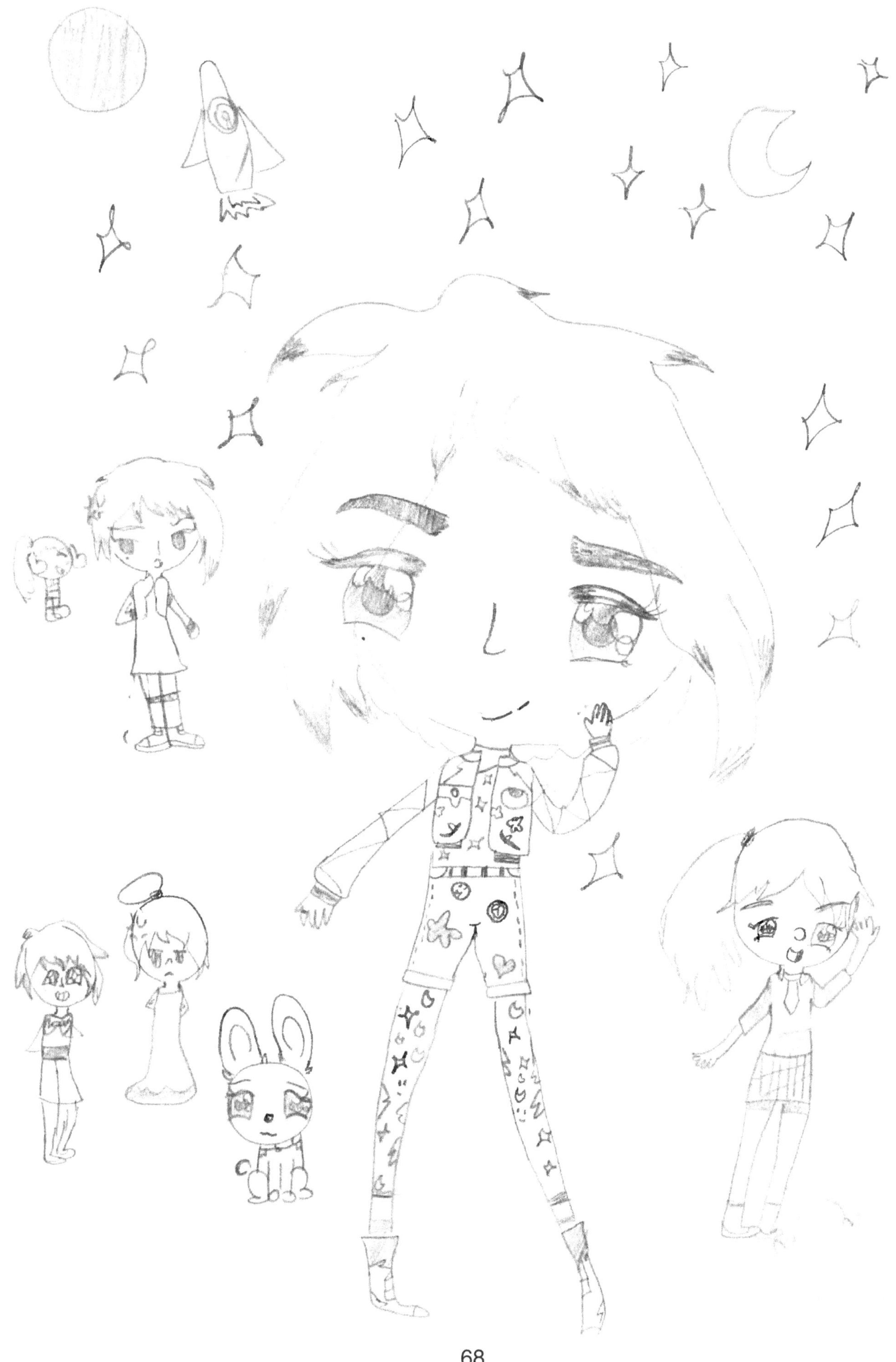

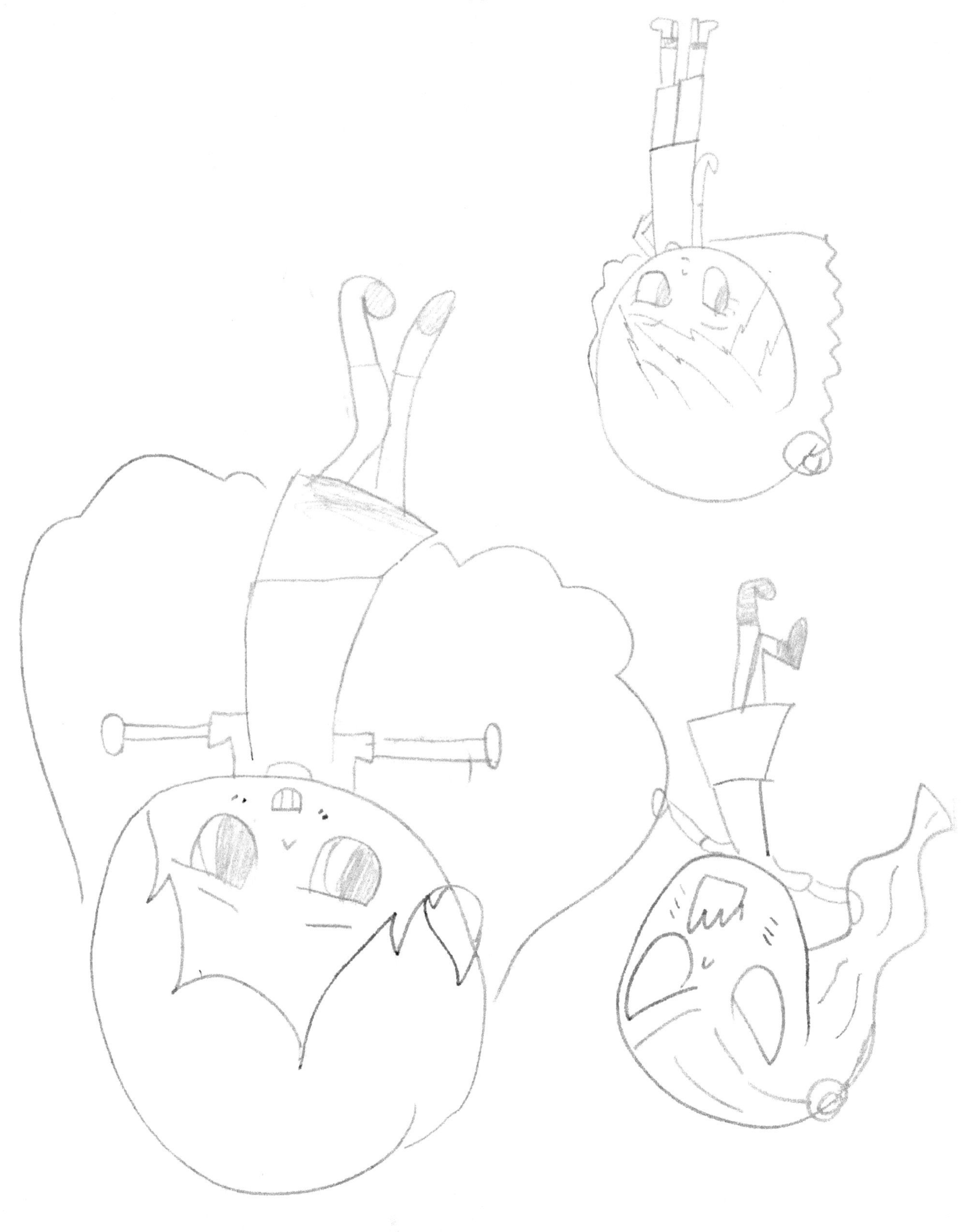

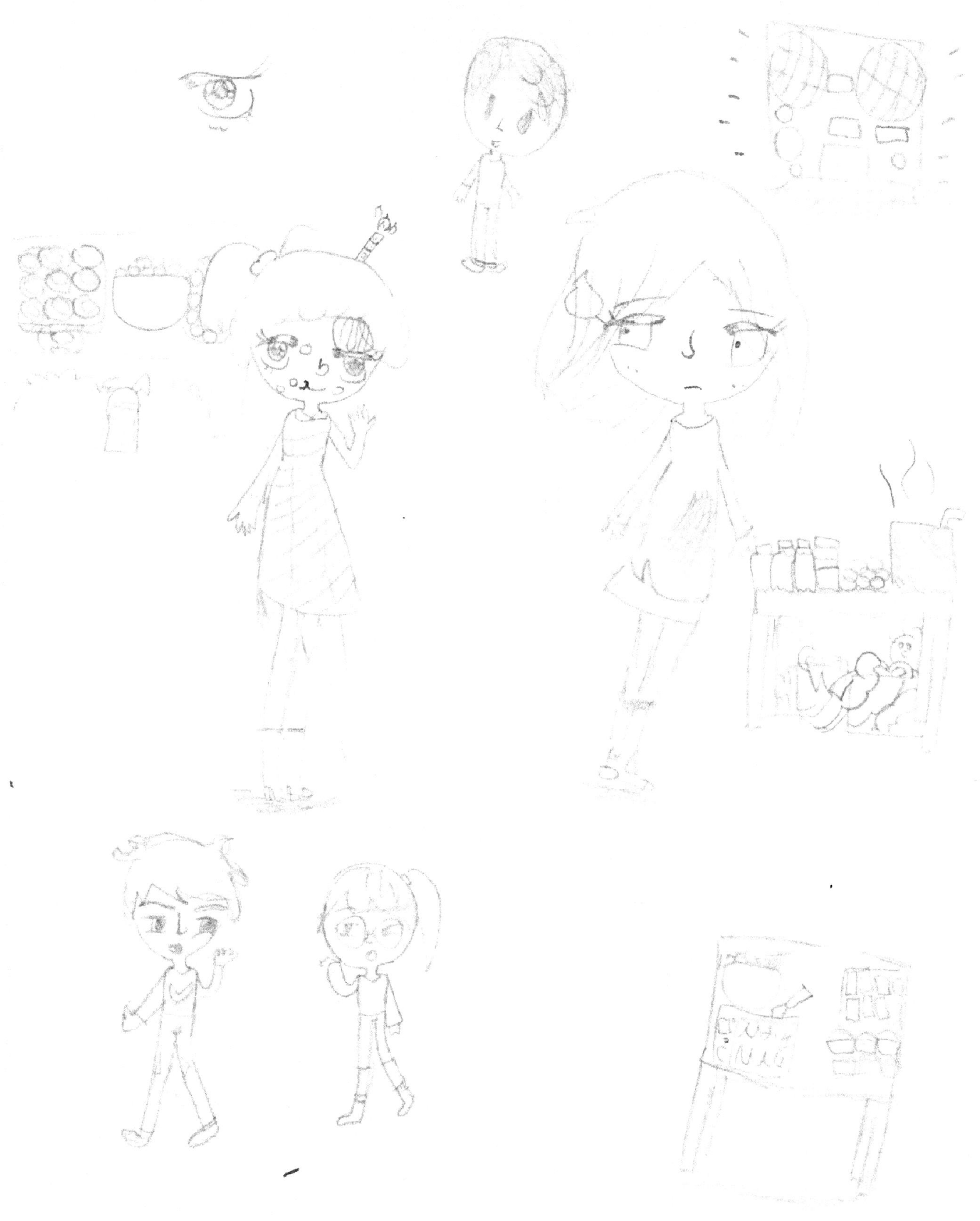

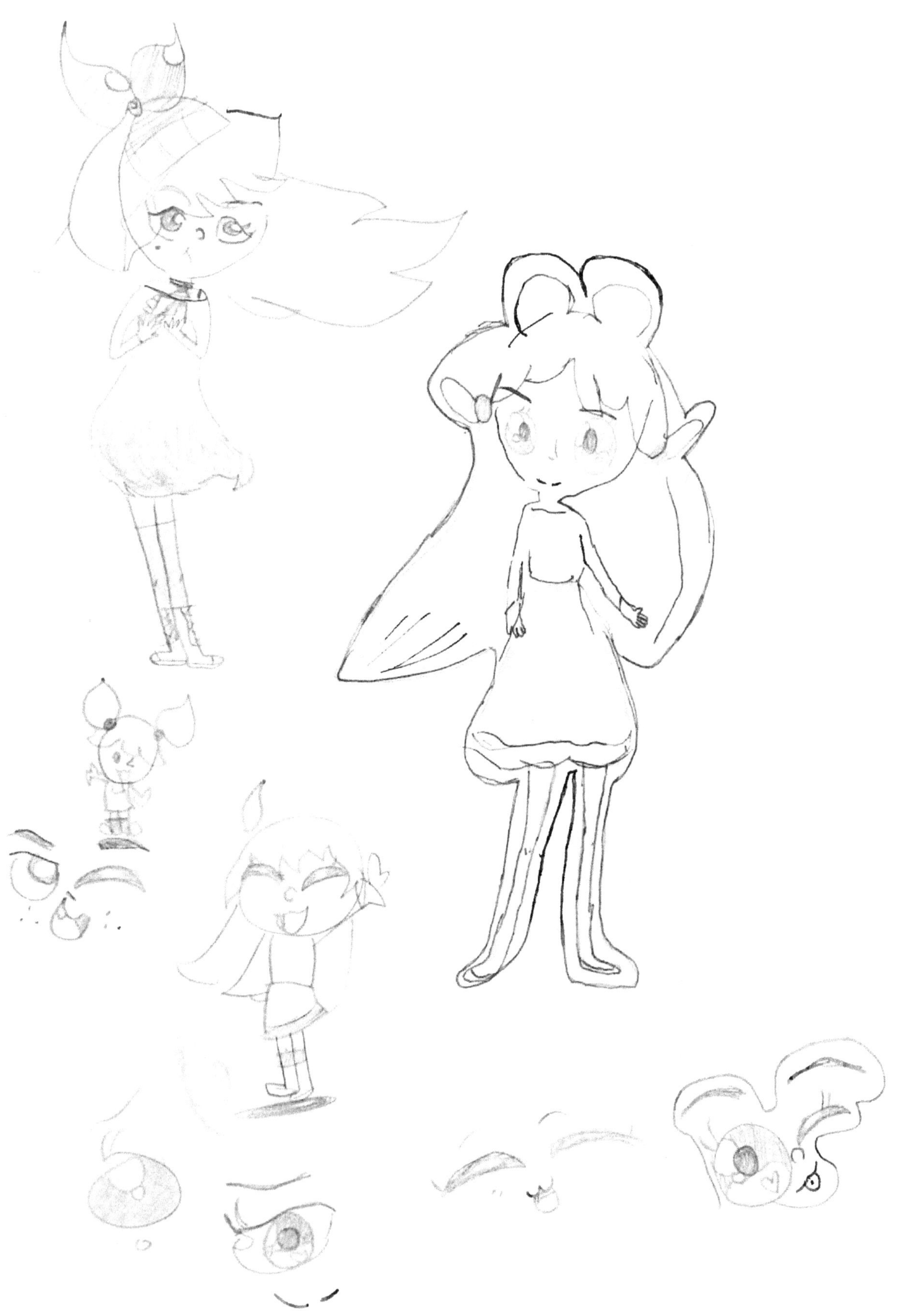

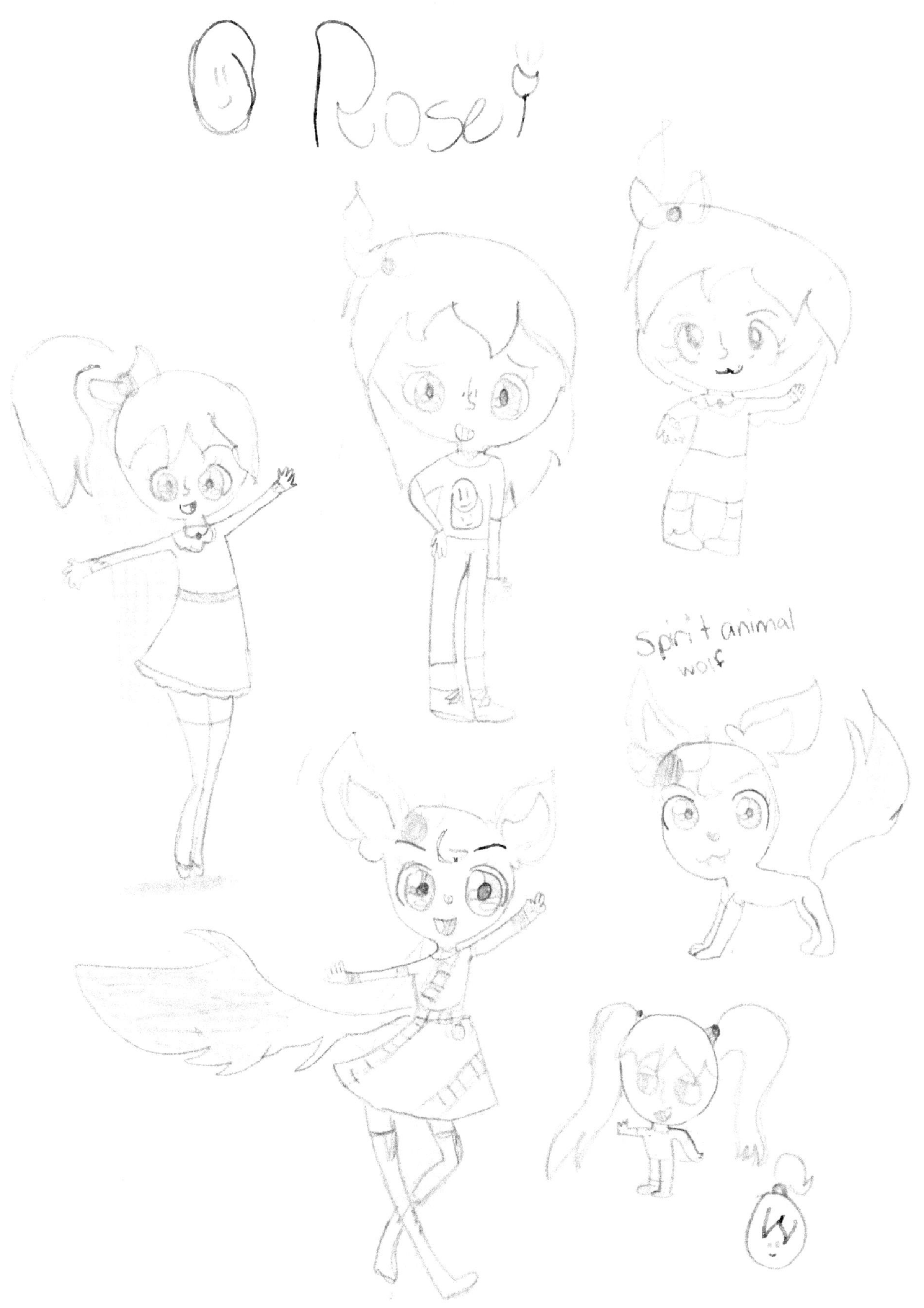
Rose
Spirit animal
wolf

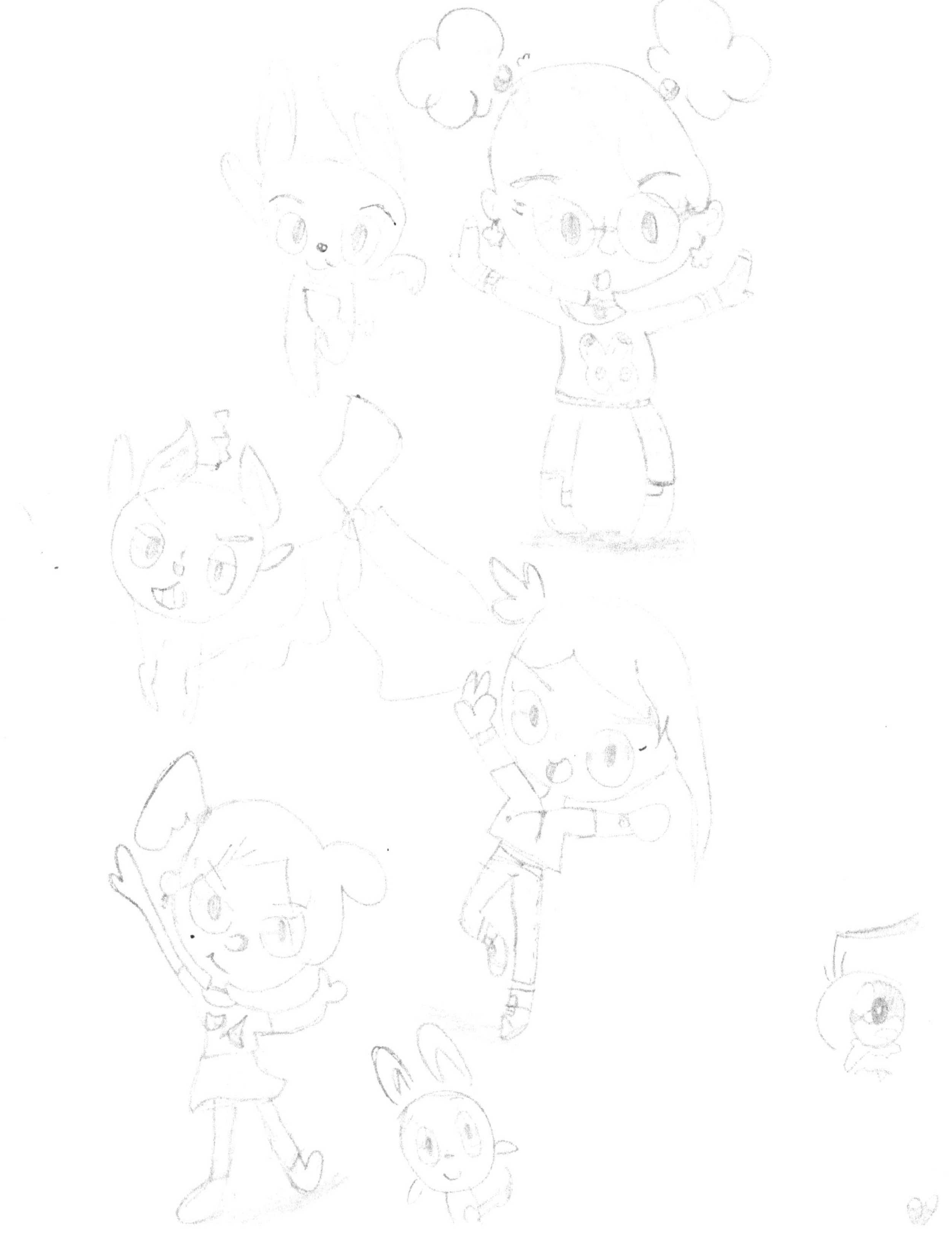

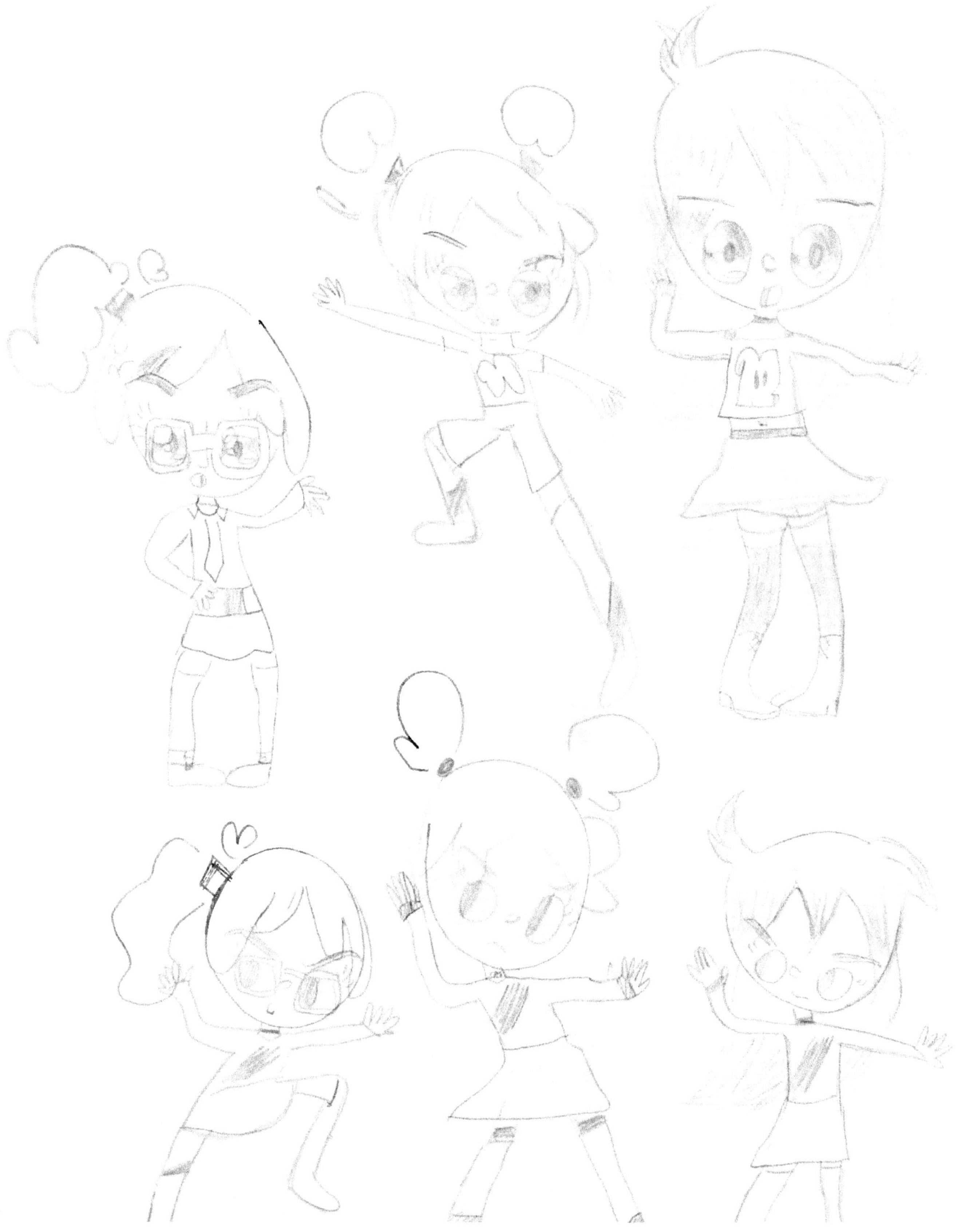

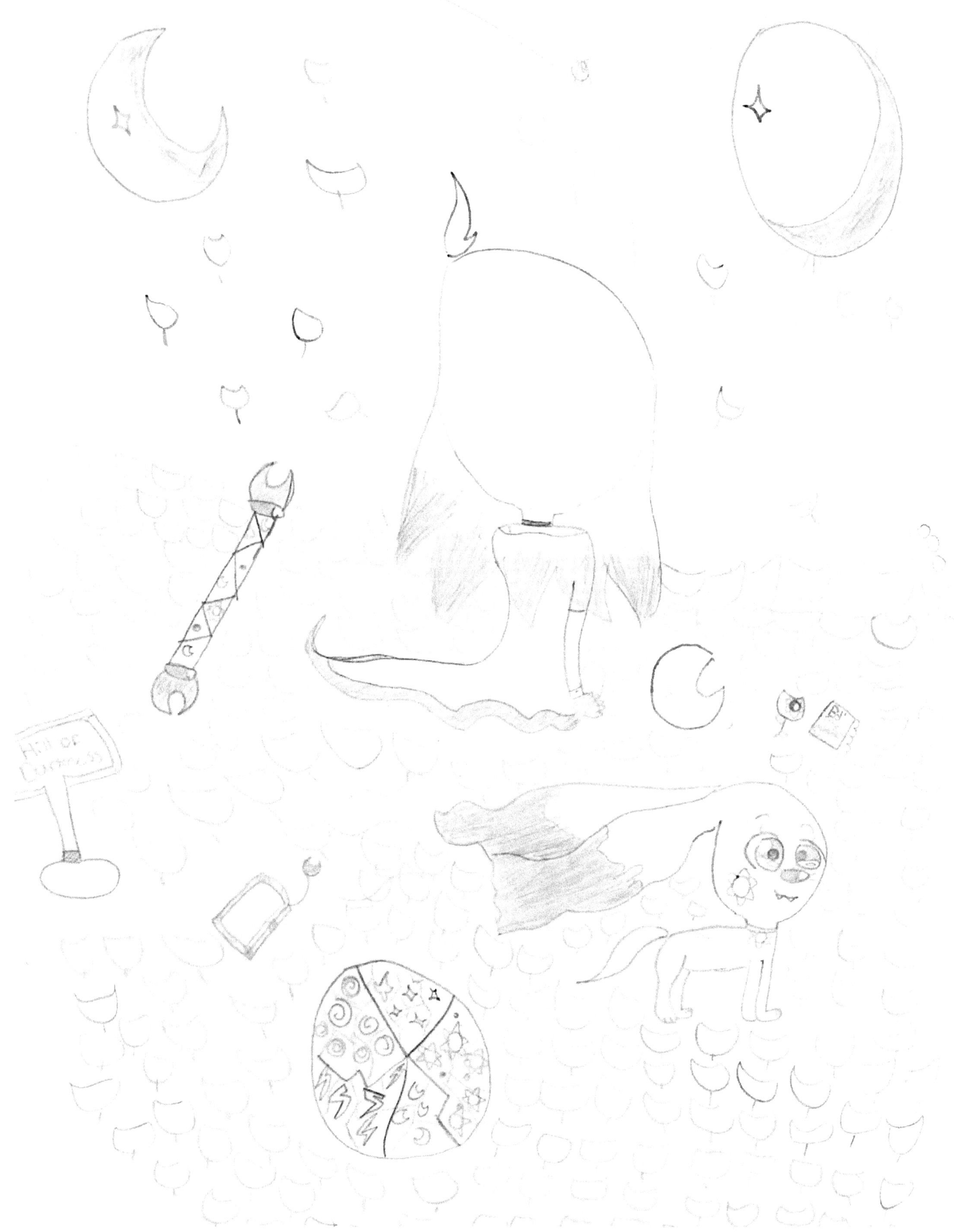

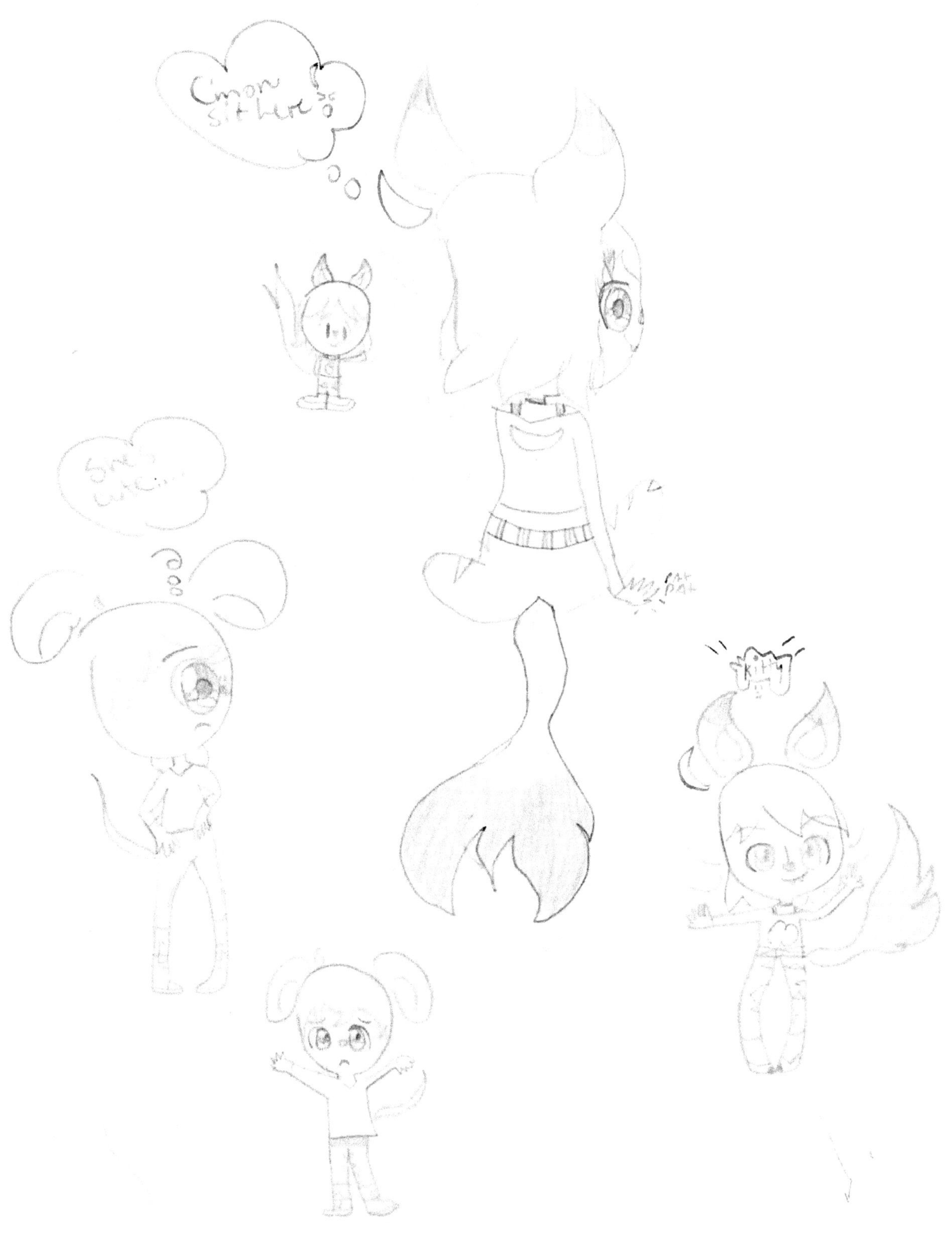
C'mon sit here

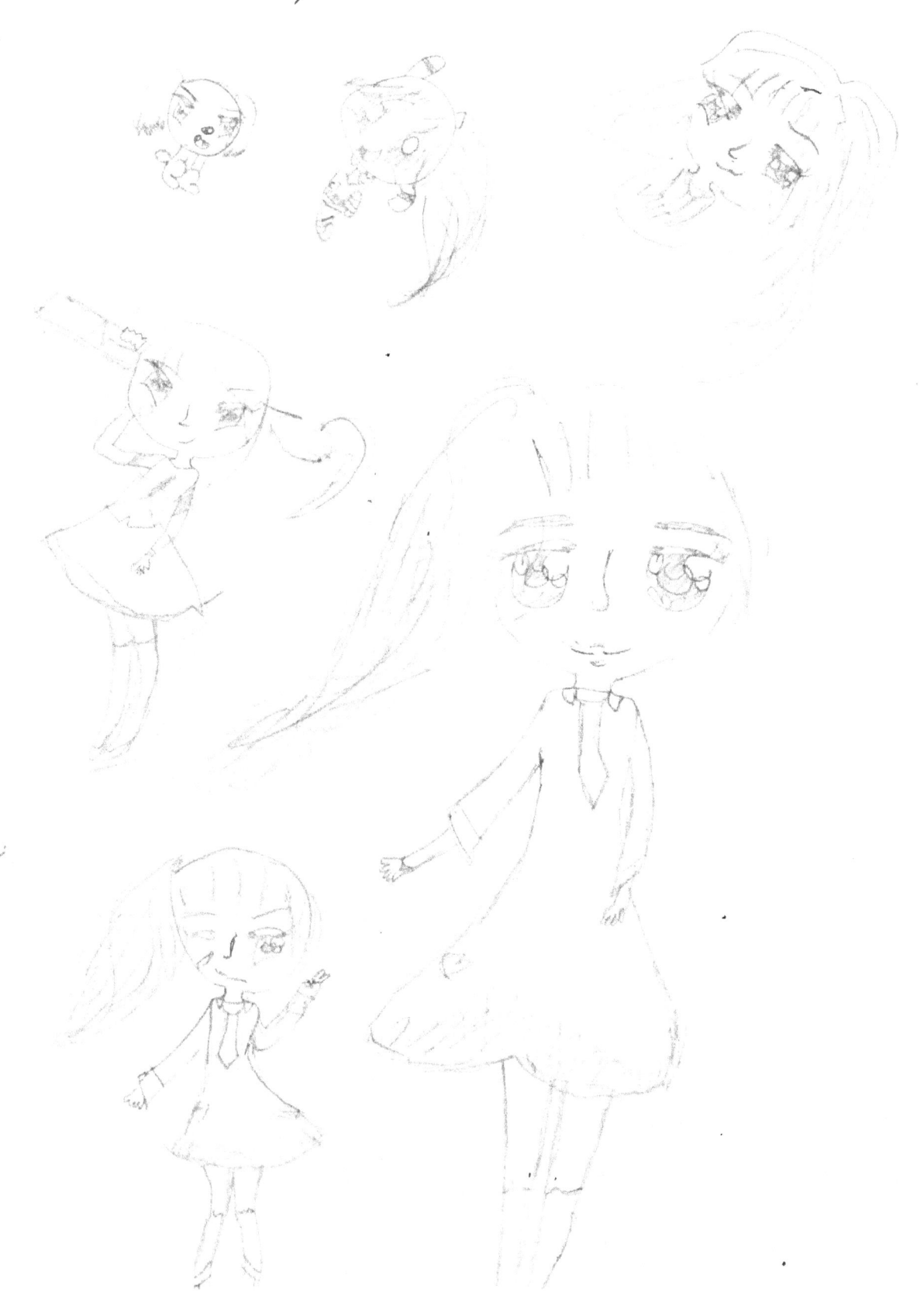

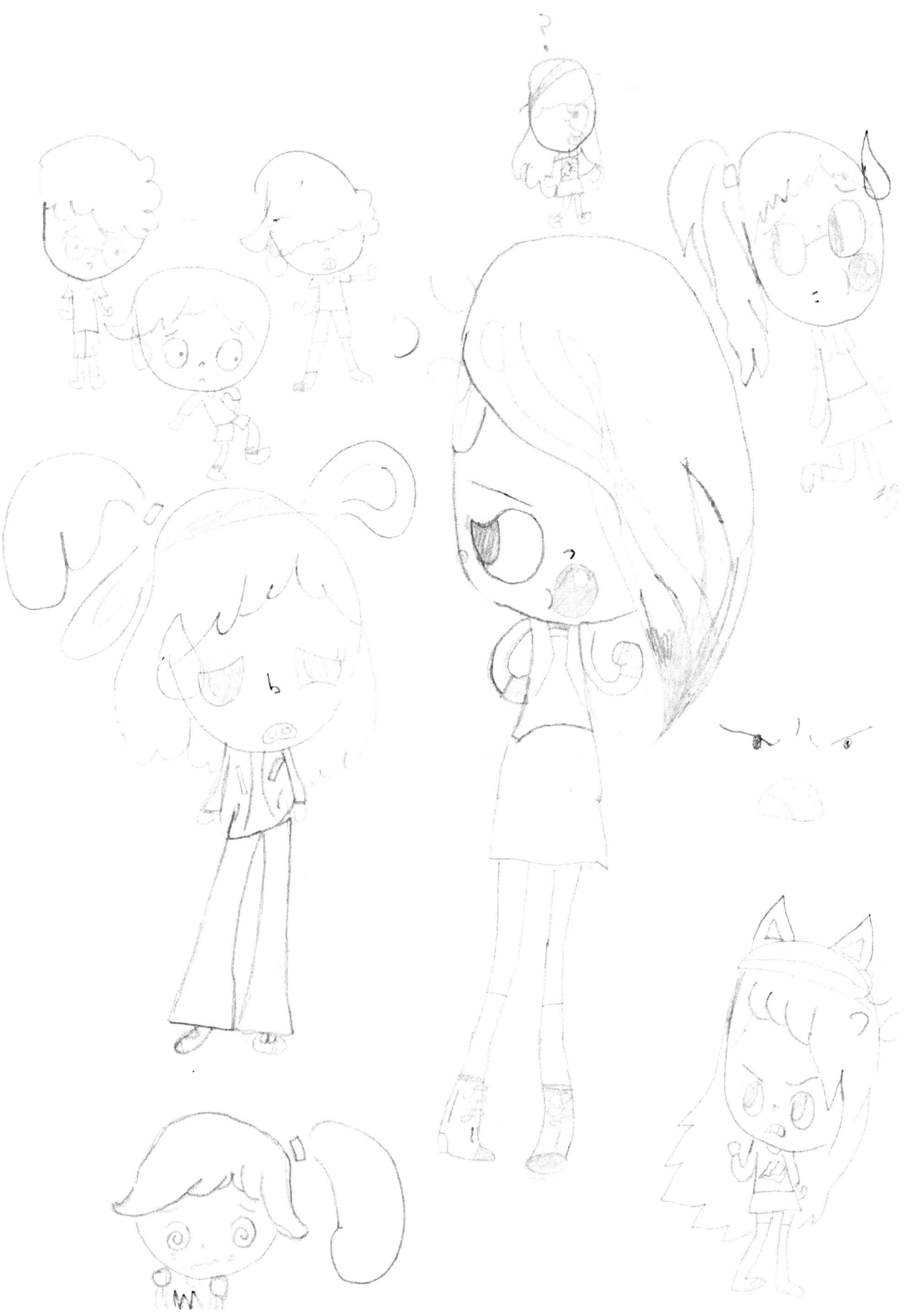

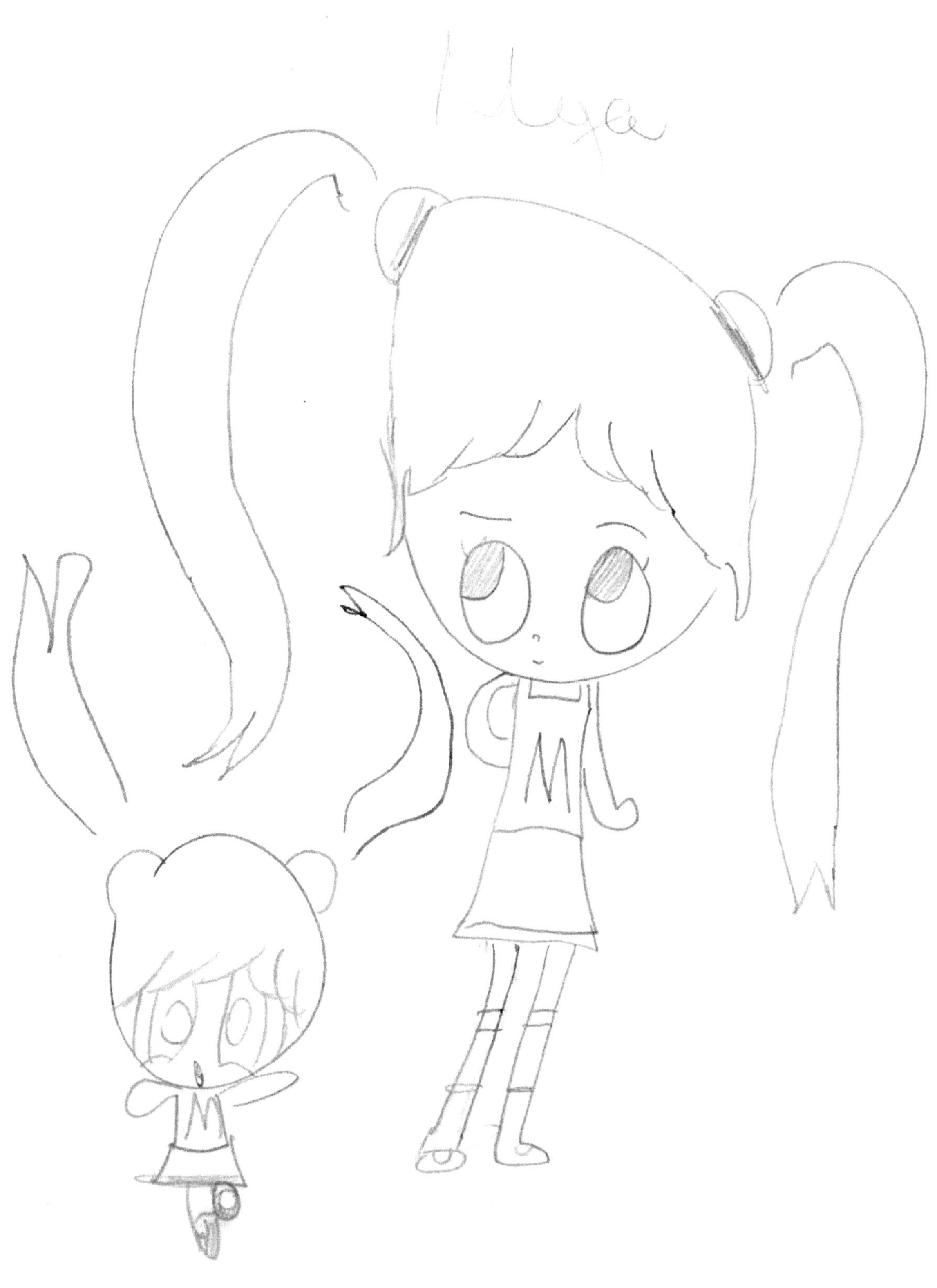

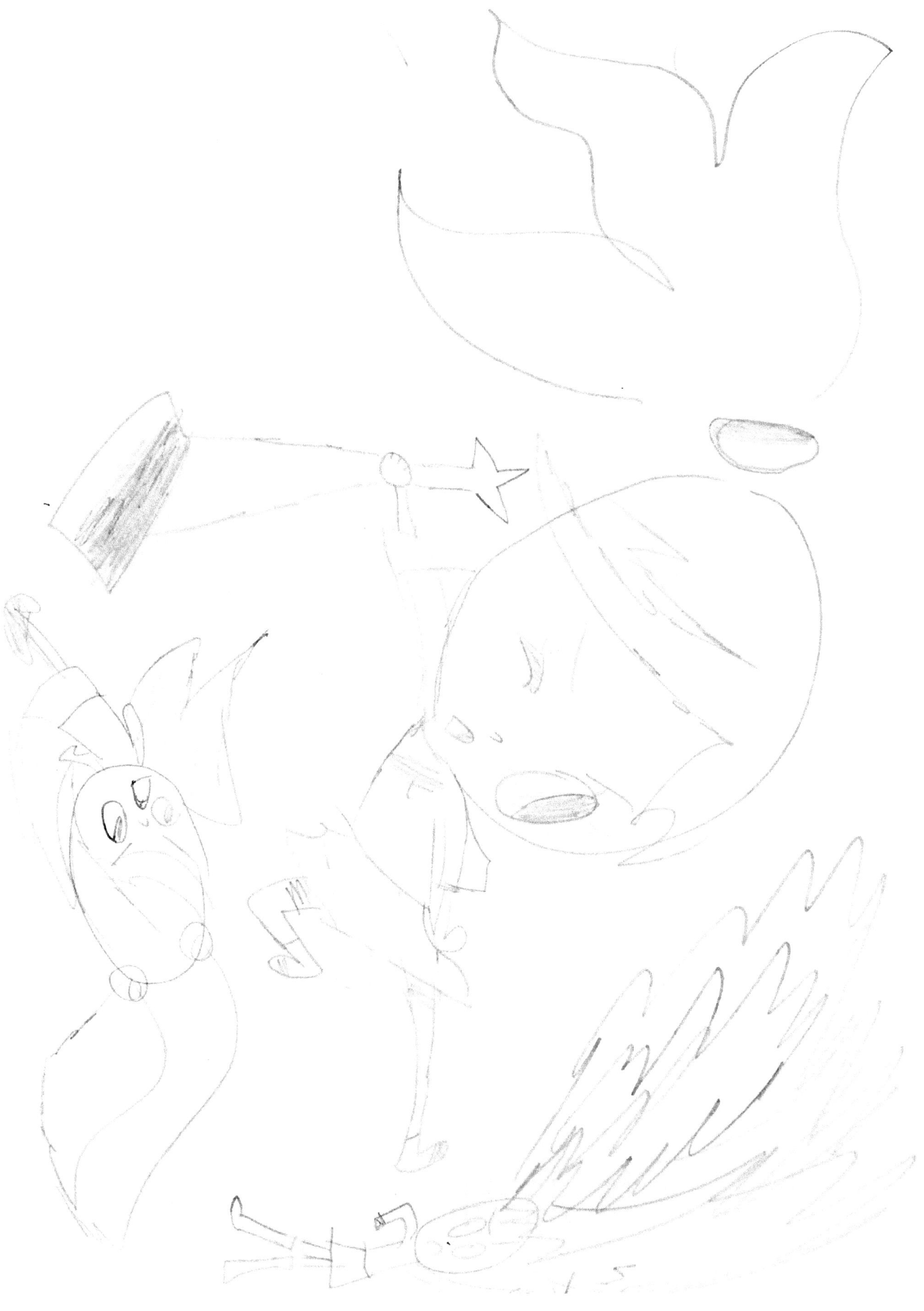

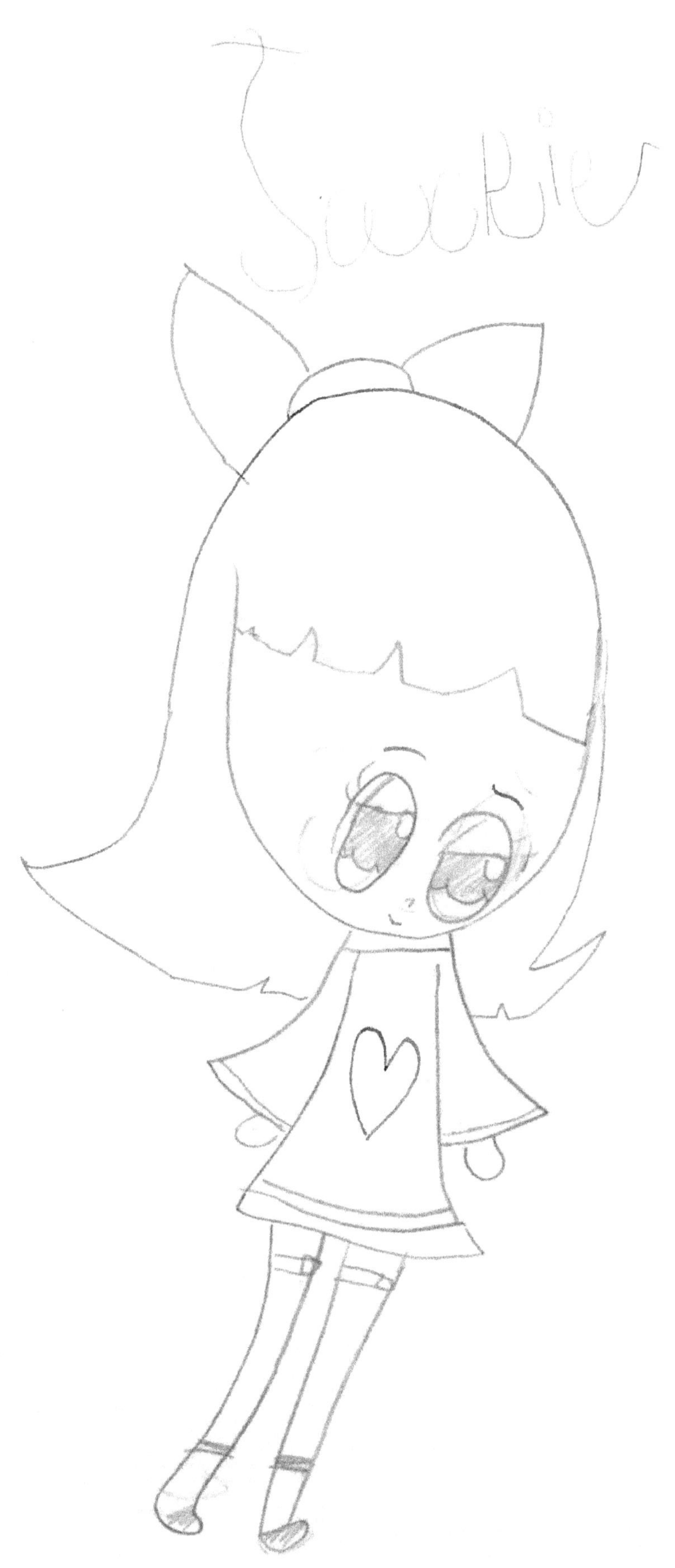

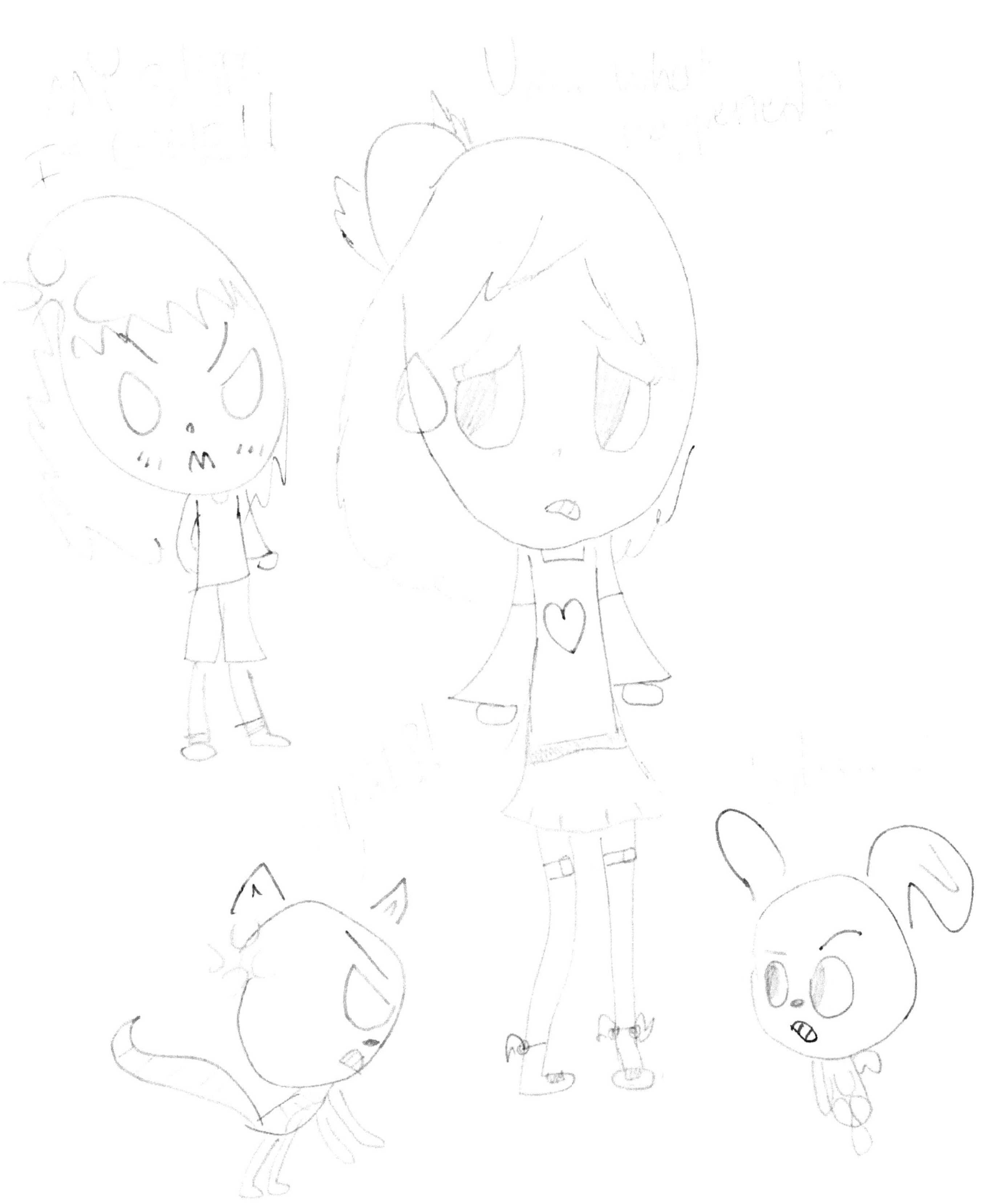

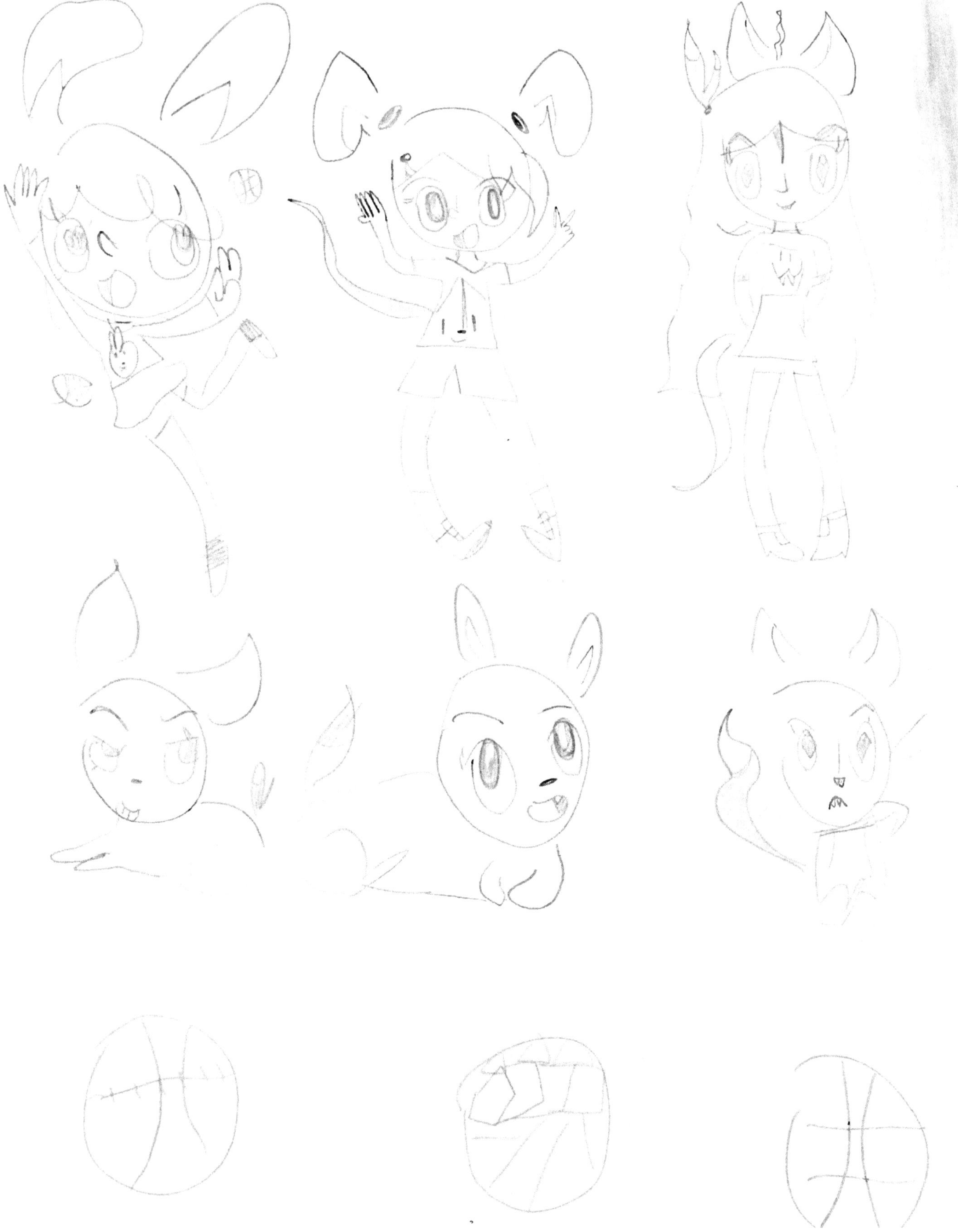

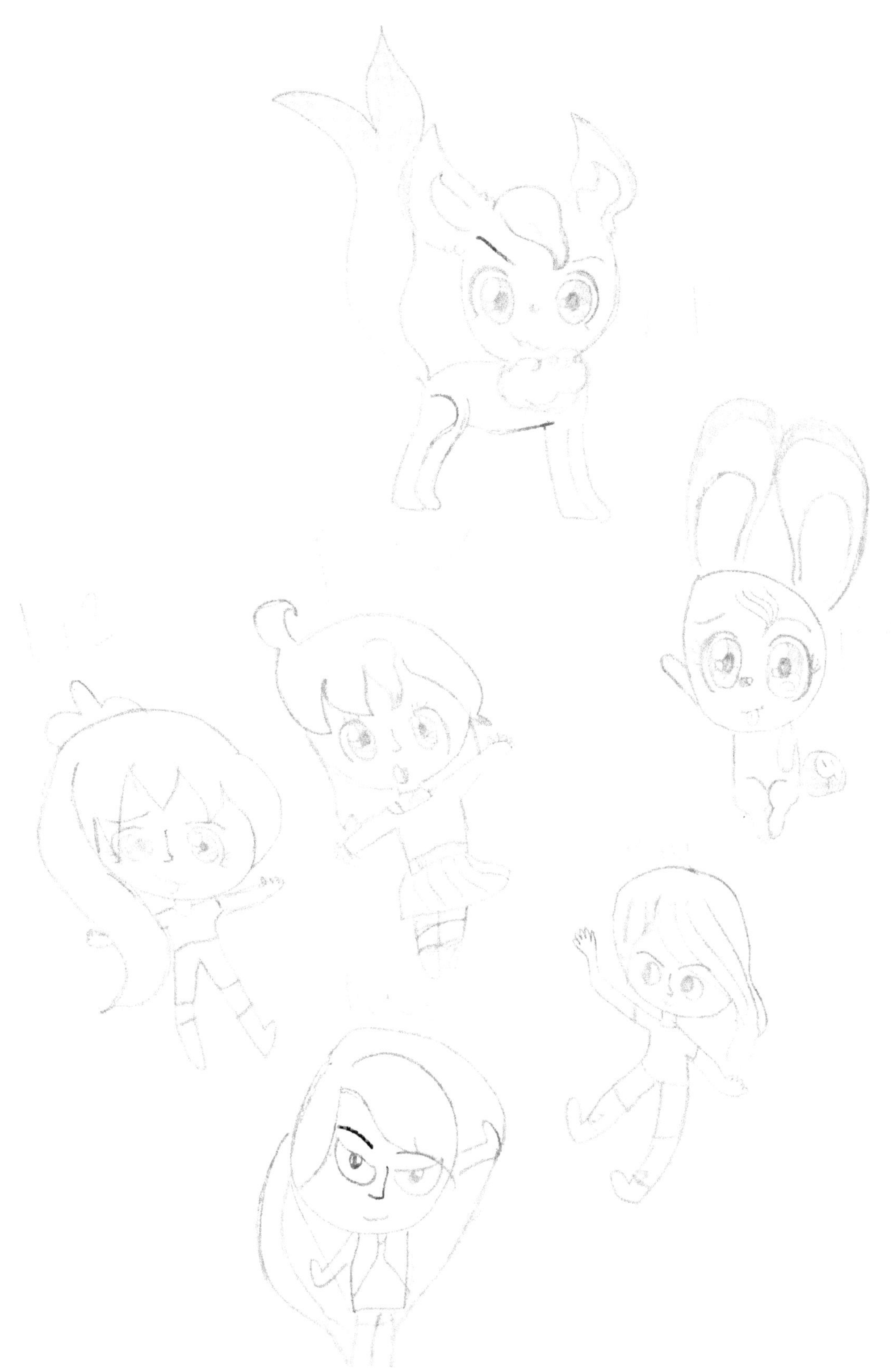

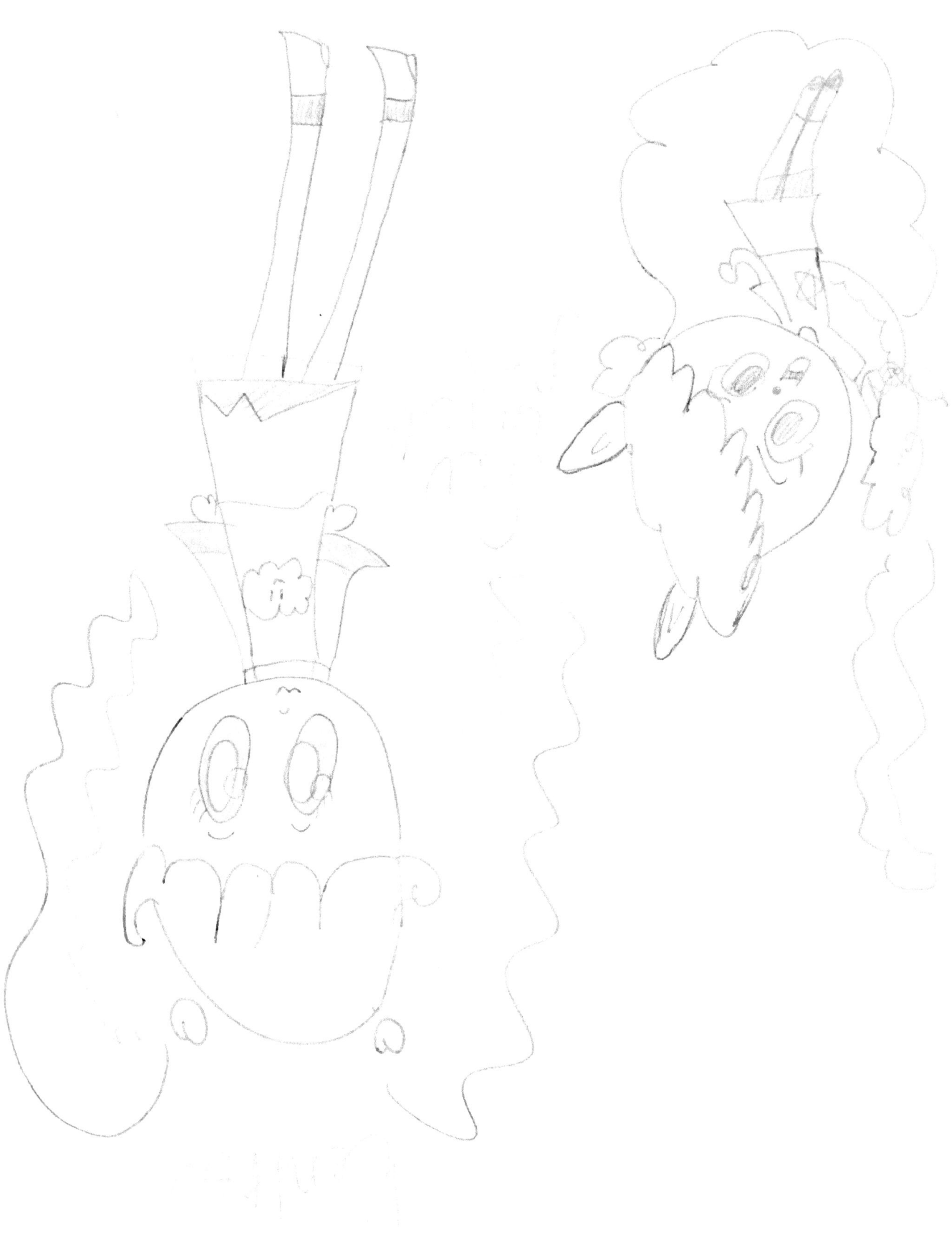

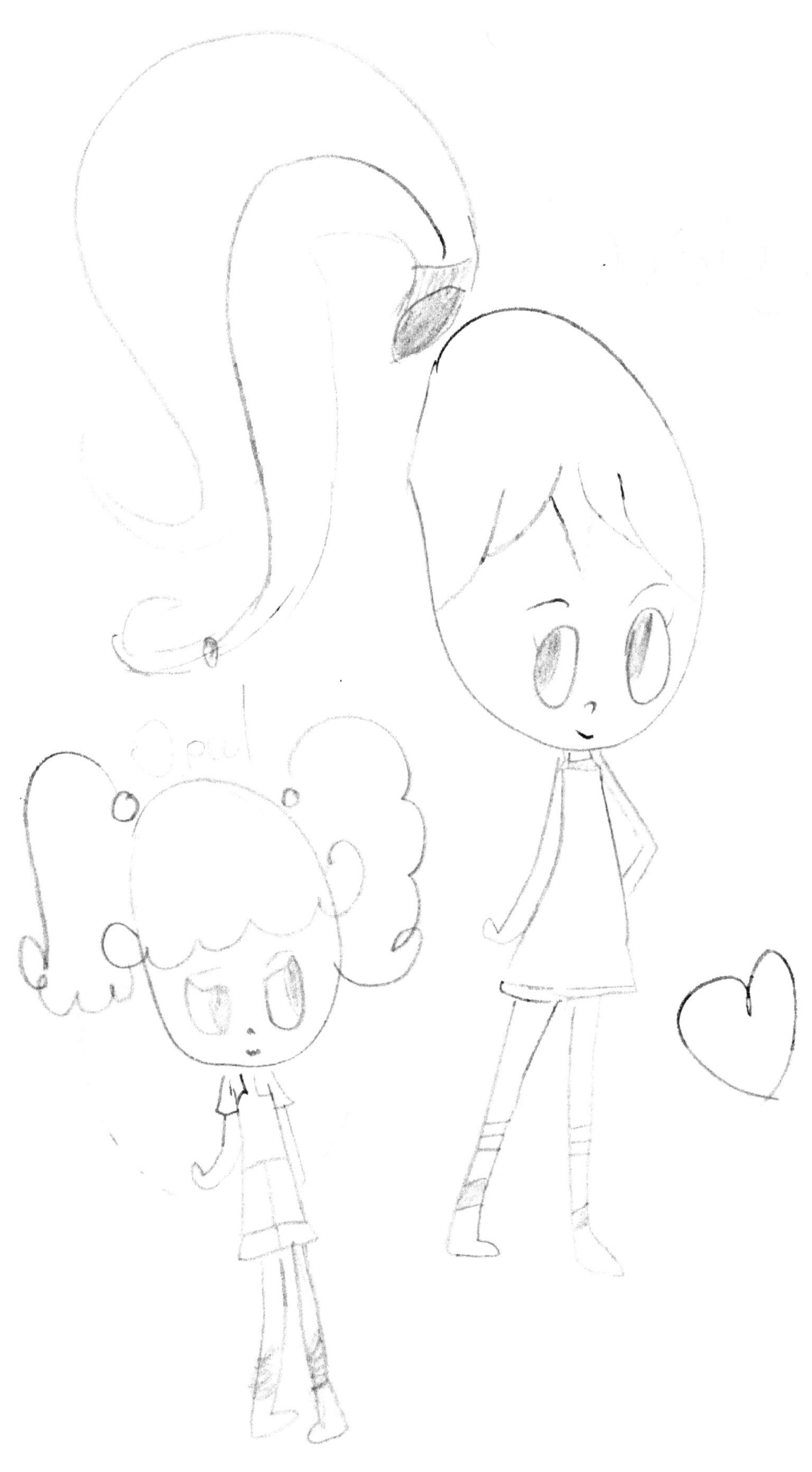
Opal

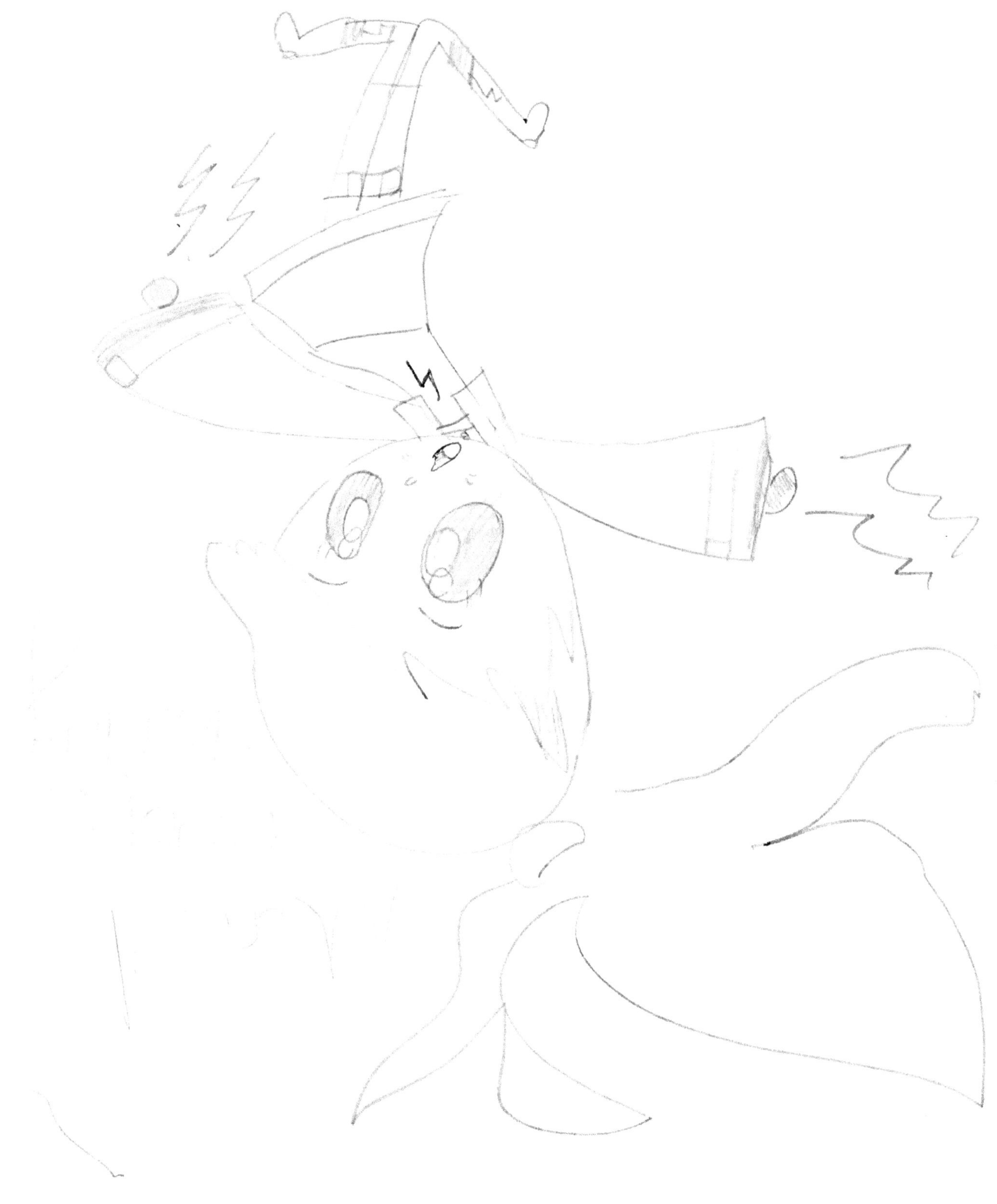

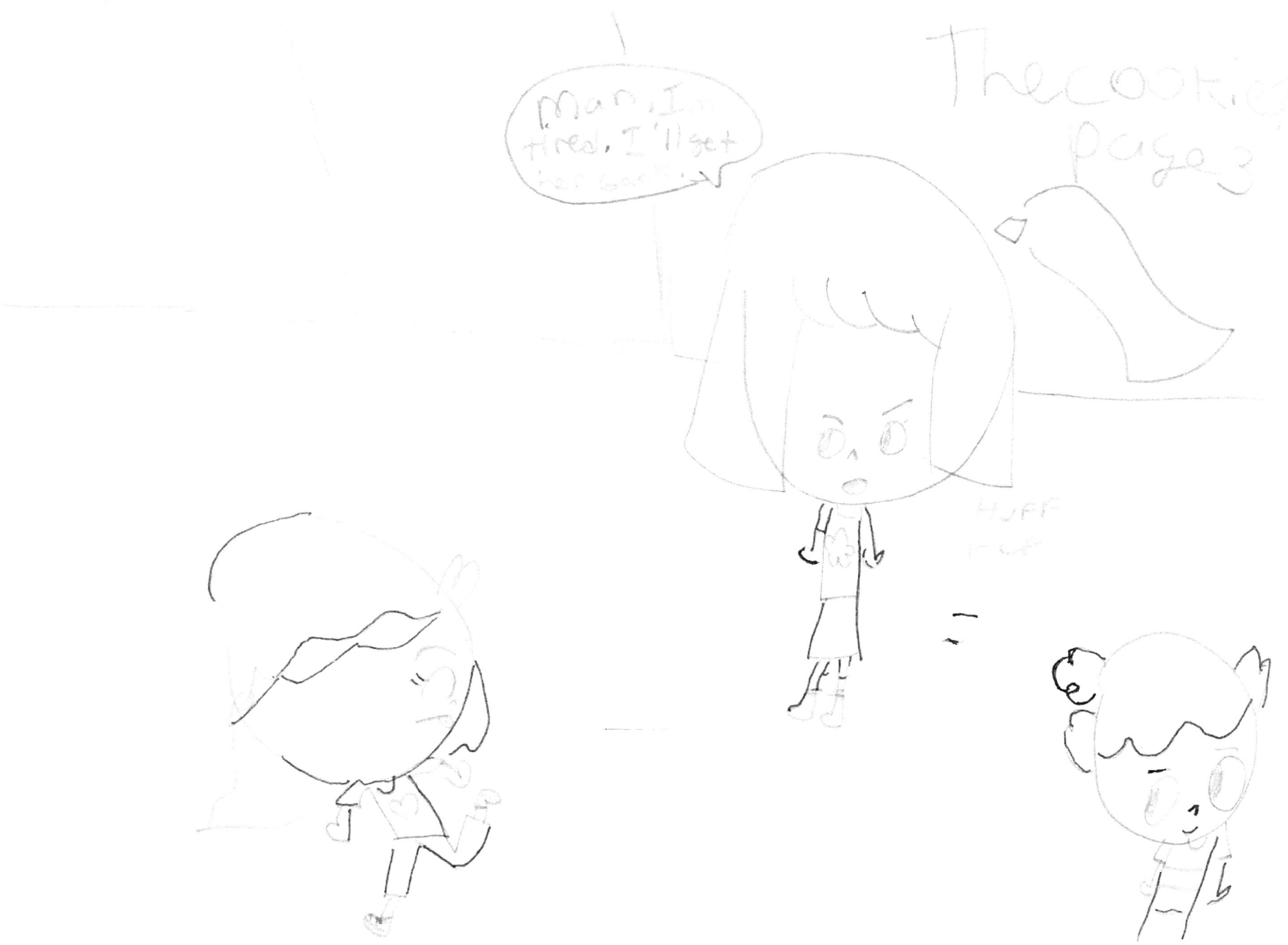
The cookie
page 3
Man, I'm
tired, I'll get
her back!
HUFF
PUFF

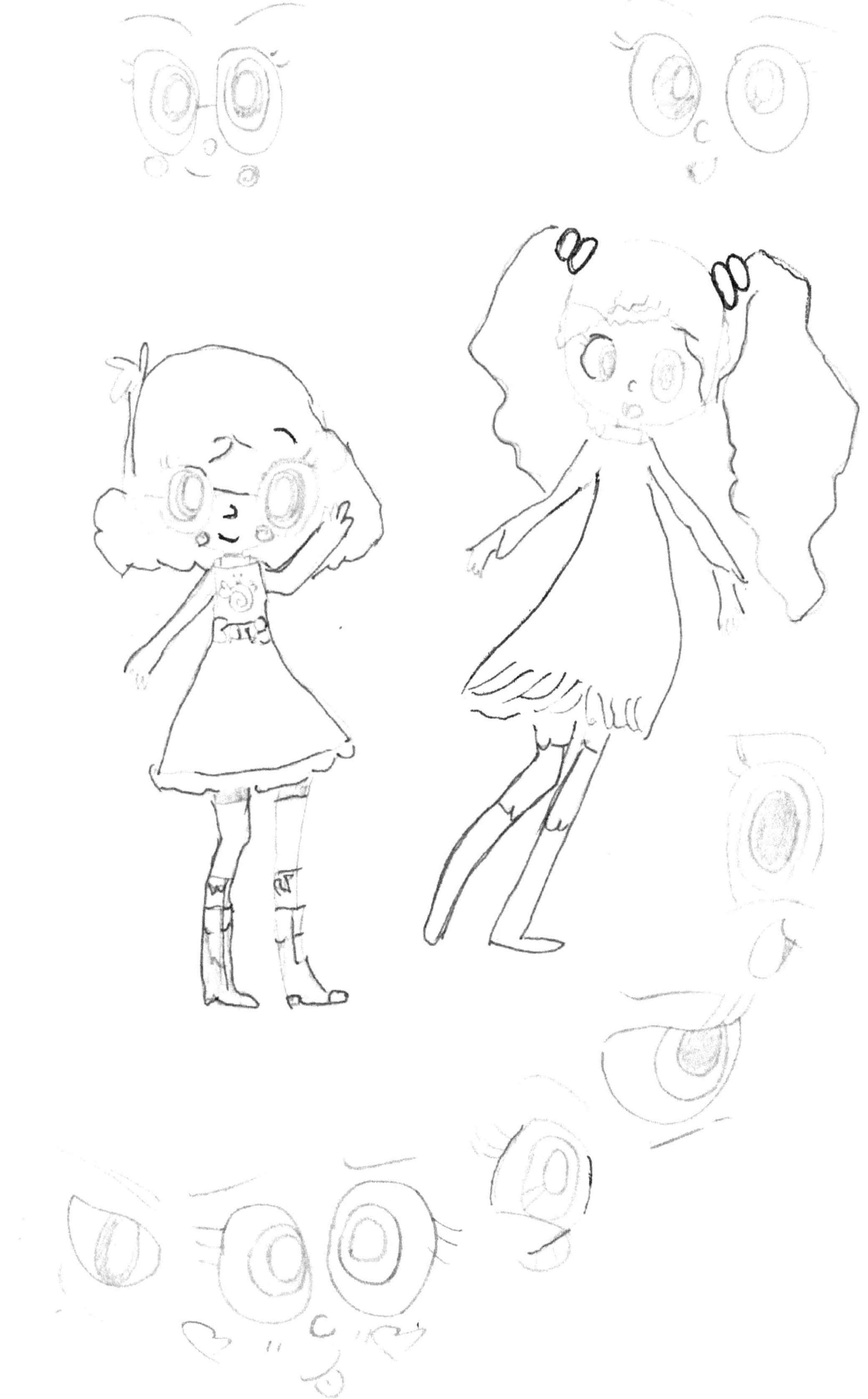

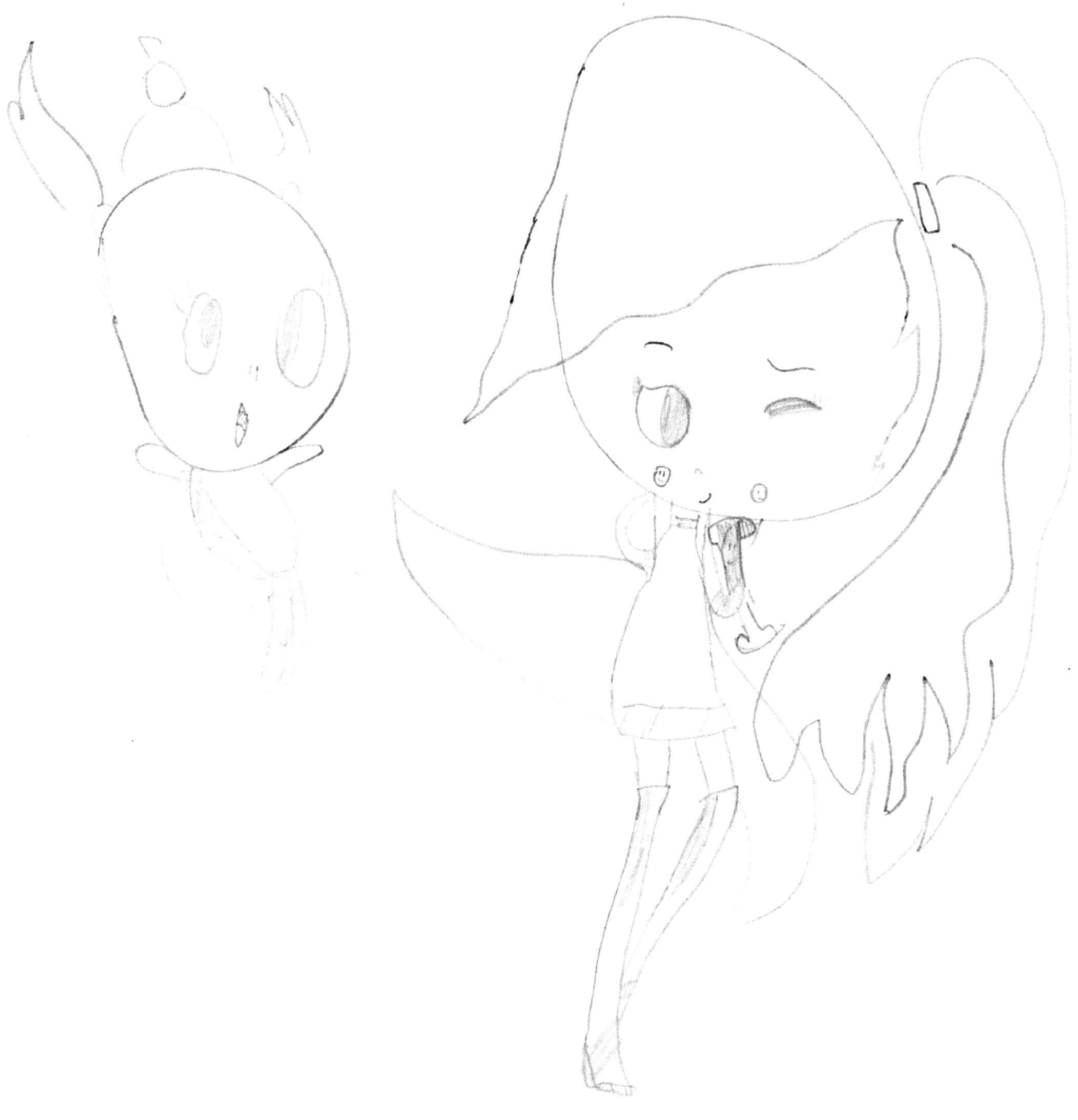

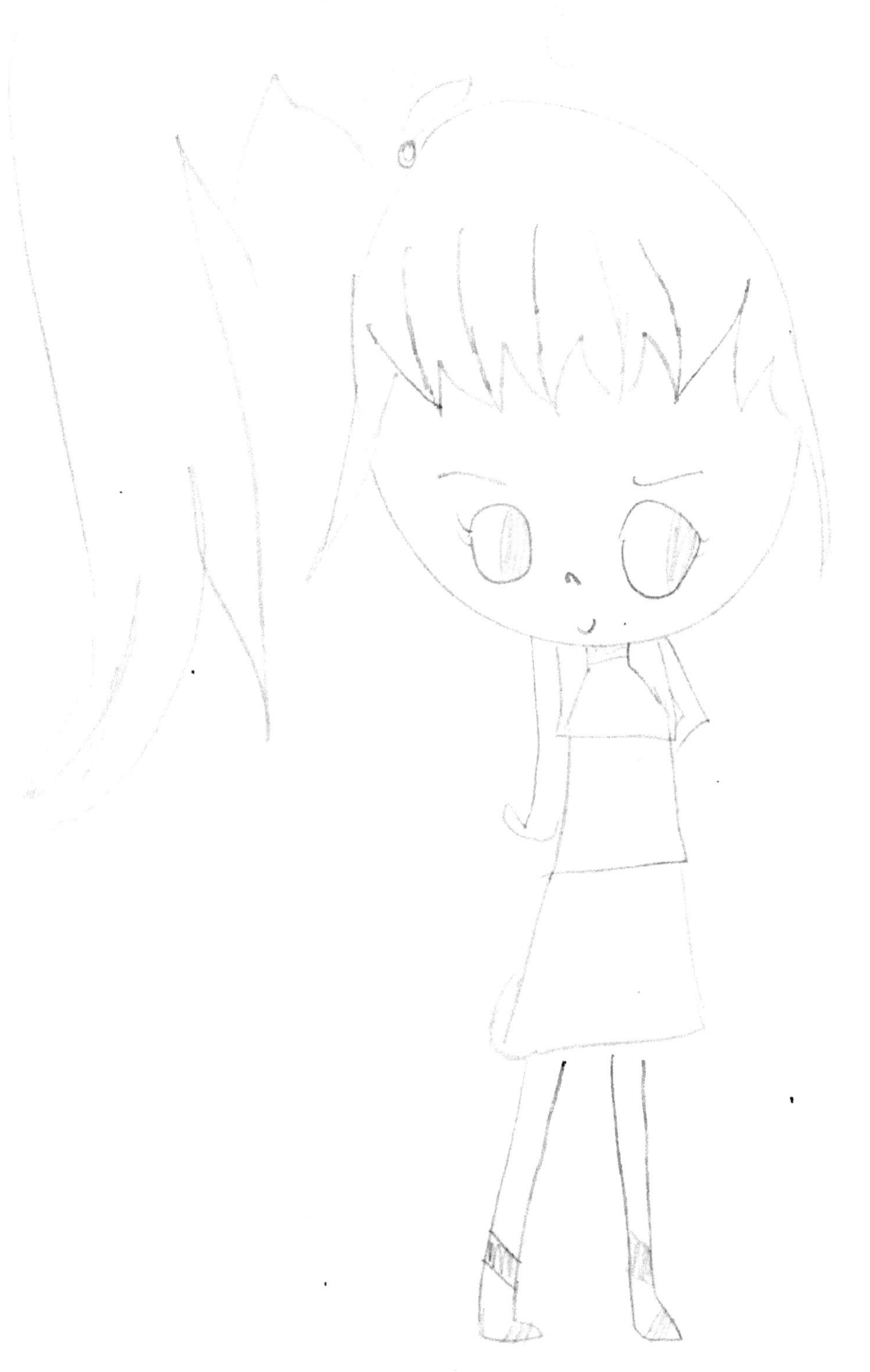

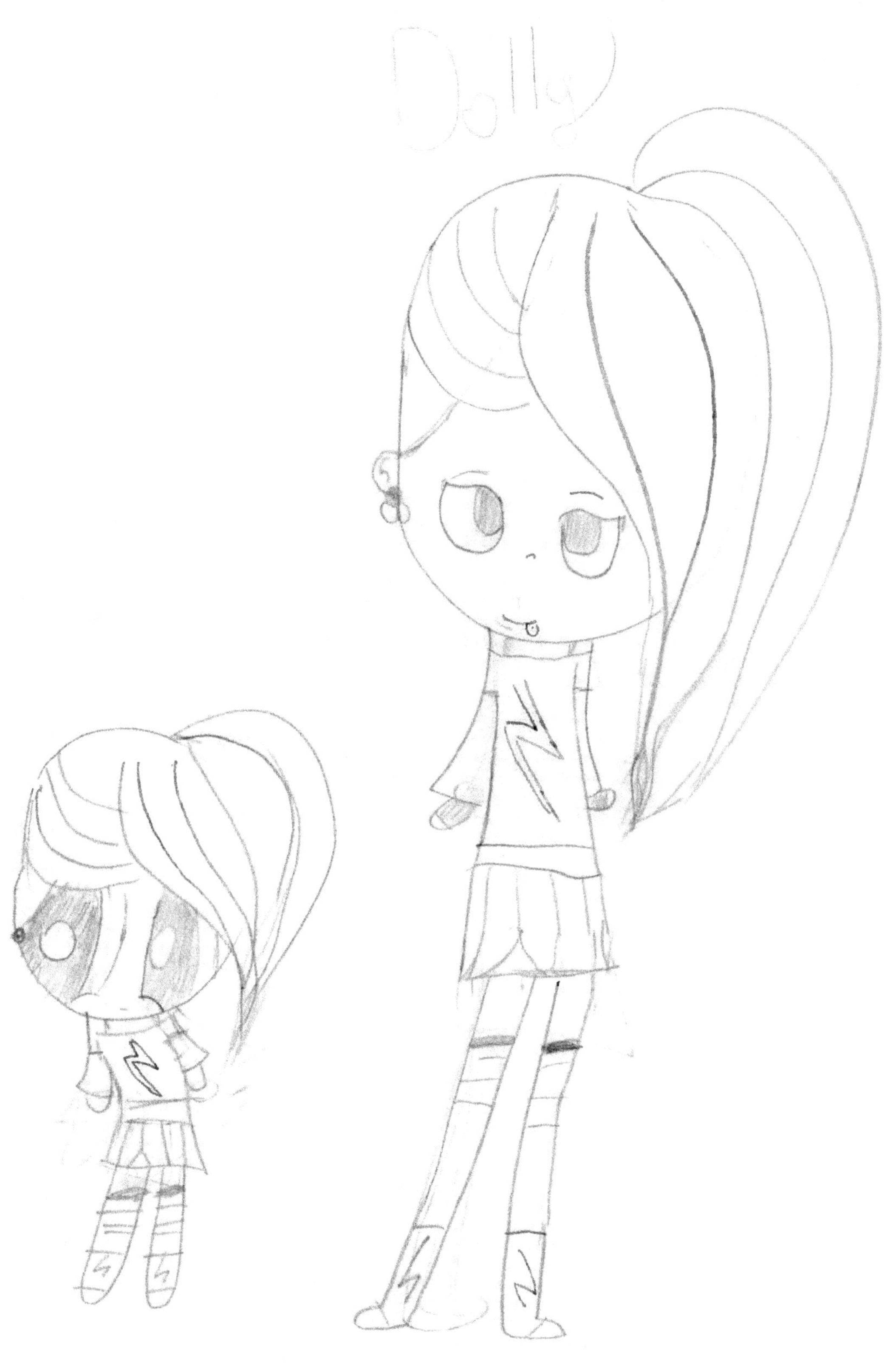
Dolly

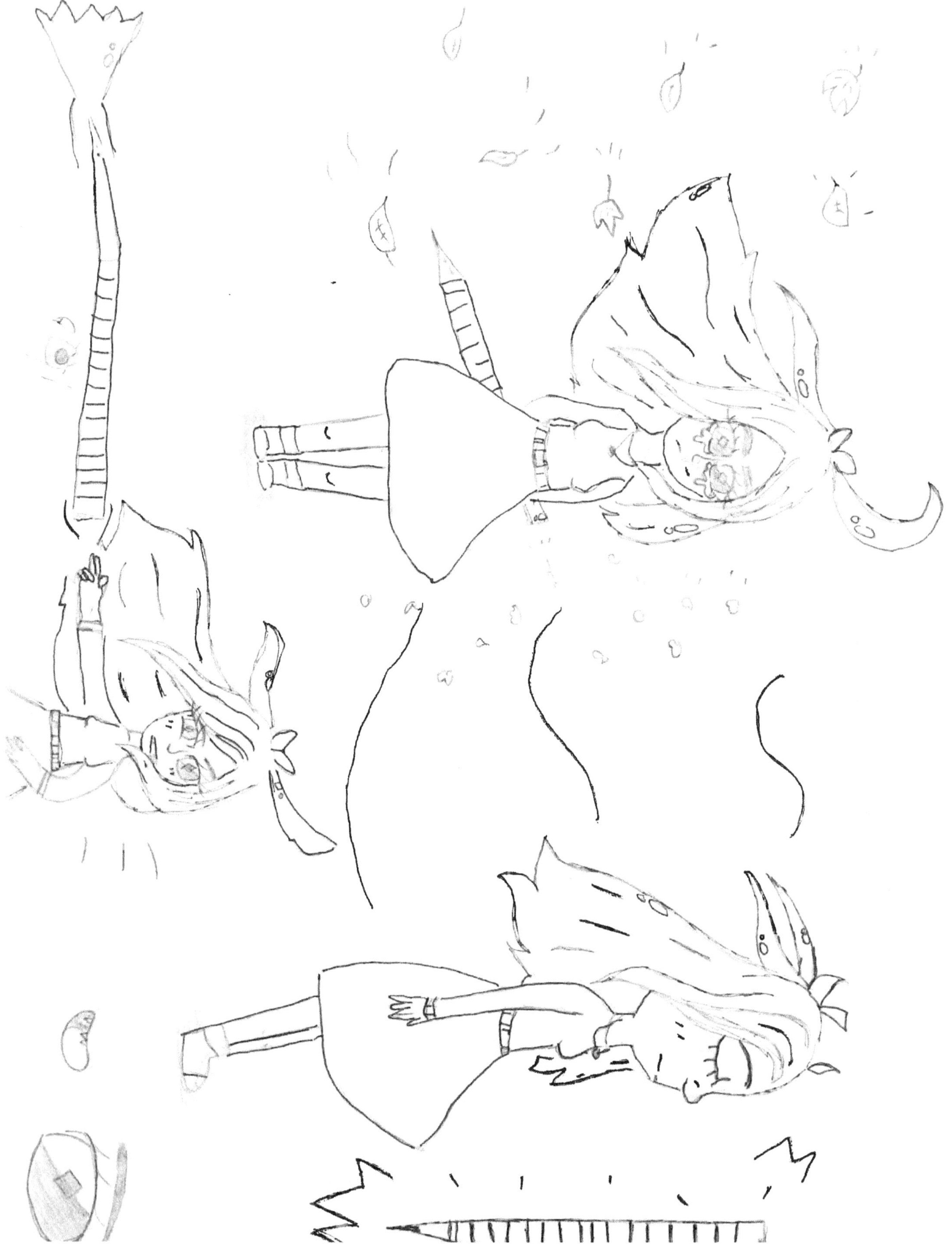

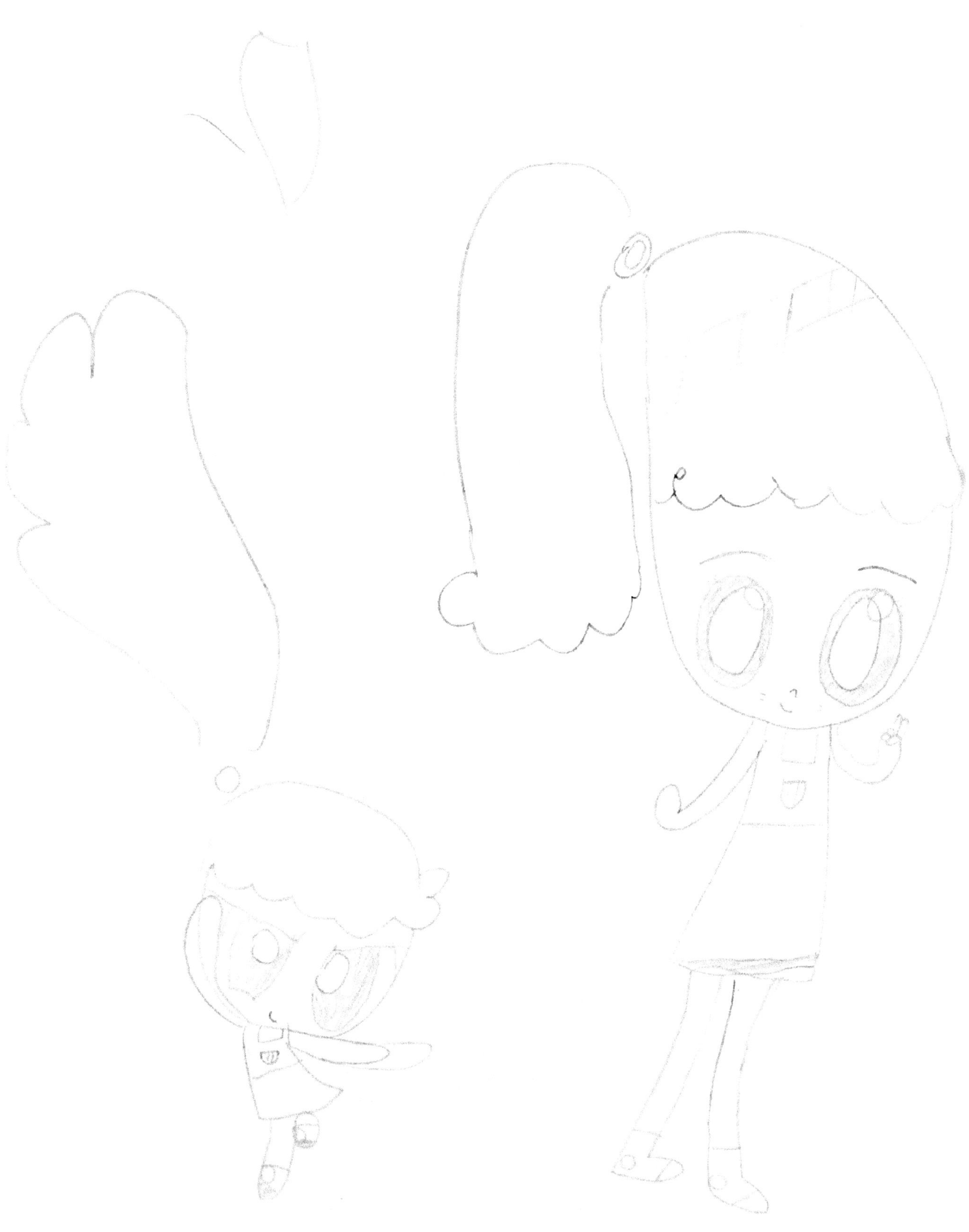

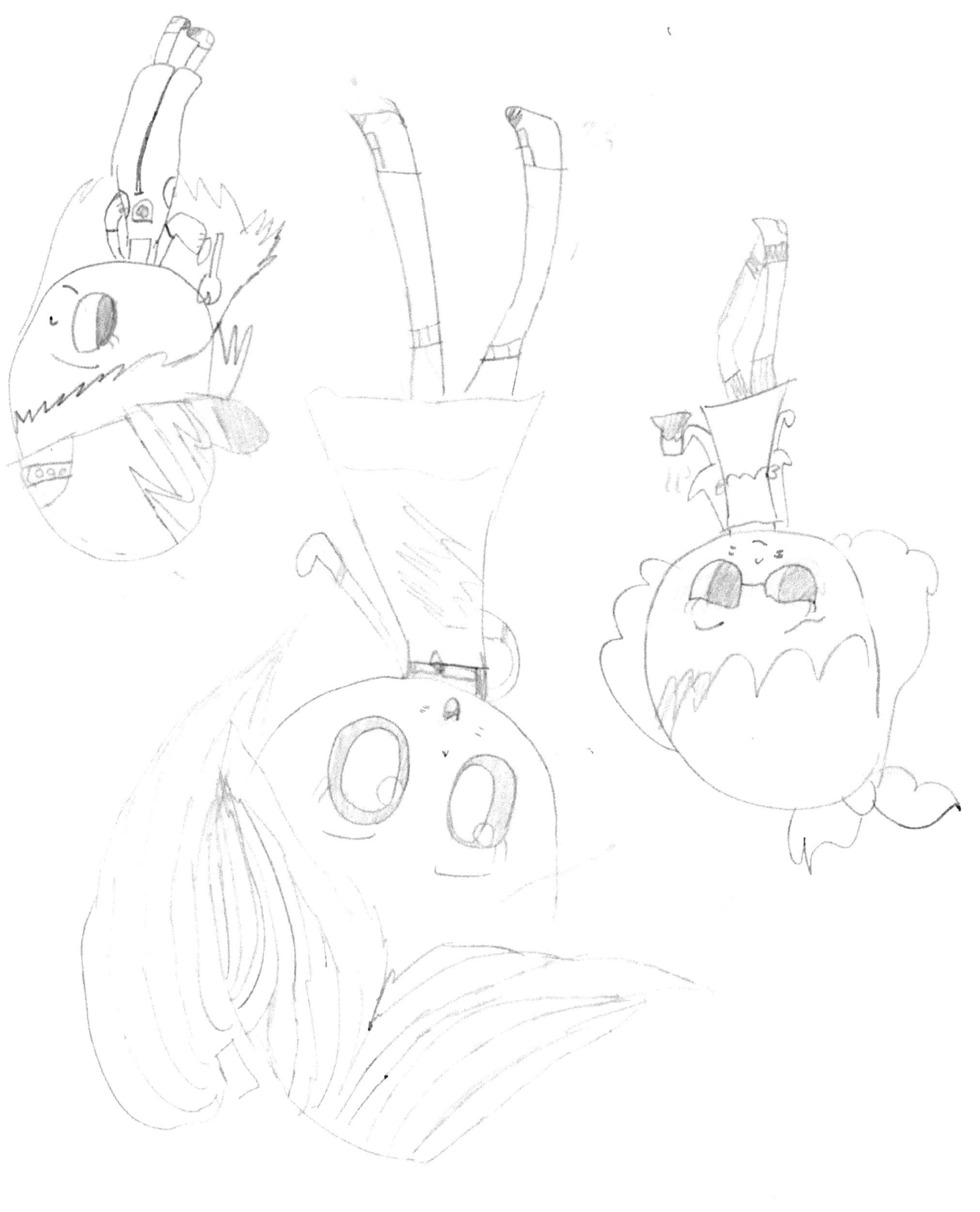

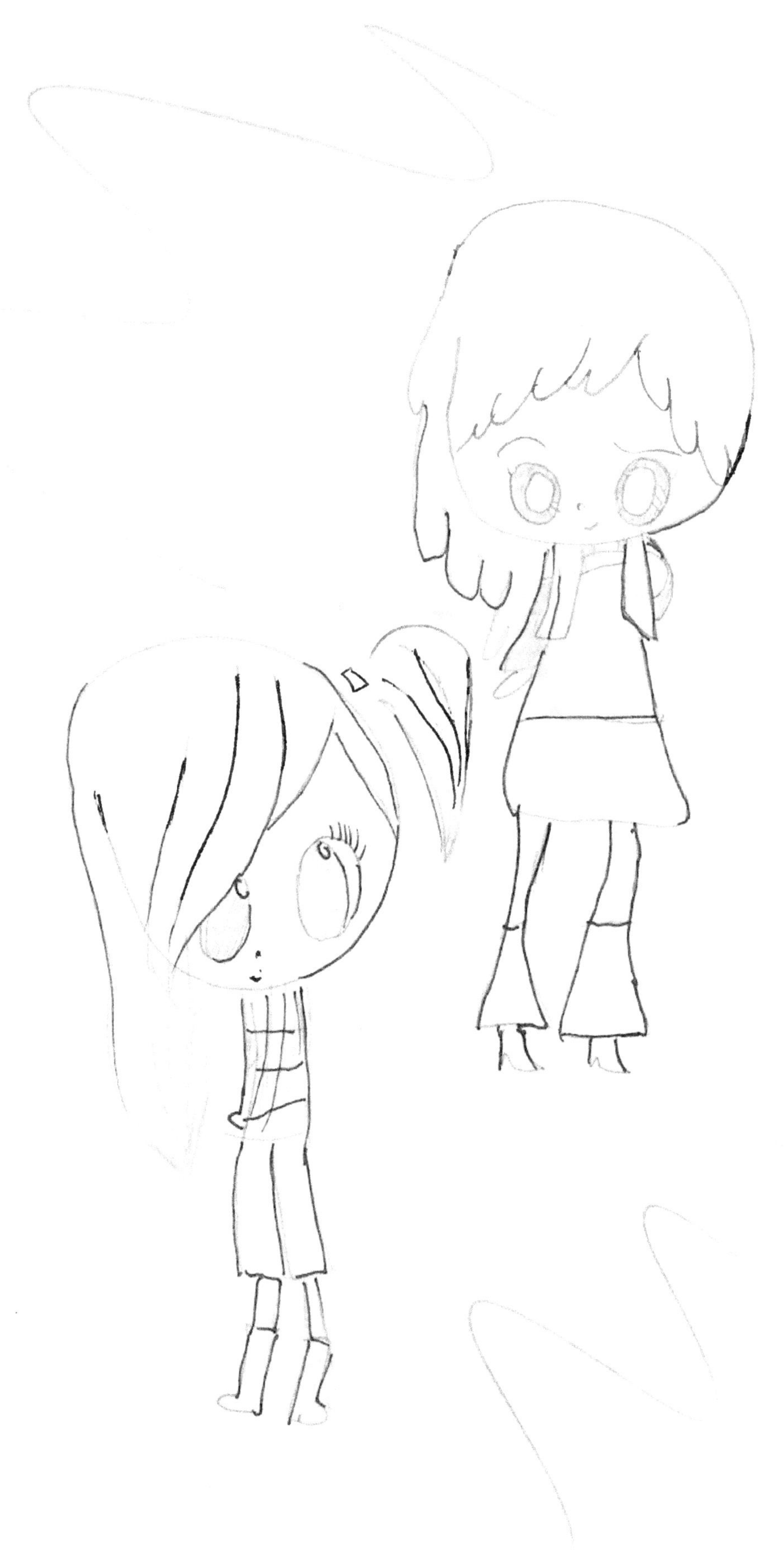

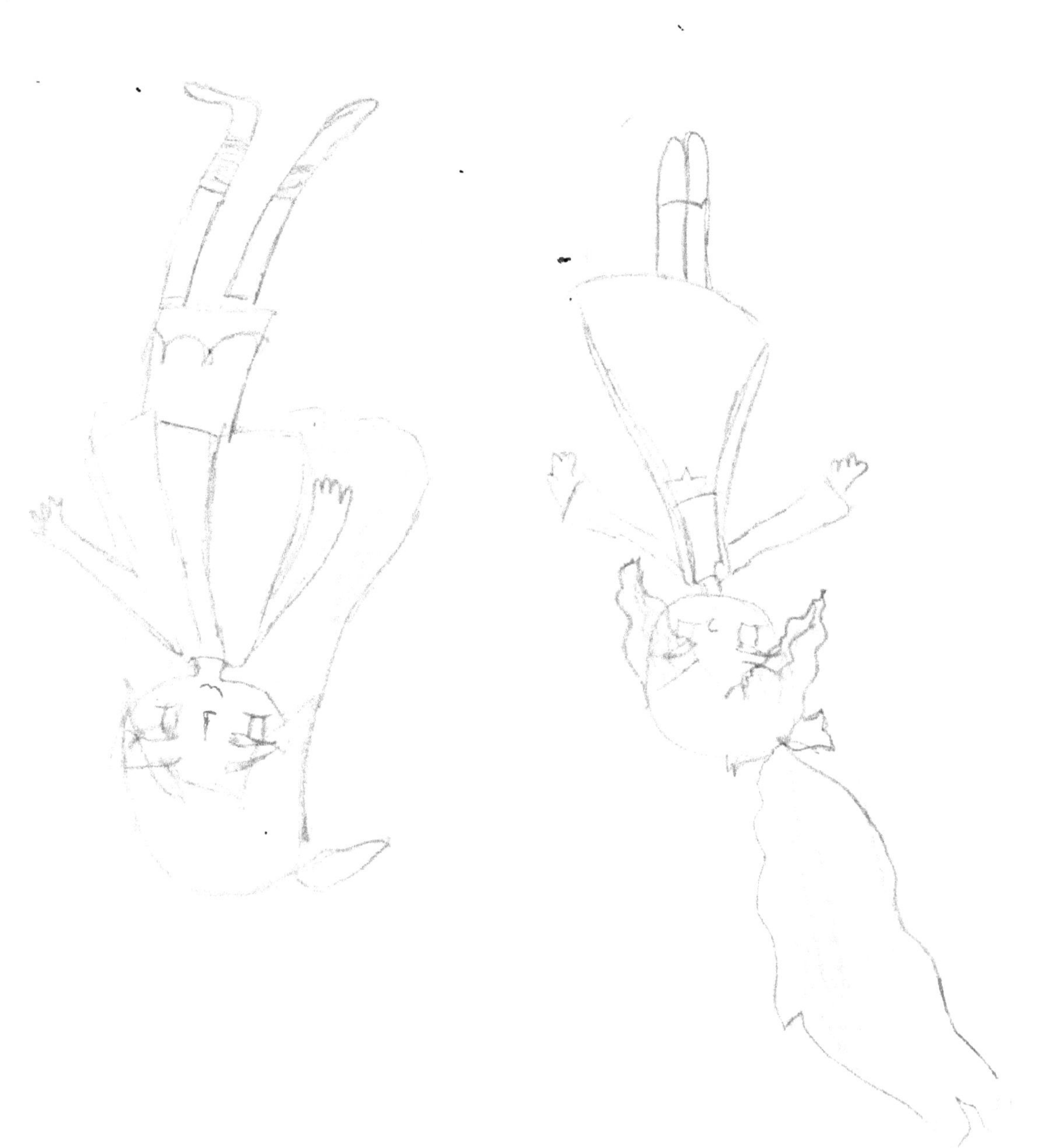

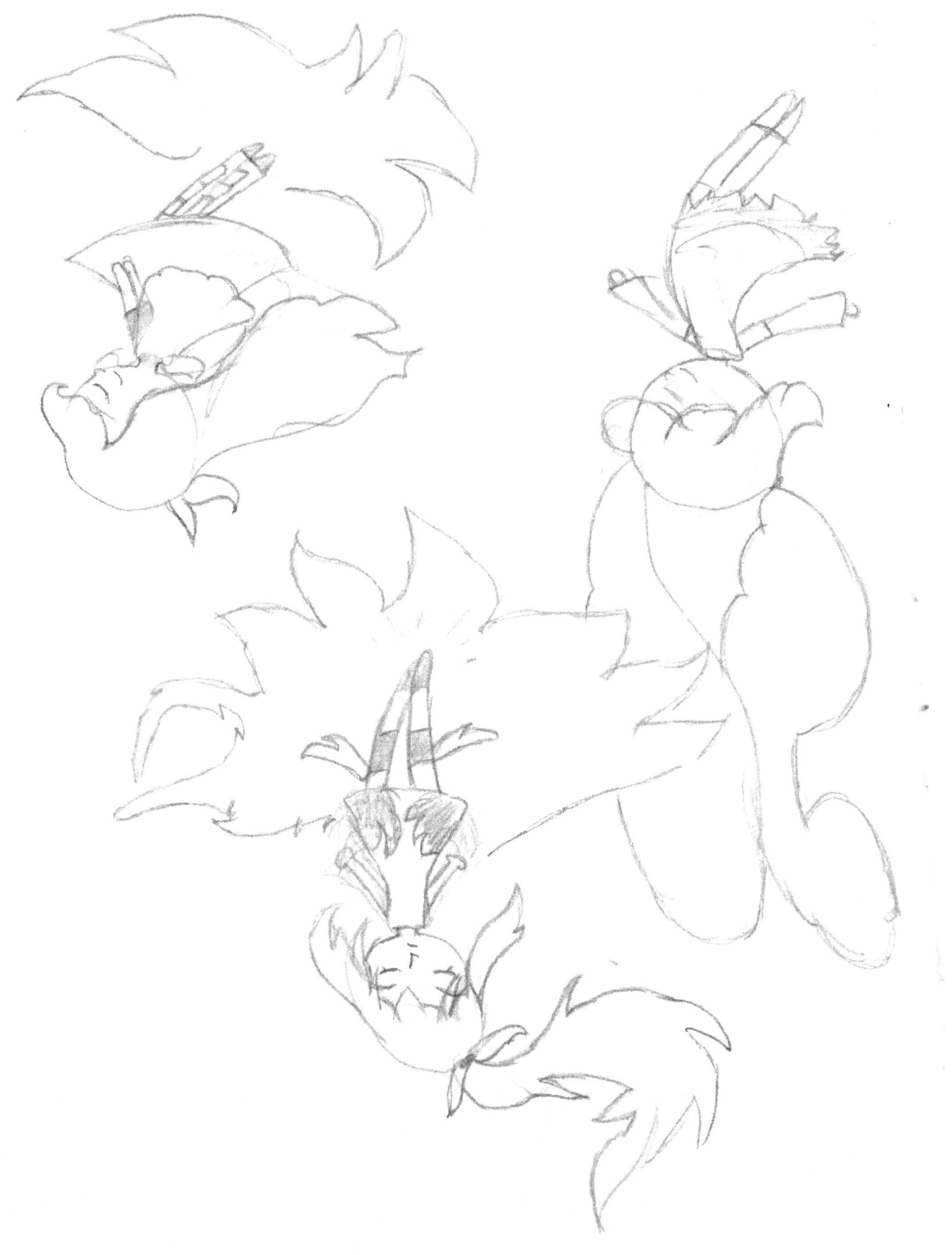

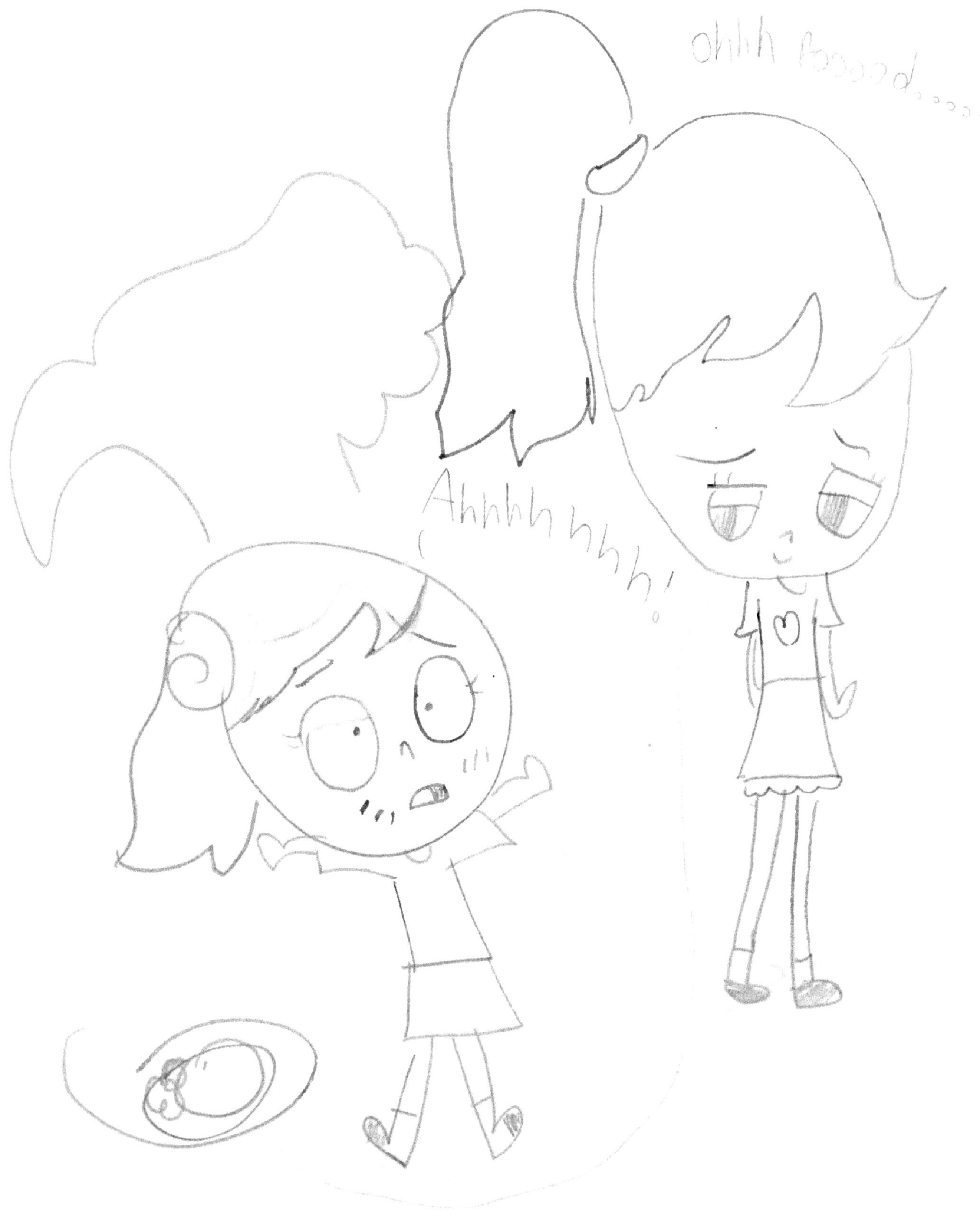
Ohhh Boooo d.....
Ahhhhhhhh!

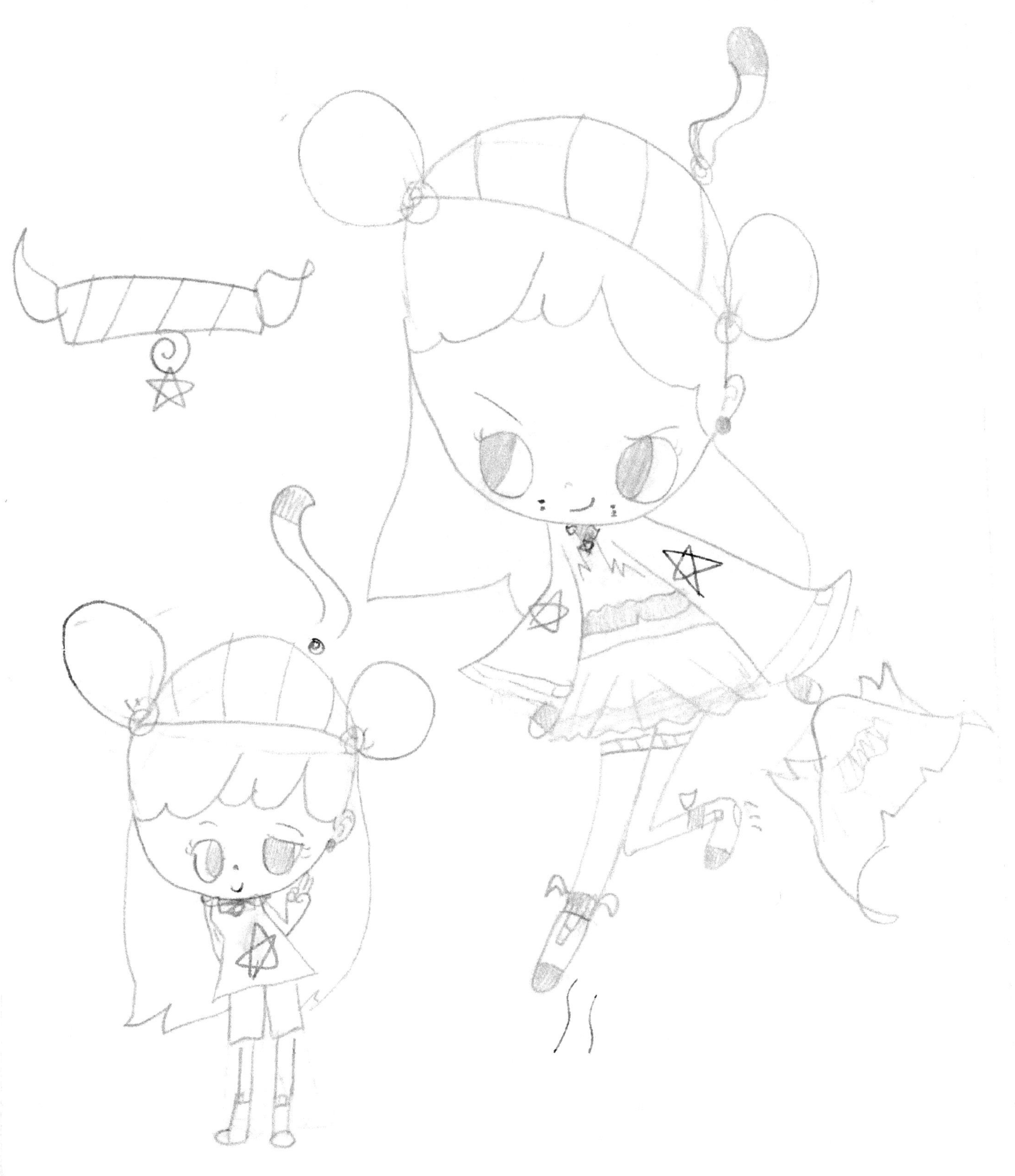

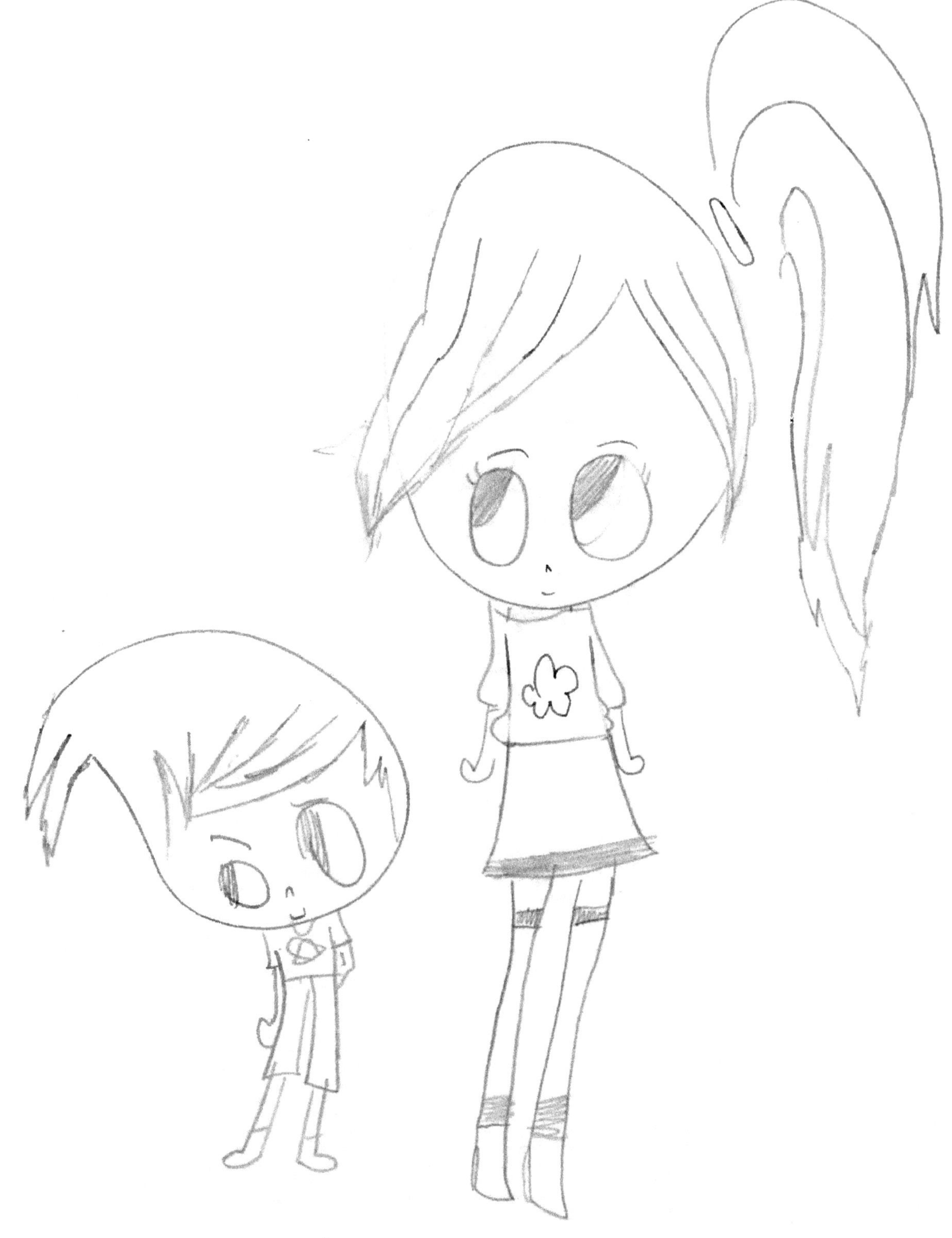

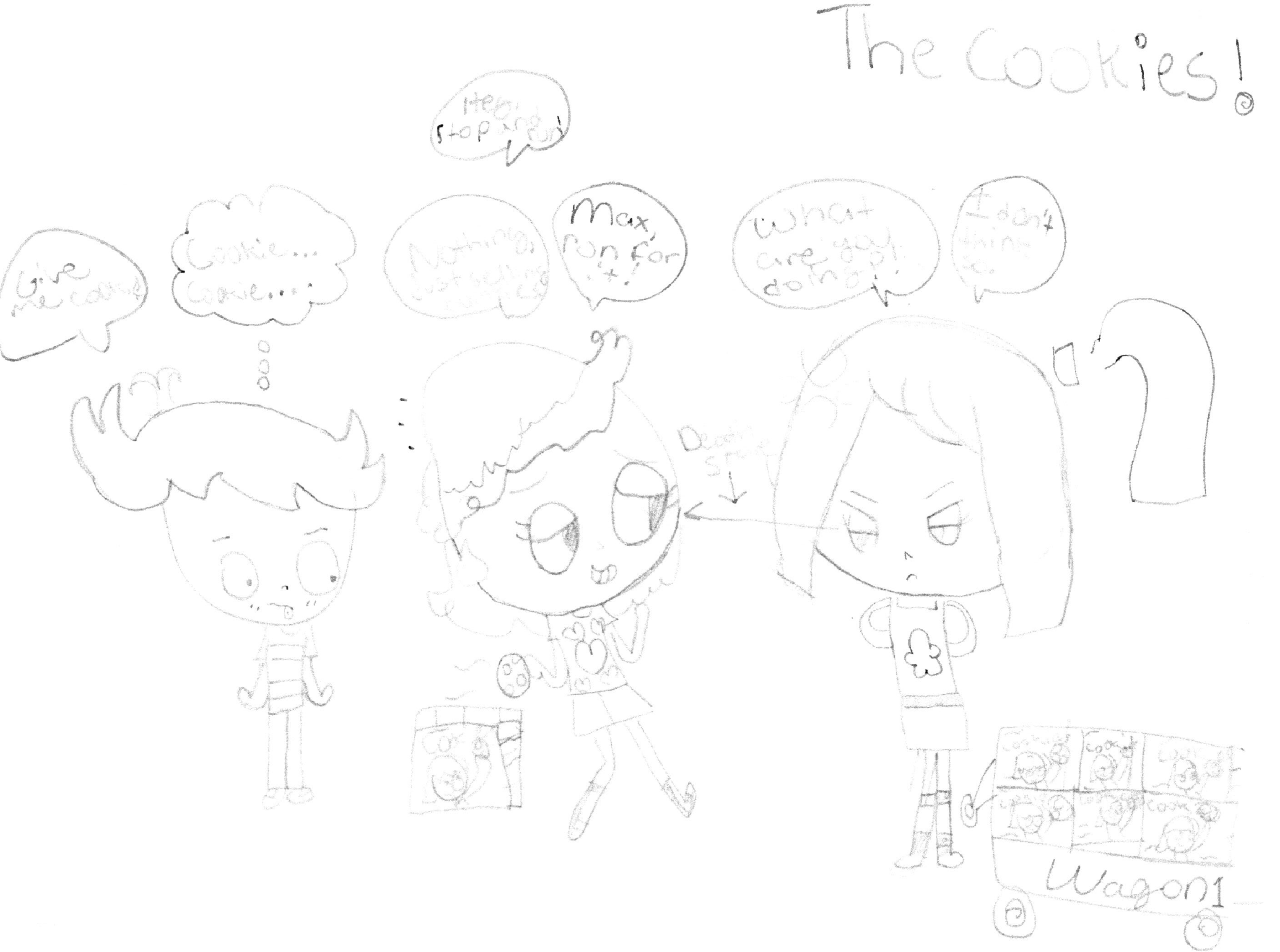
The Cookies!
Cookie....
Cookie....
Max, run for it!
What are you doing?!
Wagon1

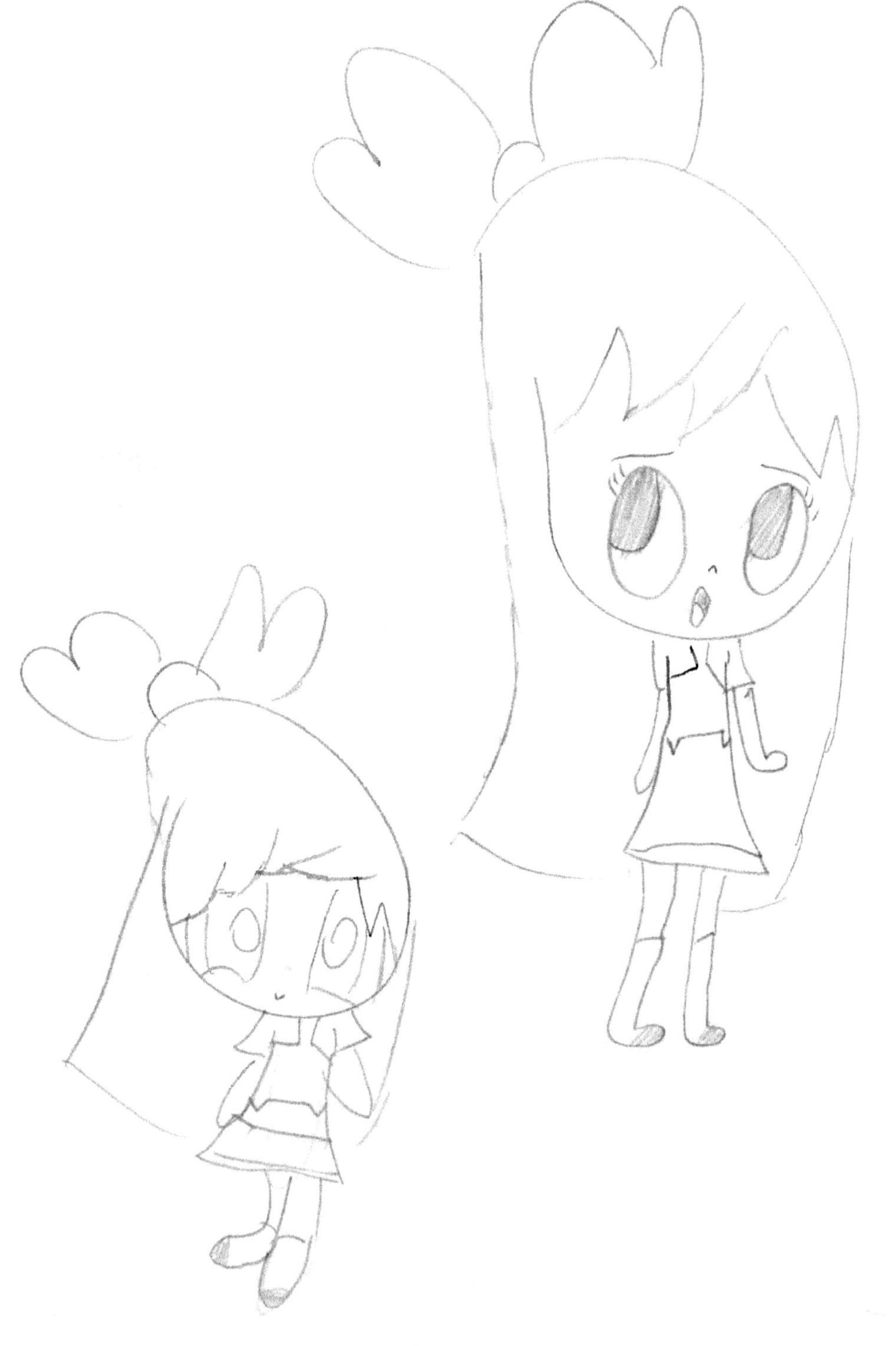

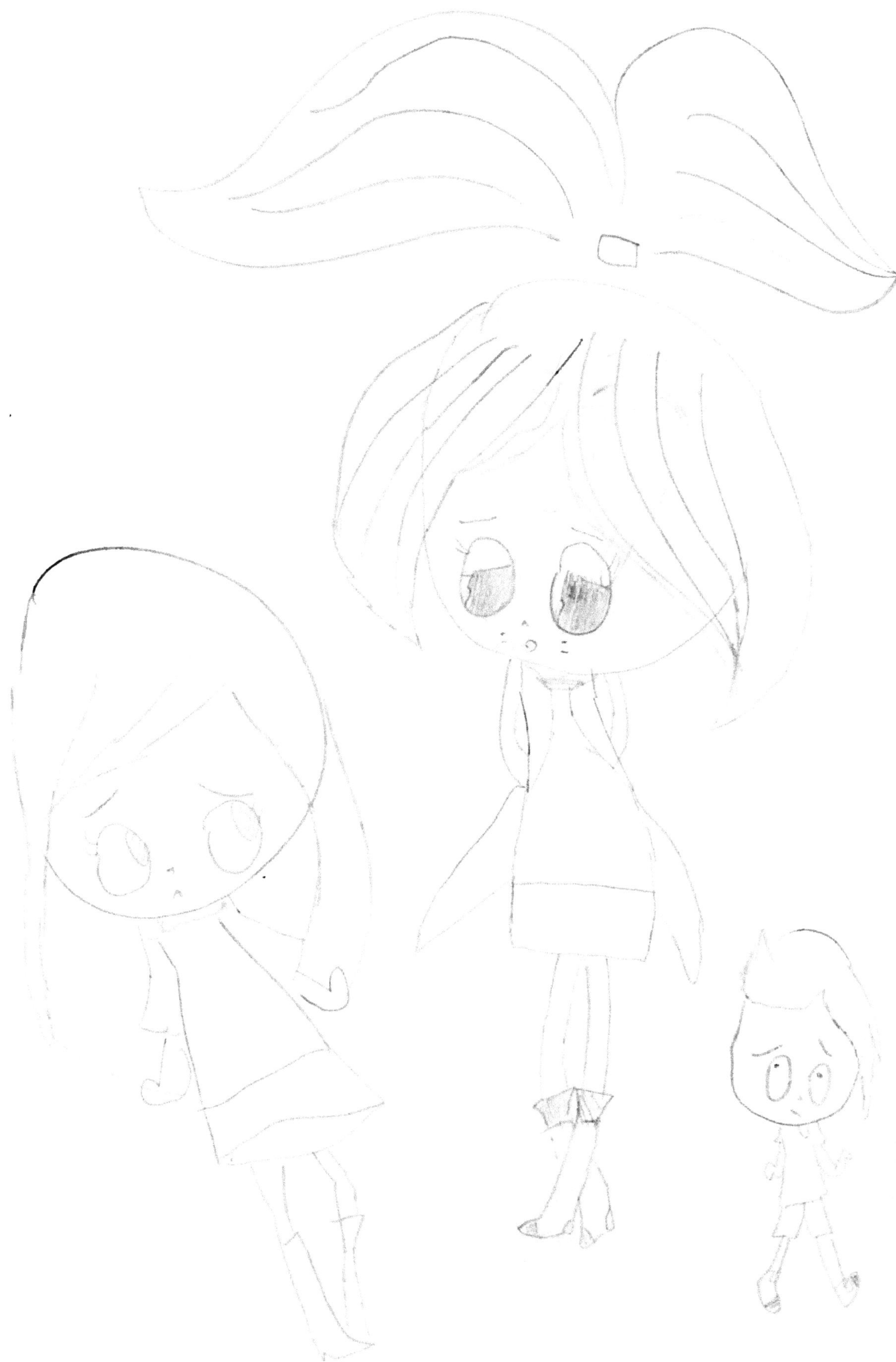

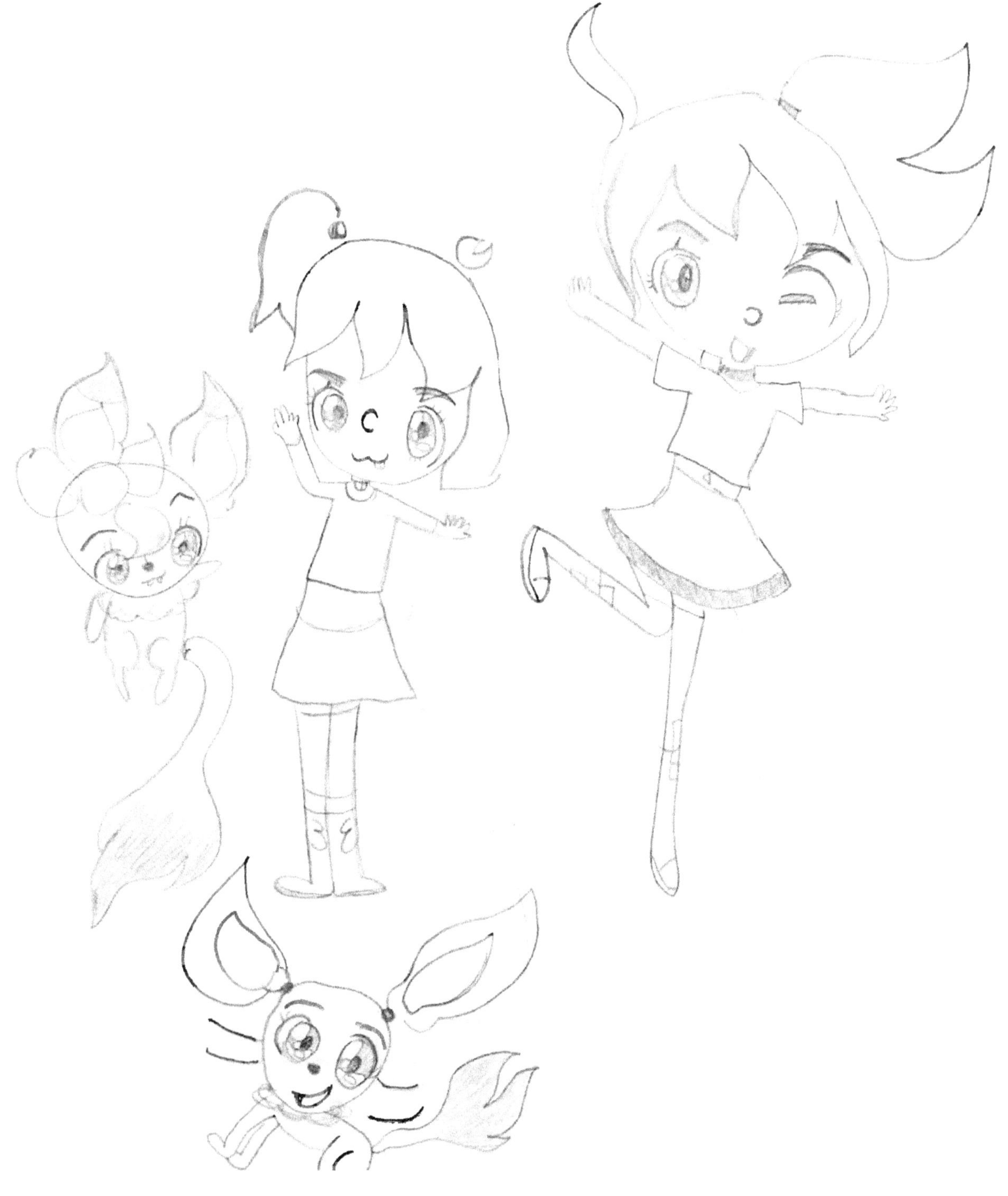

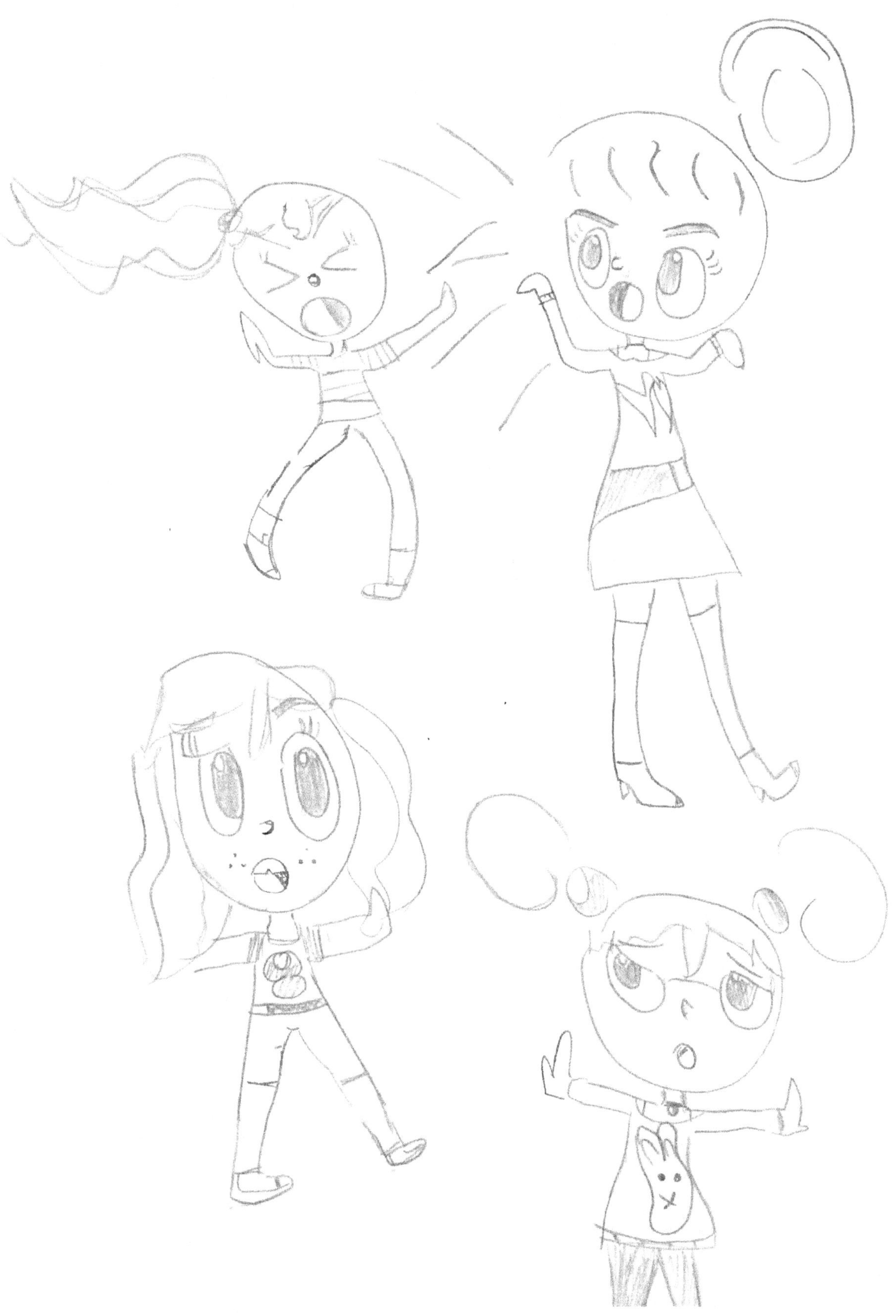

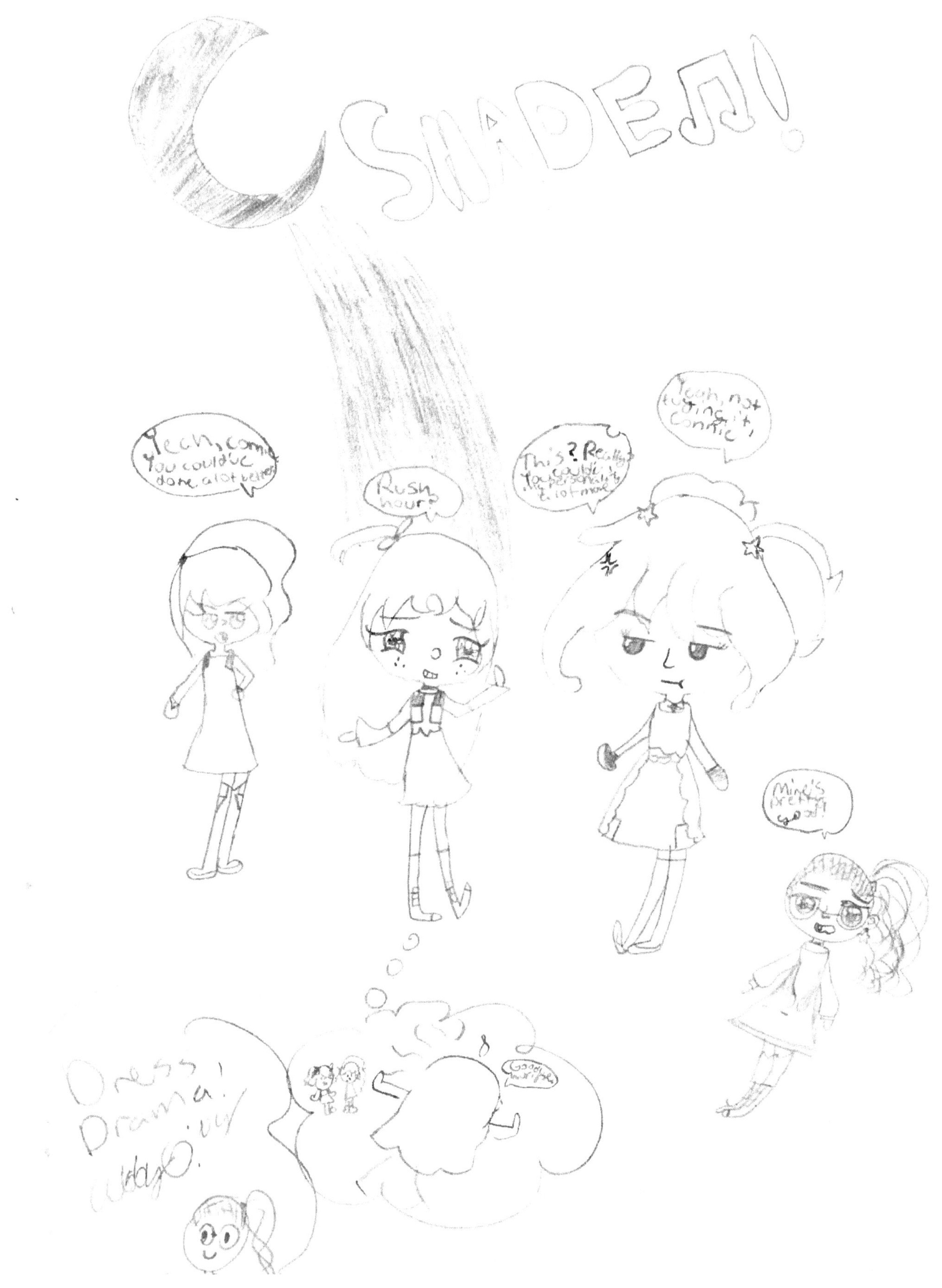
SHADE♫!
Yeah, not tuging it, Connie!
This? Really? could've your personality a lot more
Rush hour?
Mine's pretty good!
Dress! Drama!

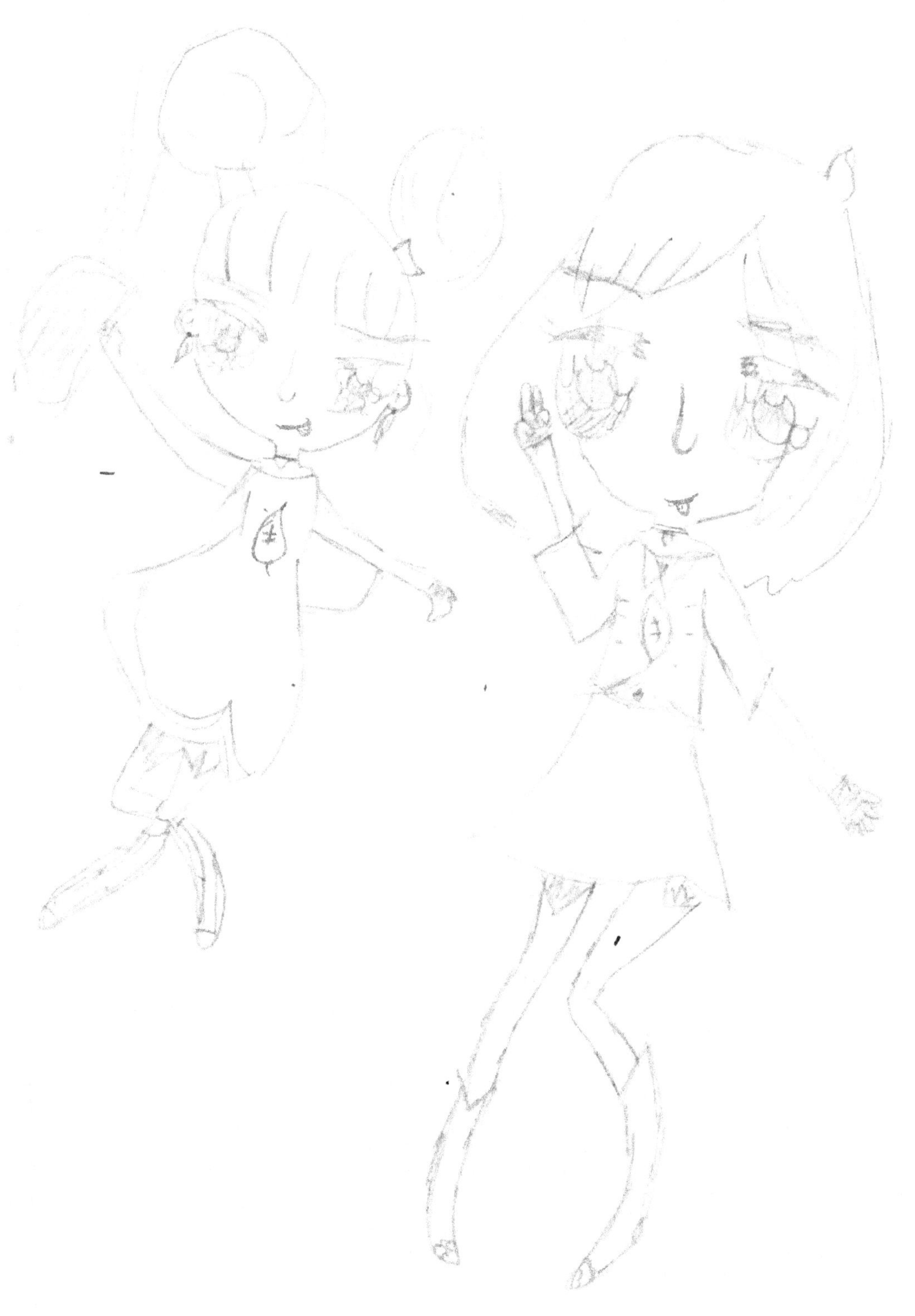

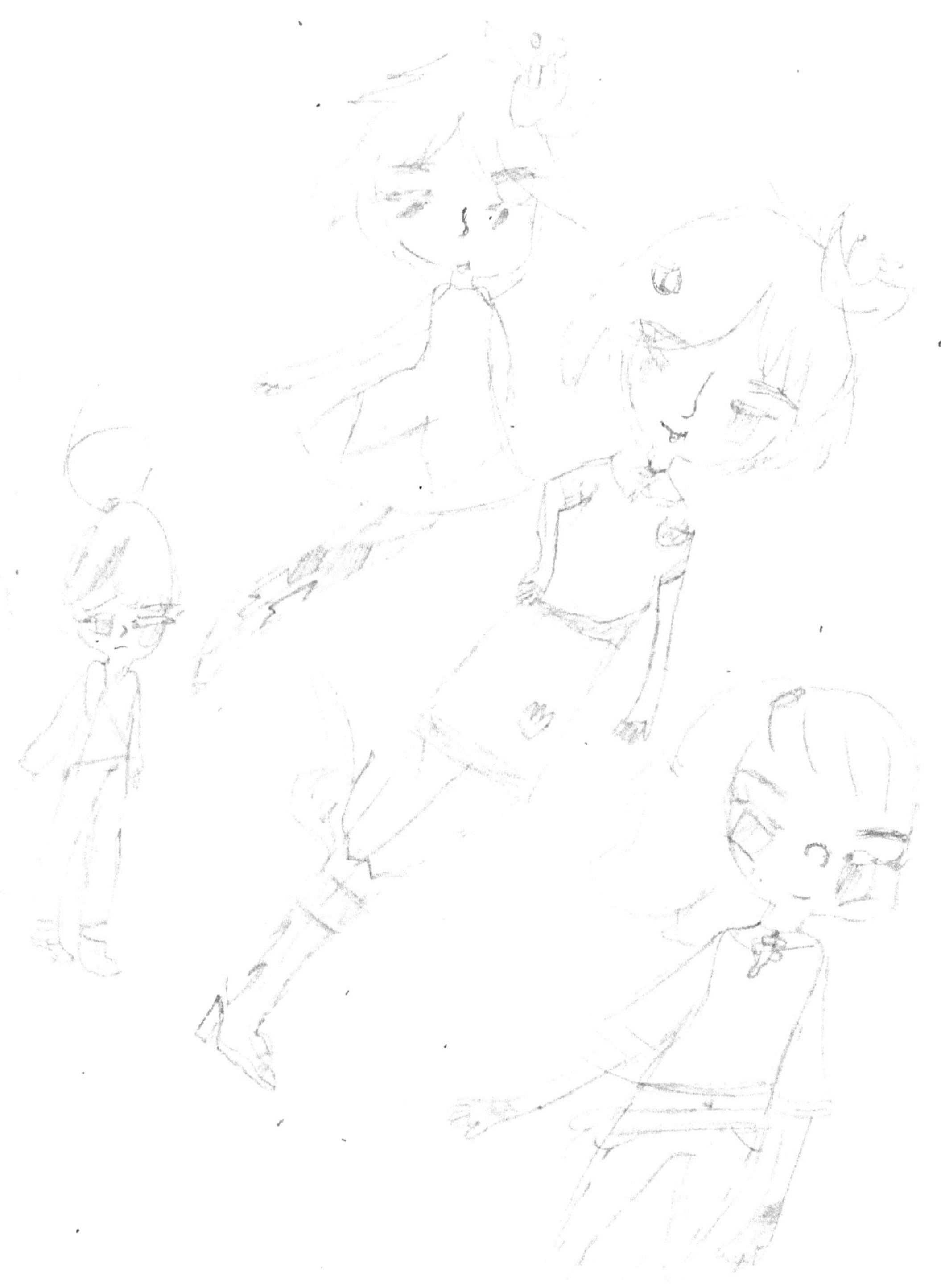

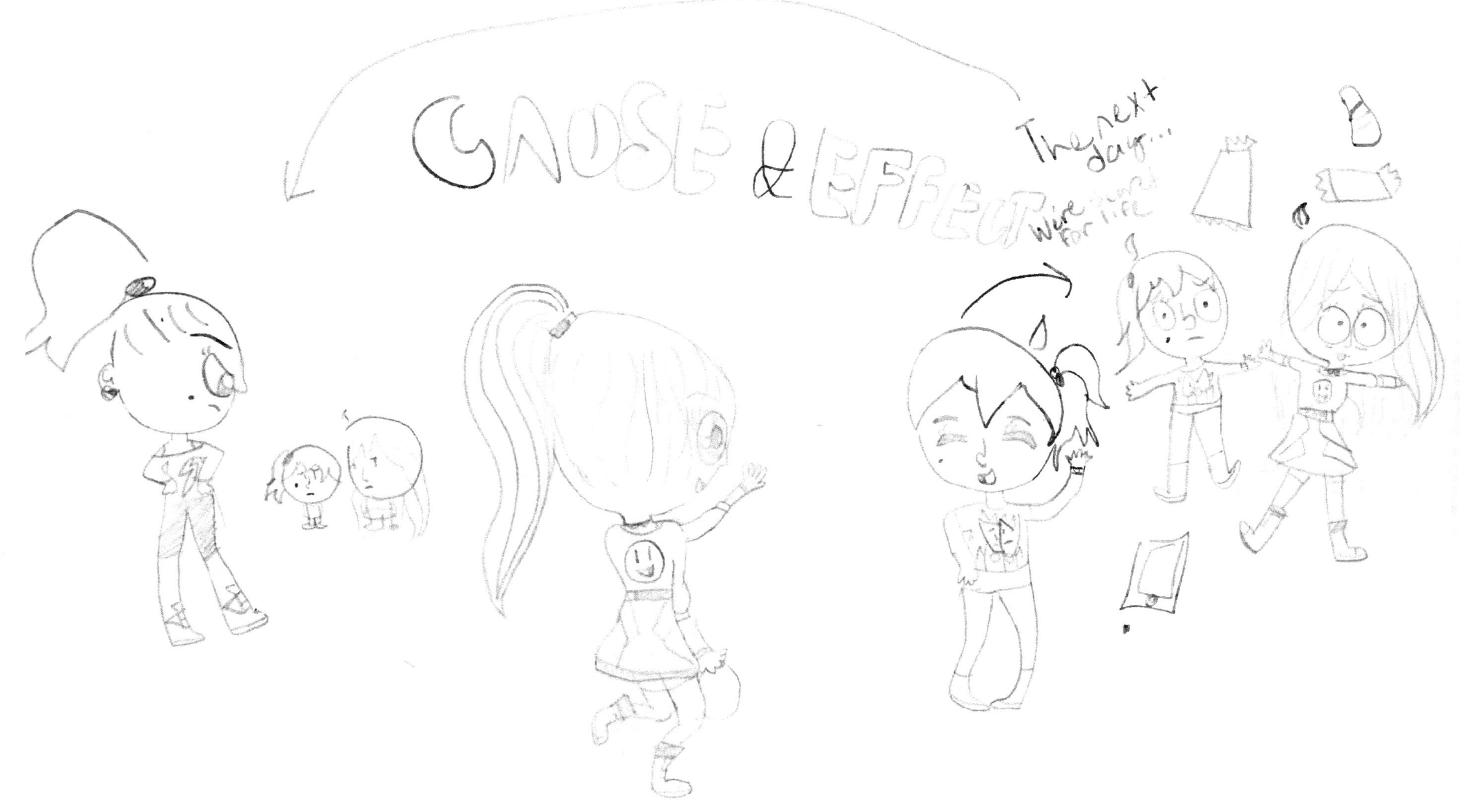

CAUSE & EFFECT
The next day...
We're friends for life

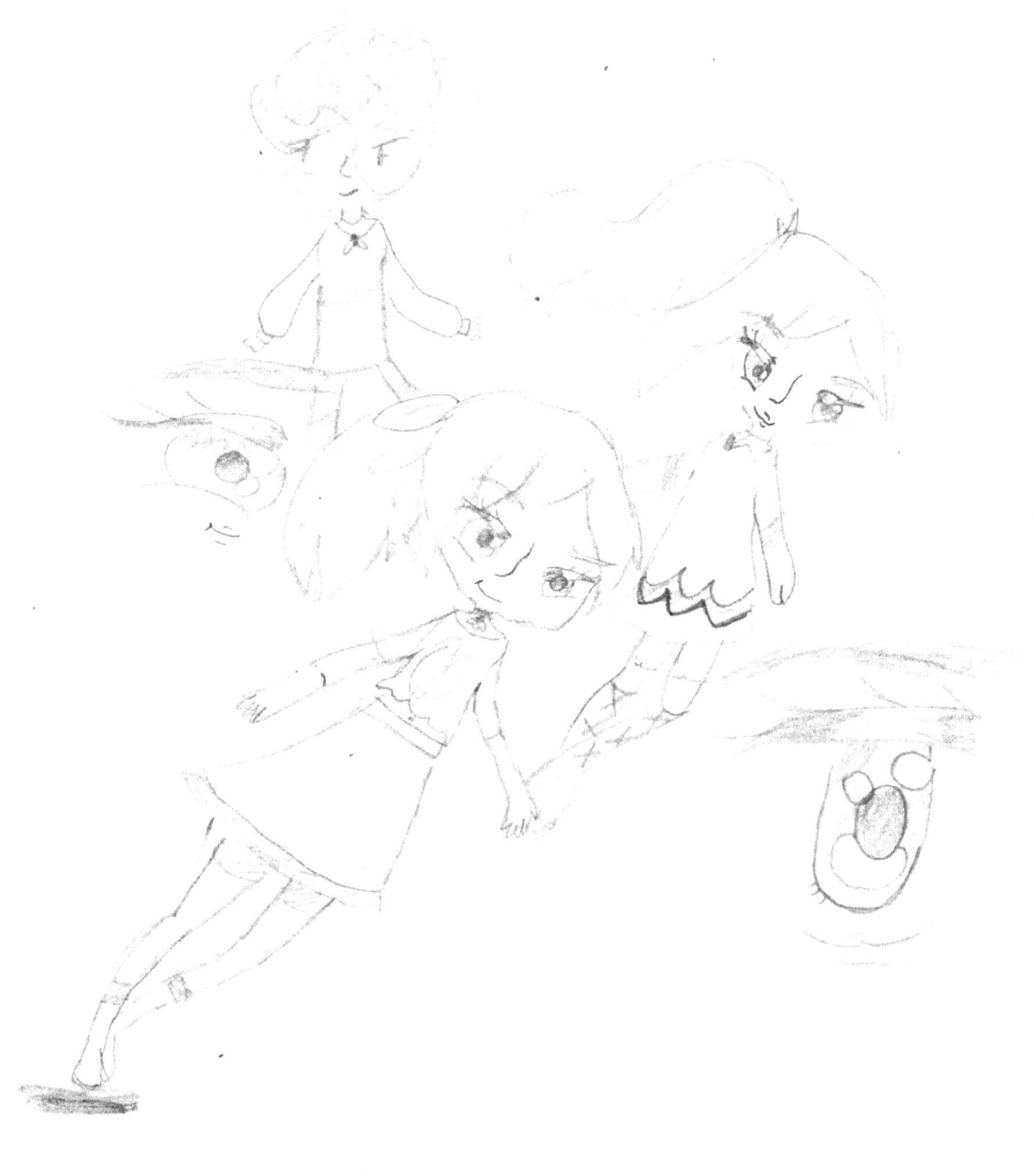

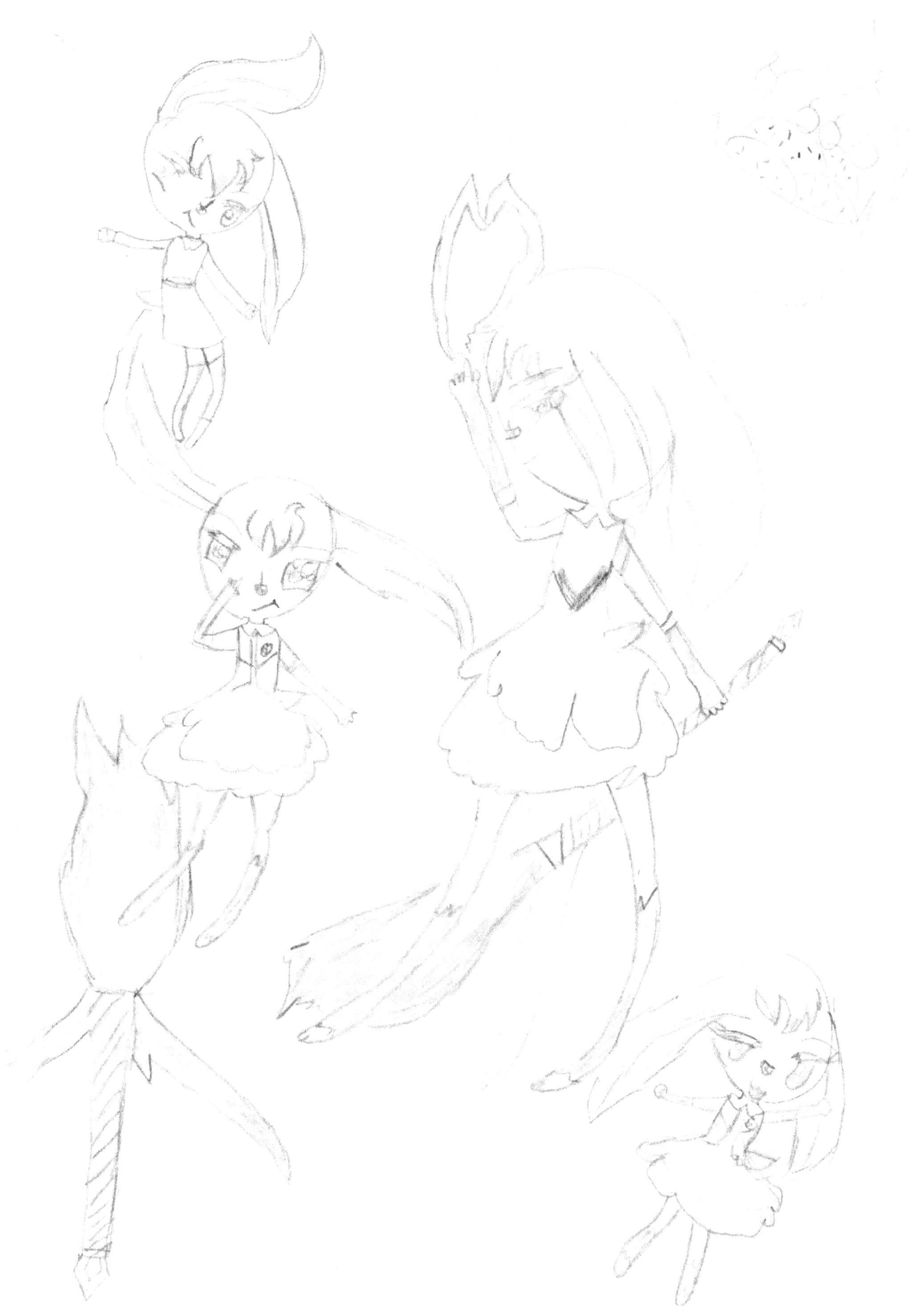

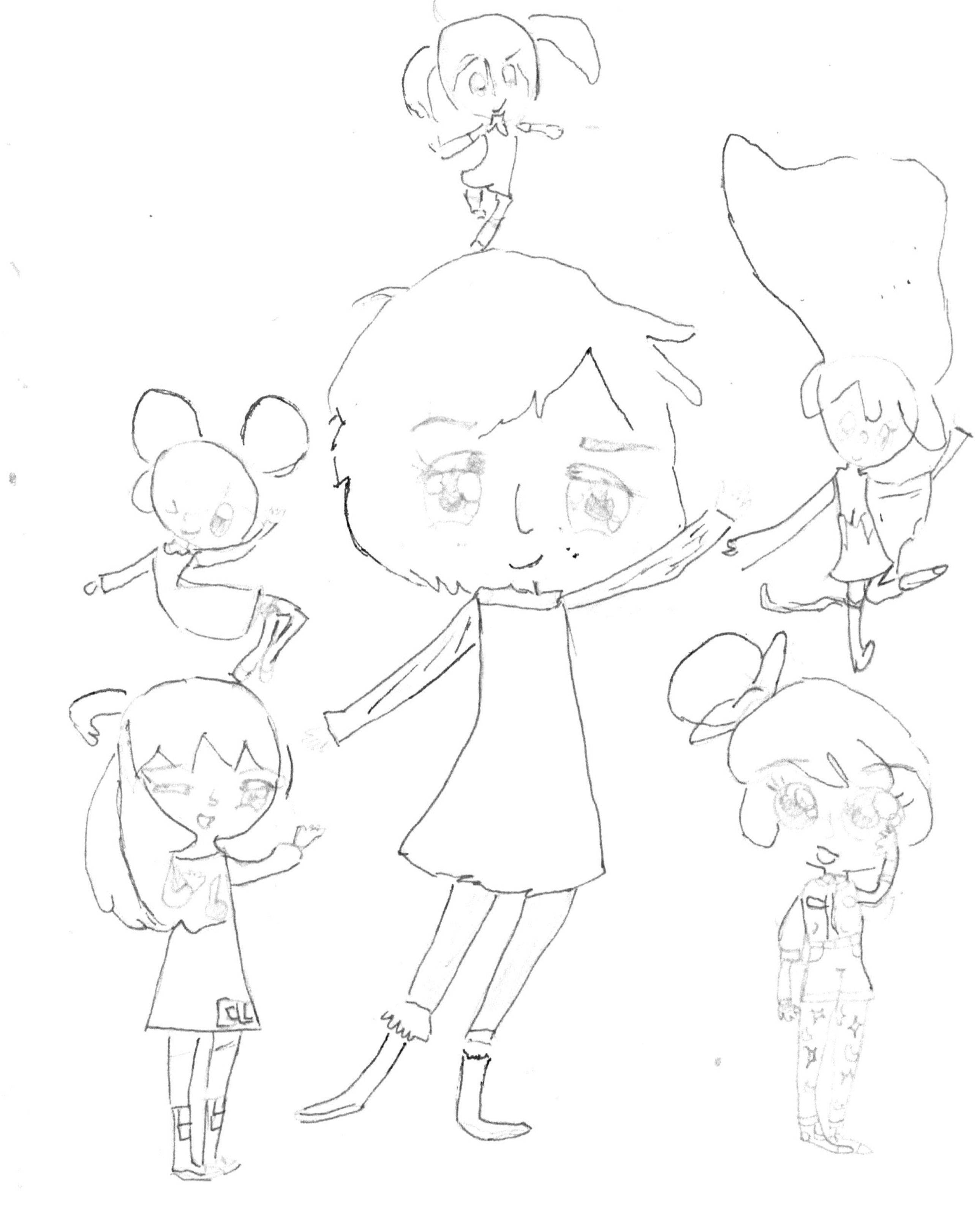

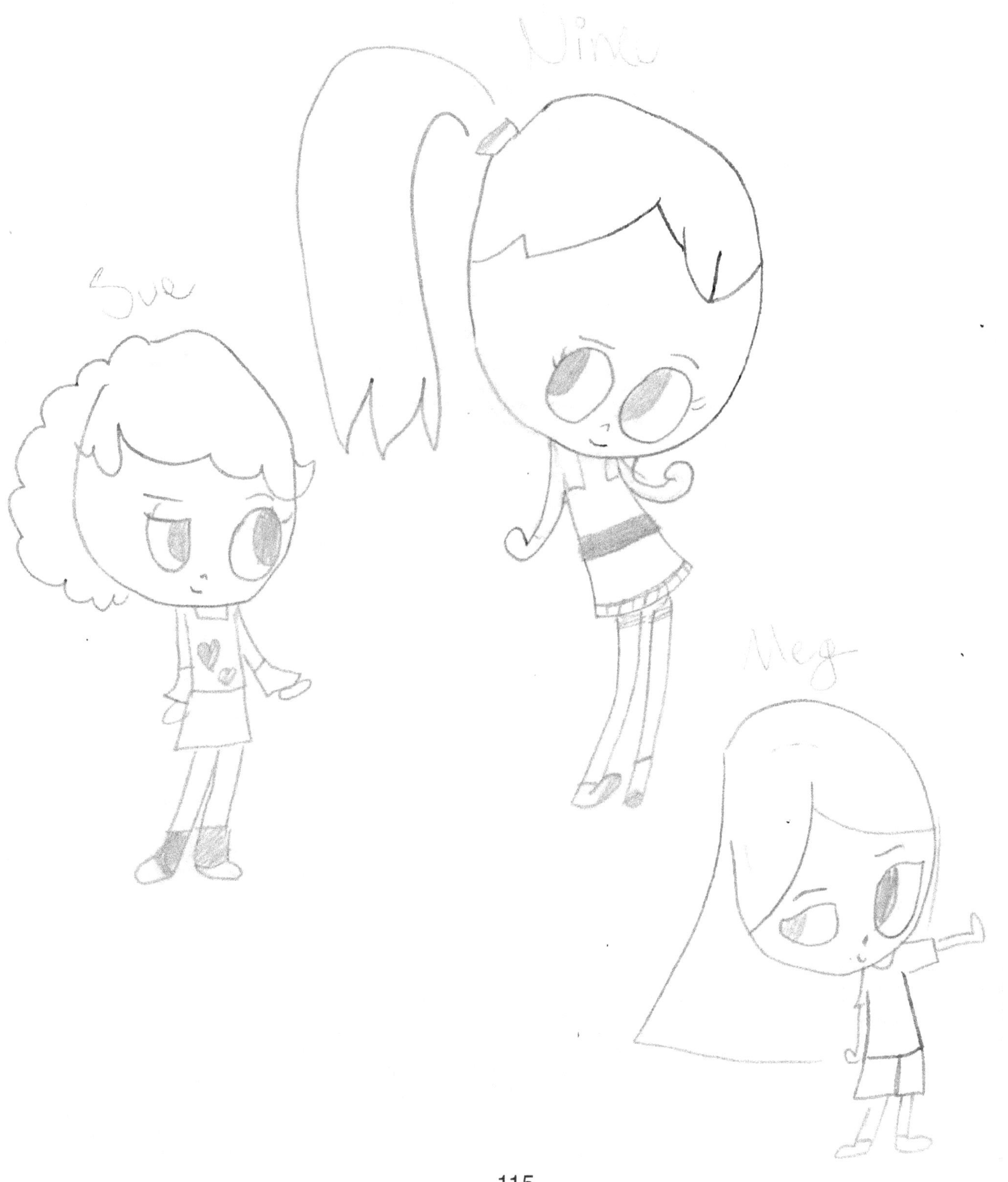
Nina
Sue
Meg

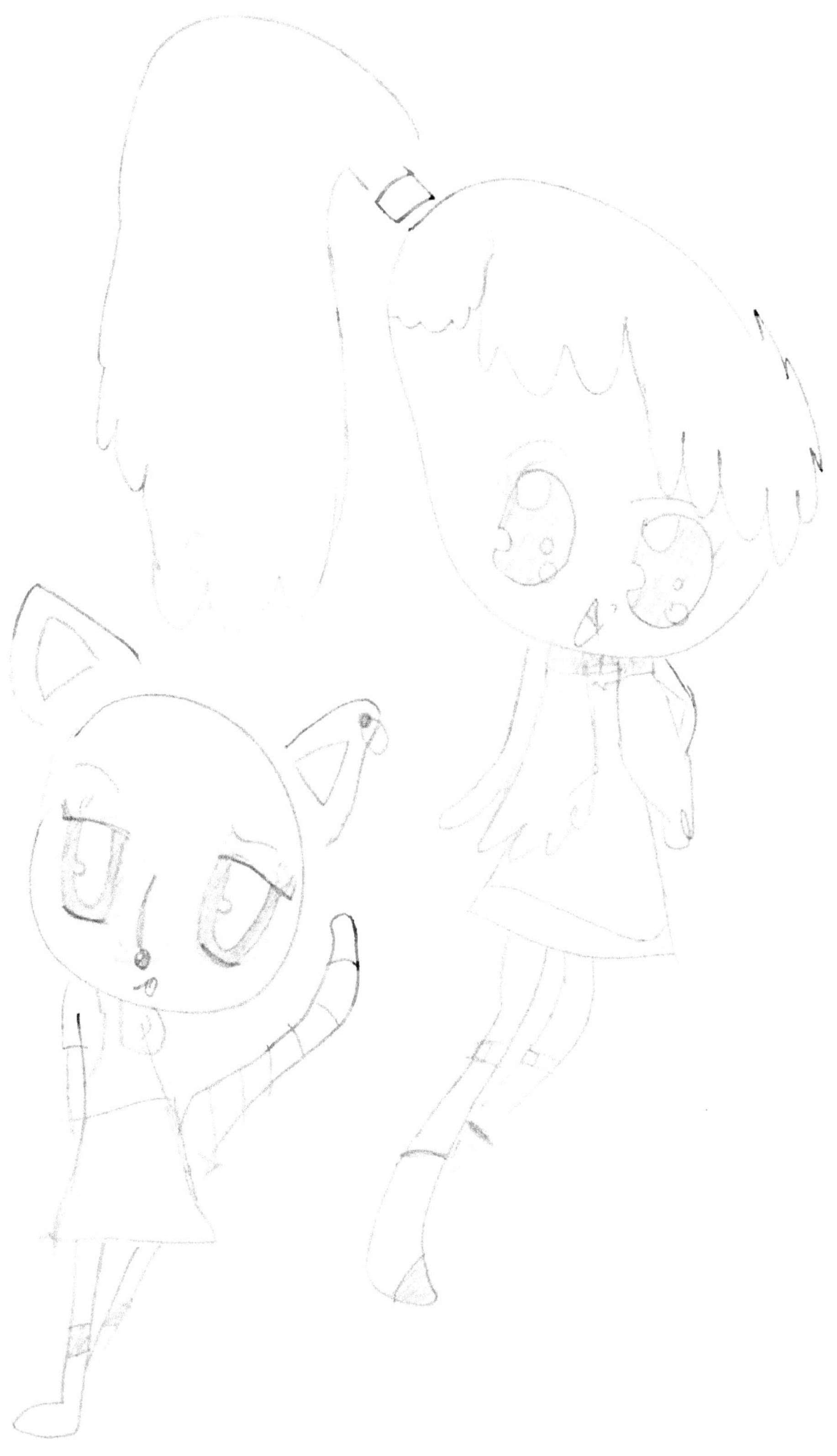

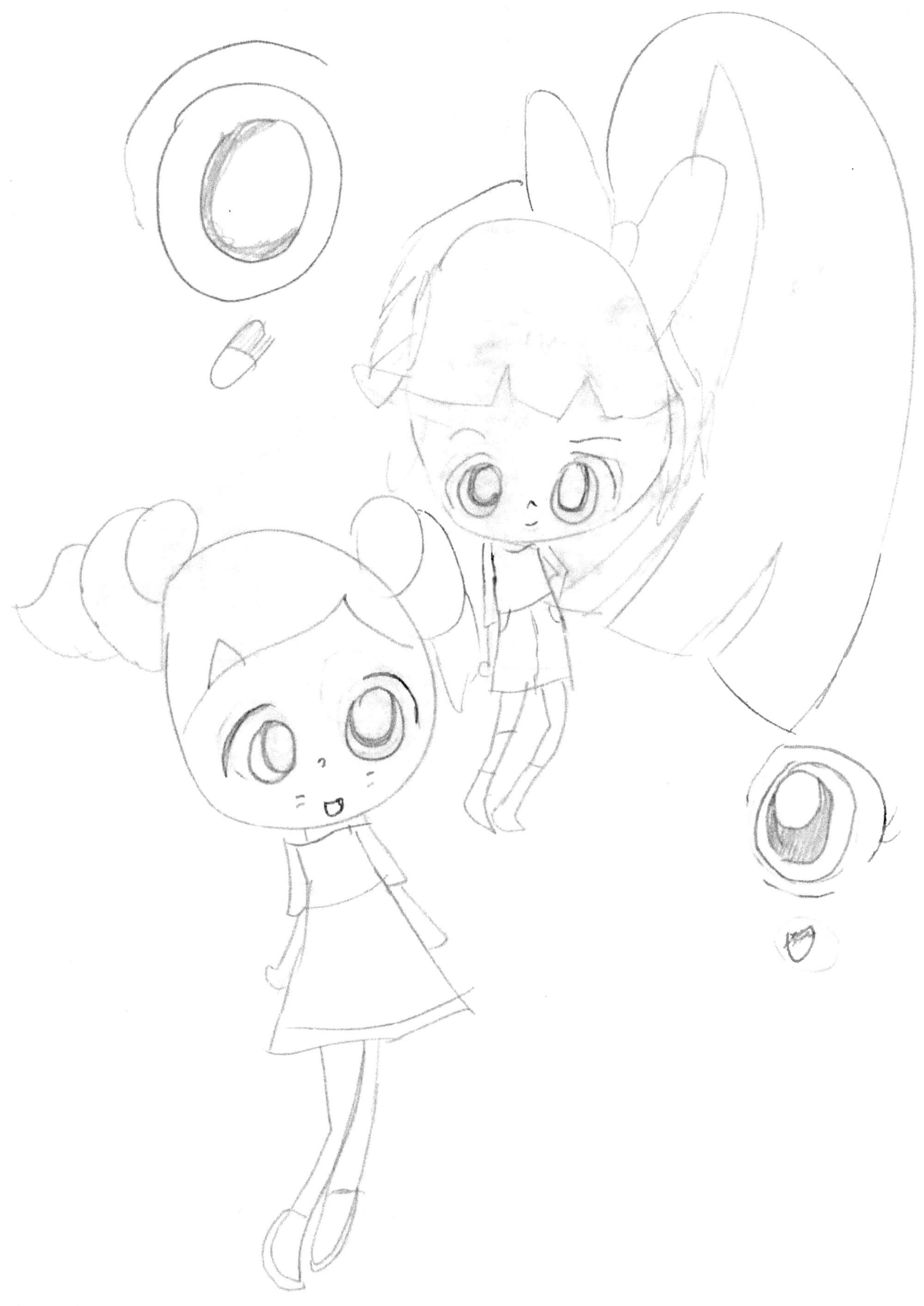

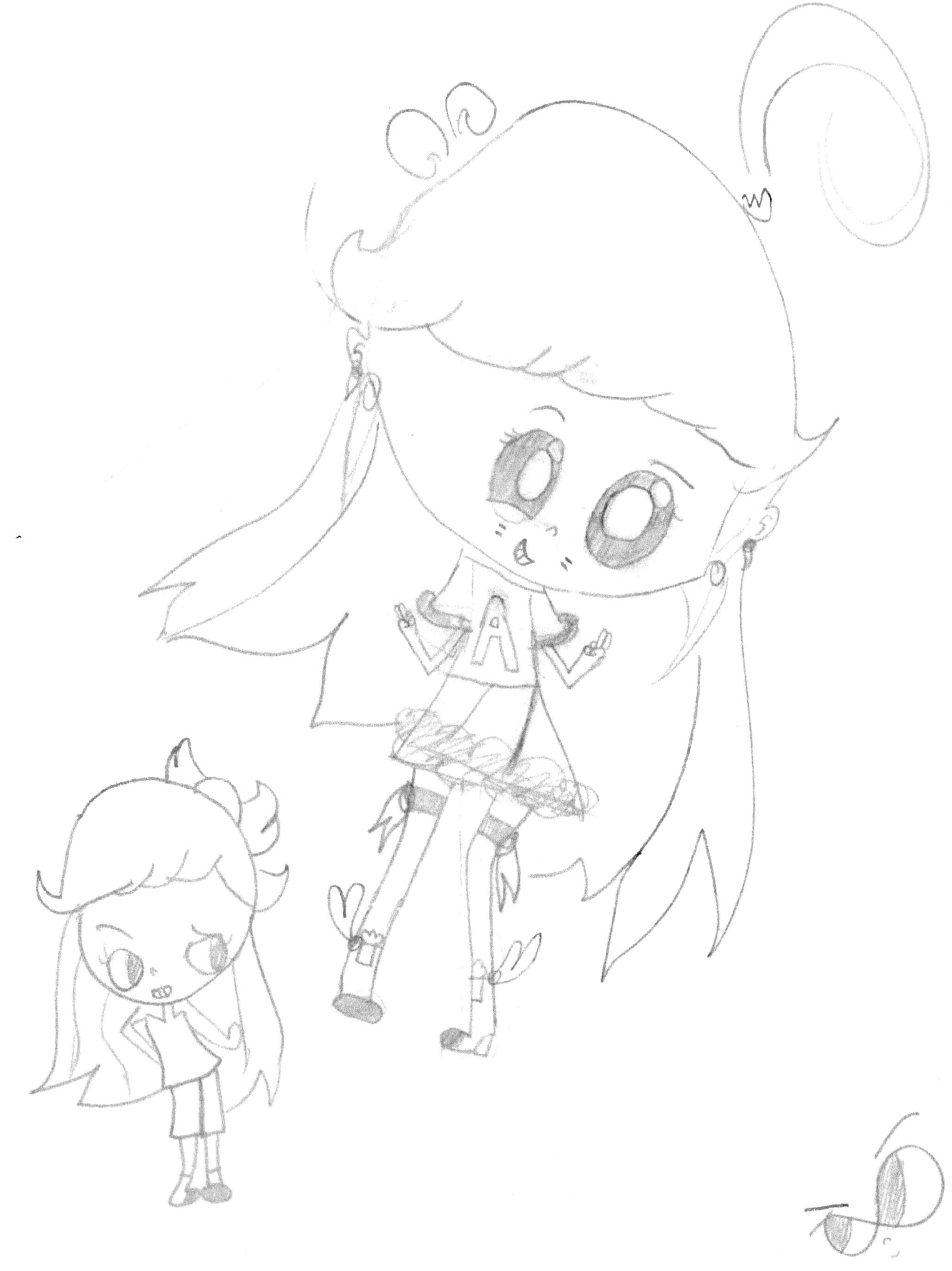

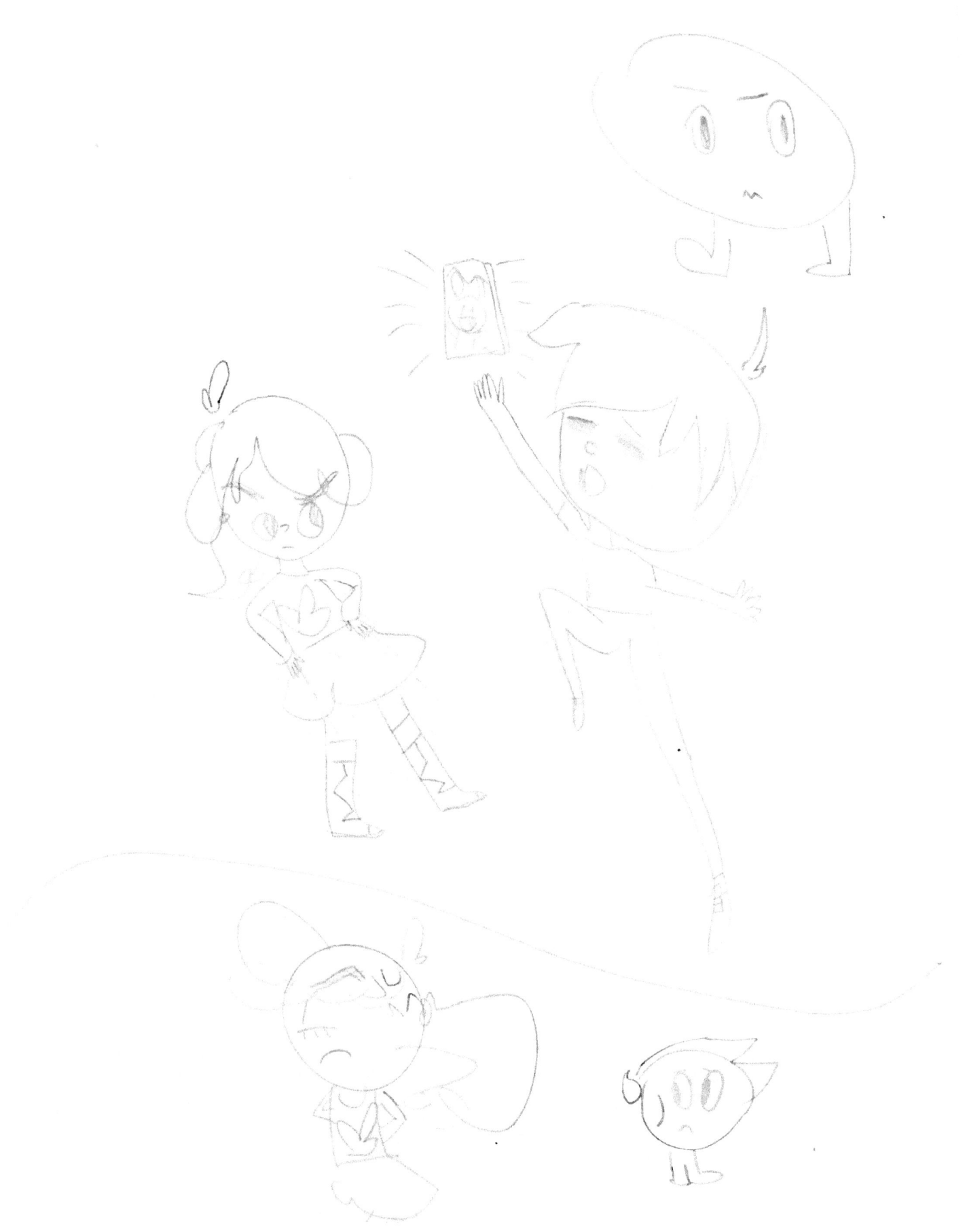

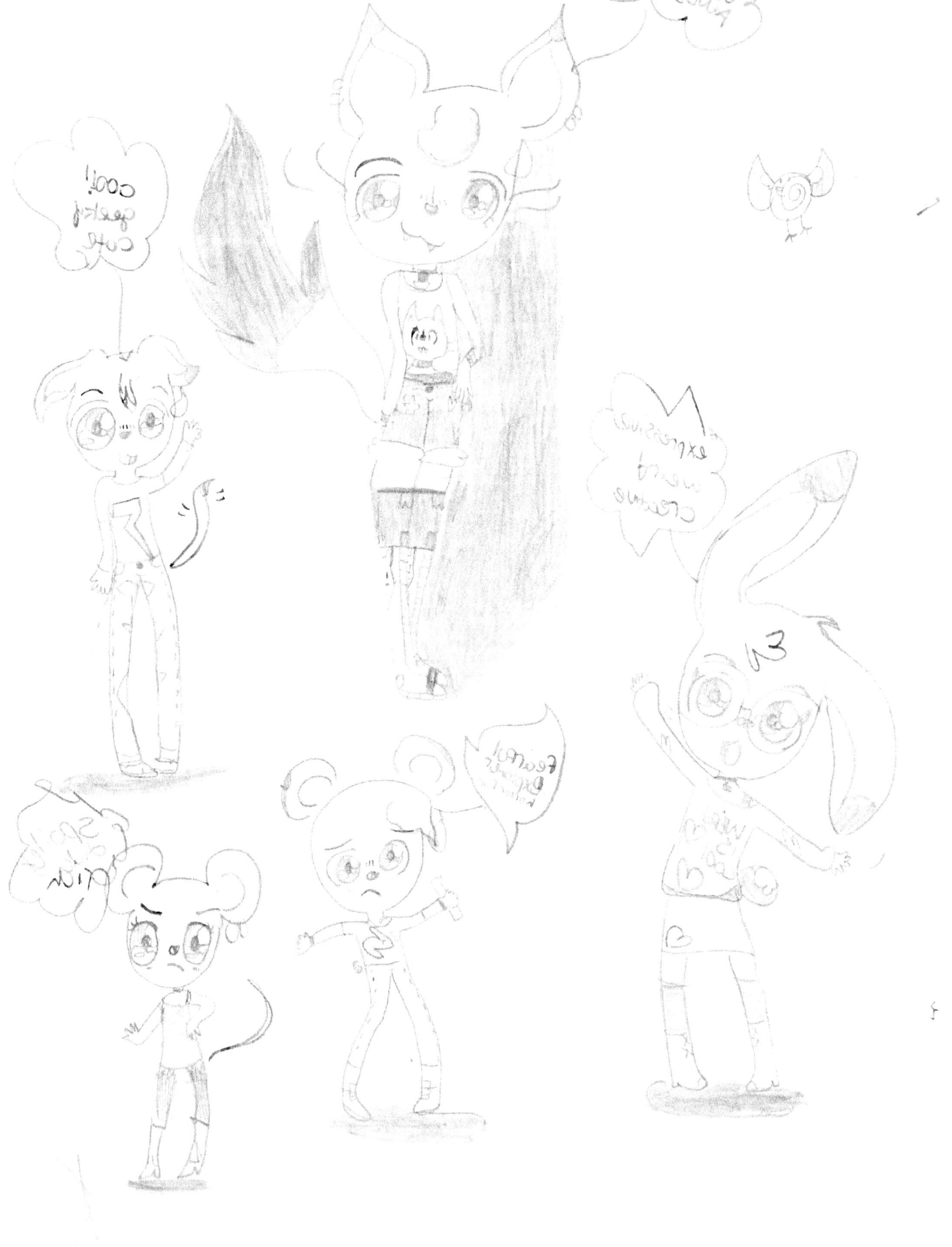

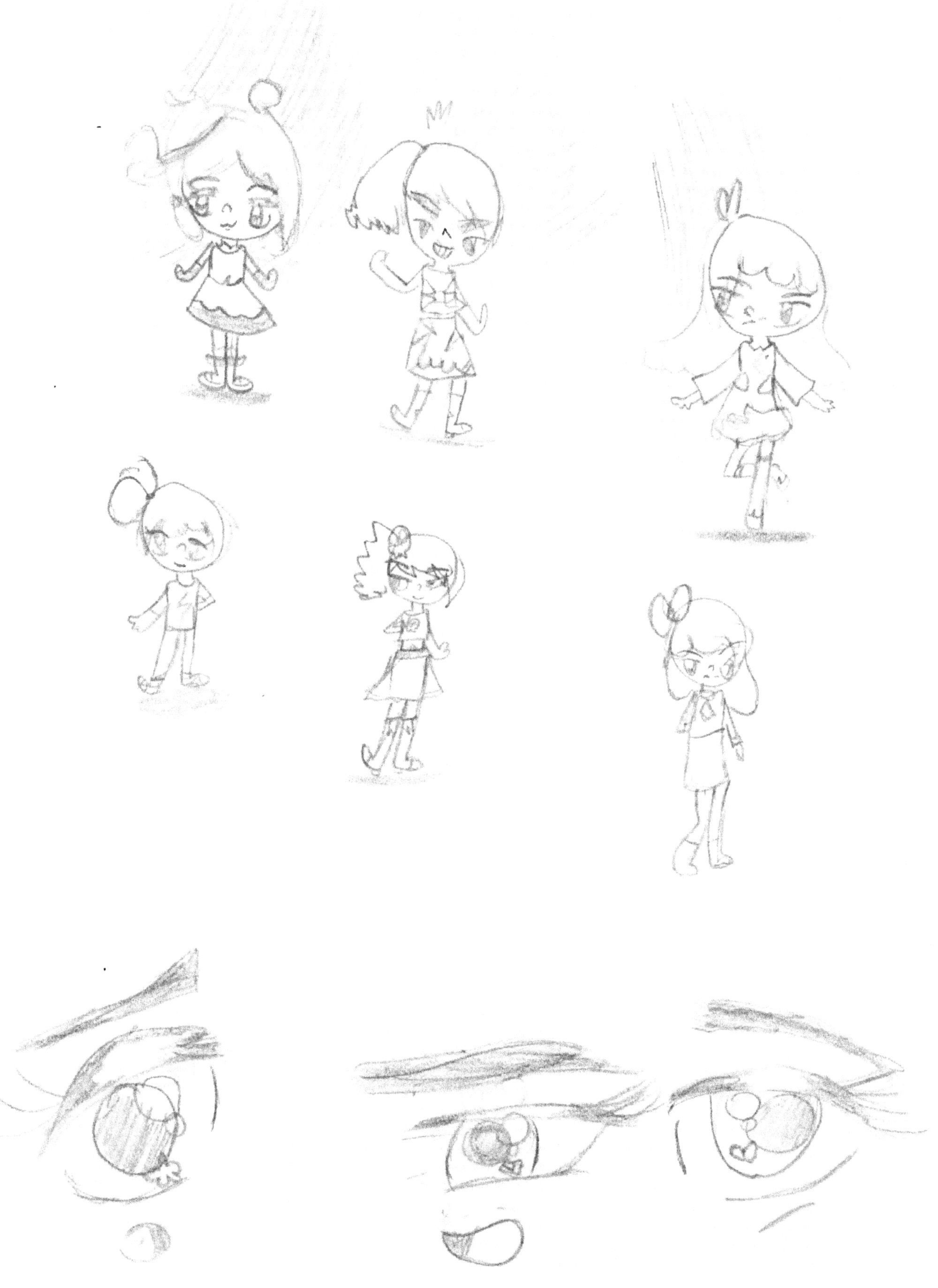

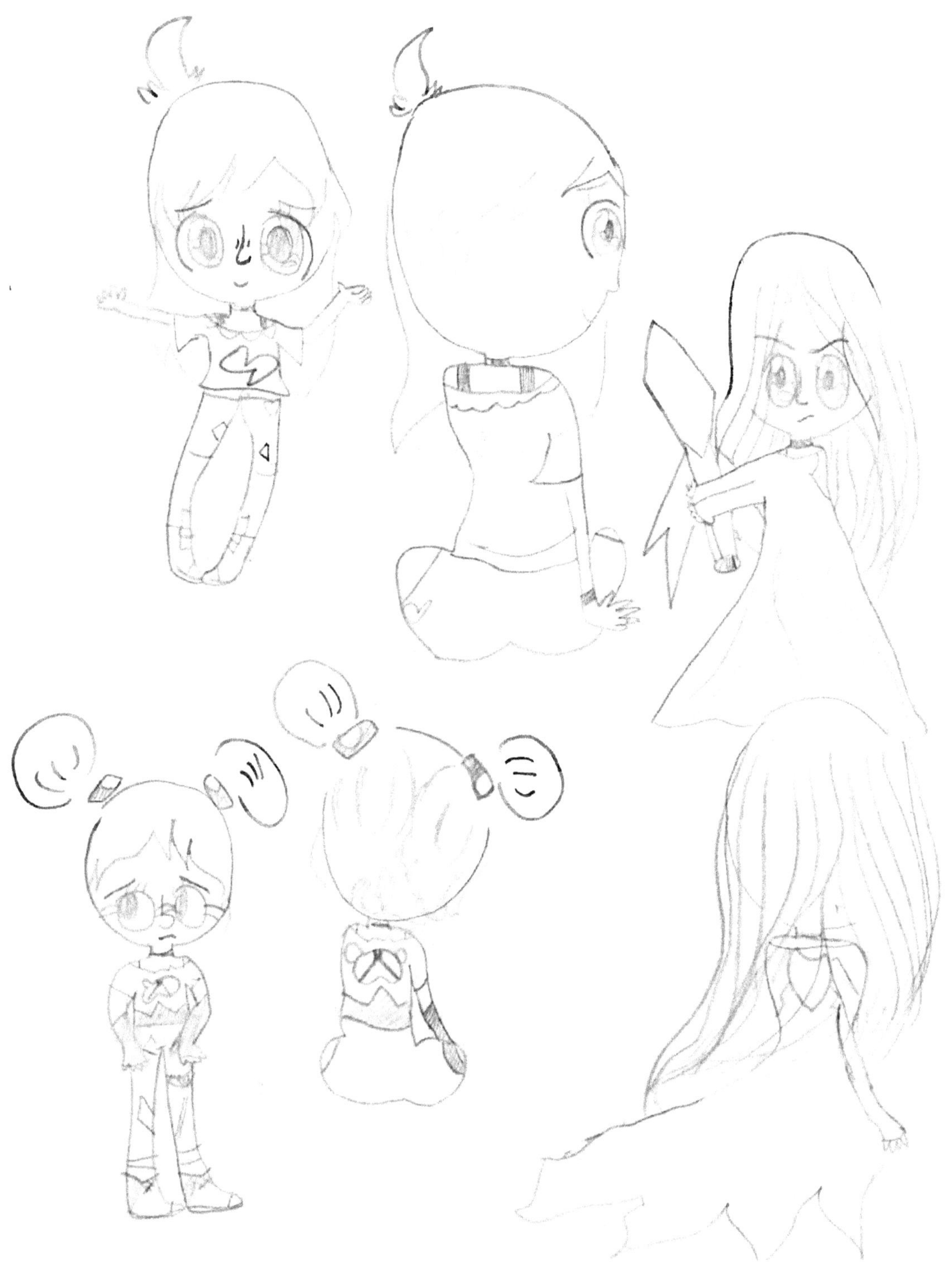

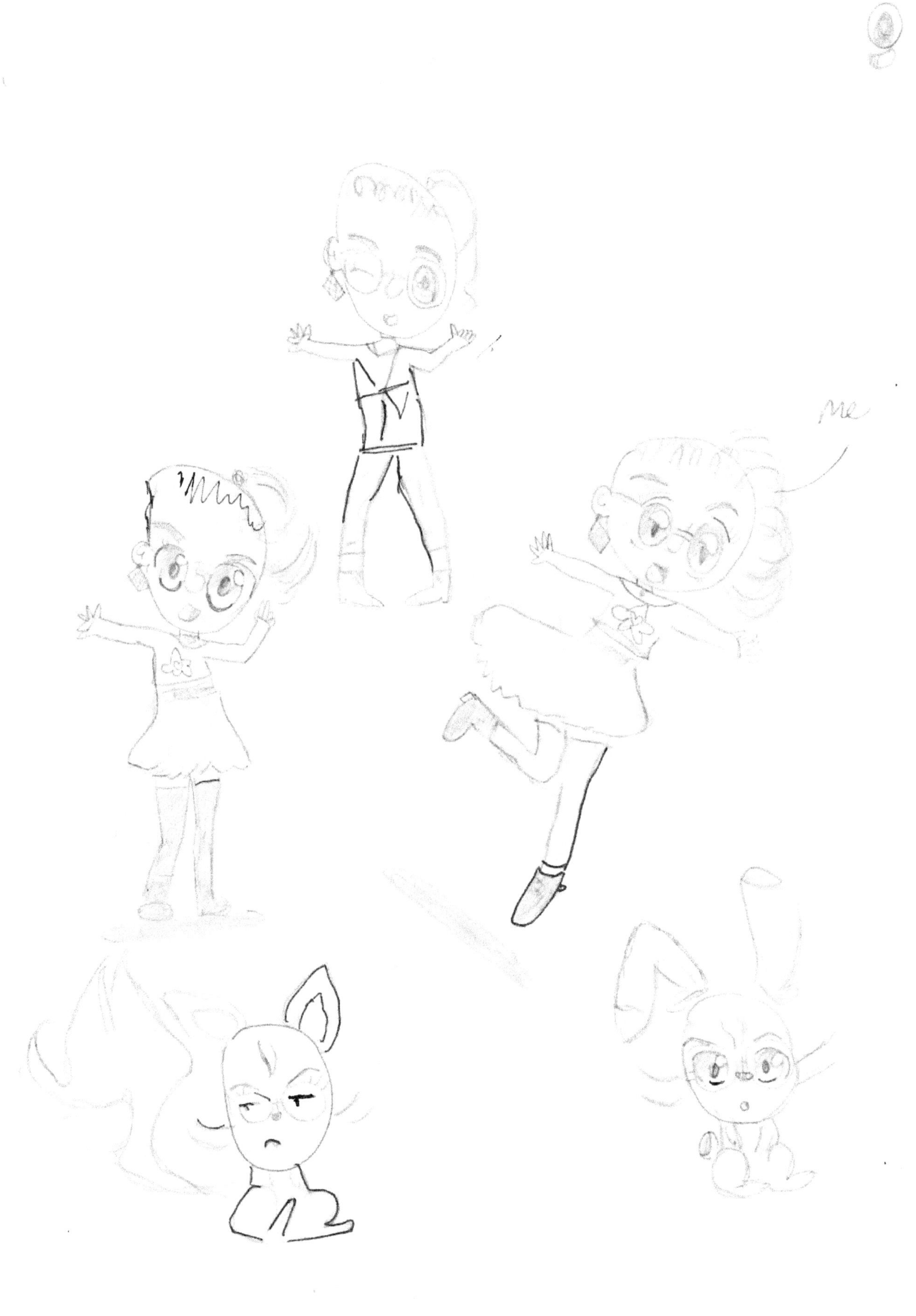

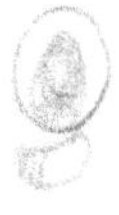

me

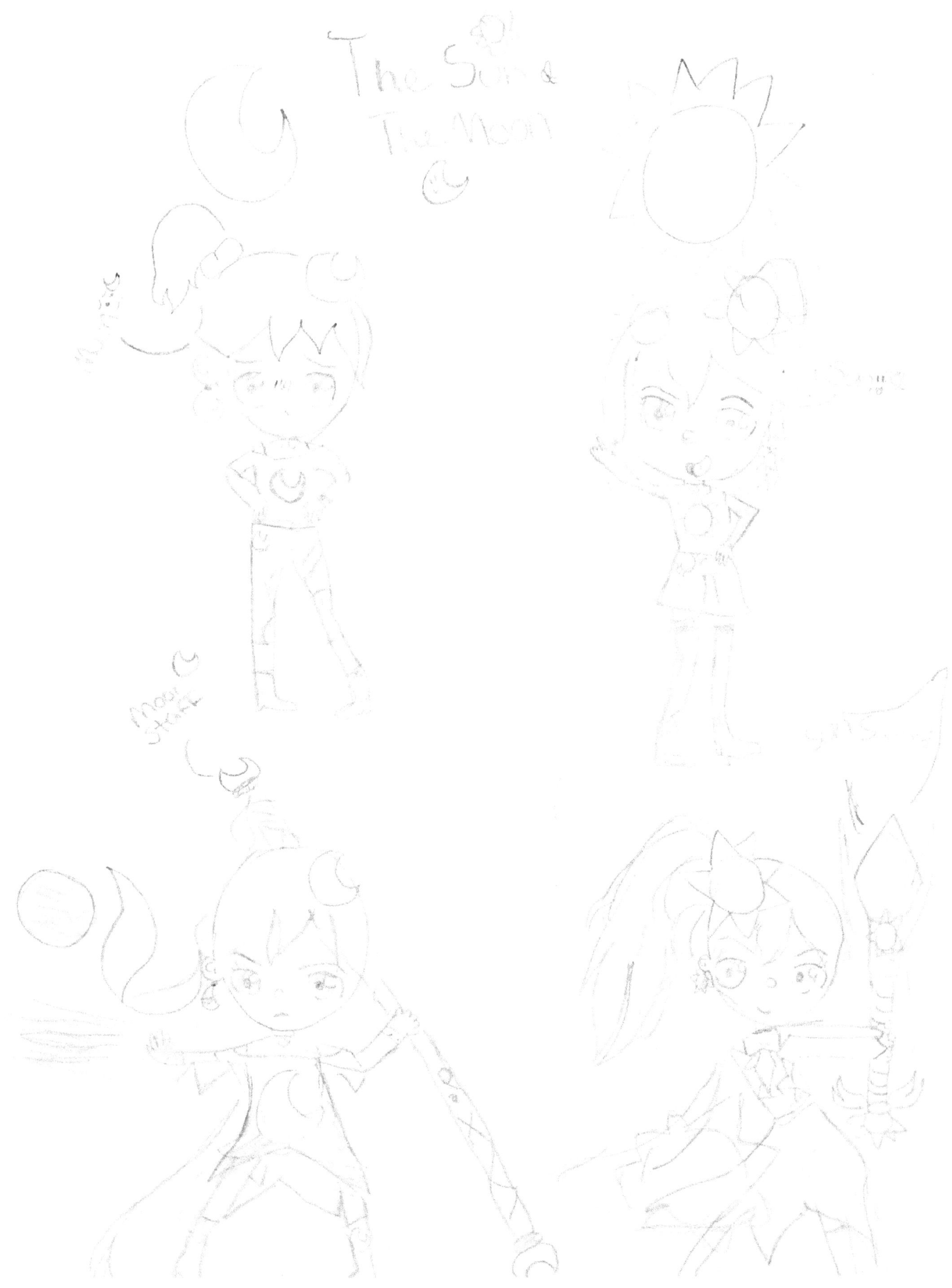
The Sun &
The Moon
Moon
Staff

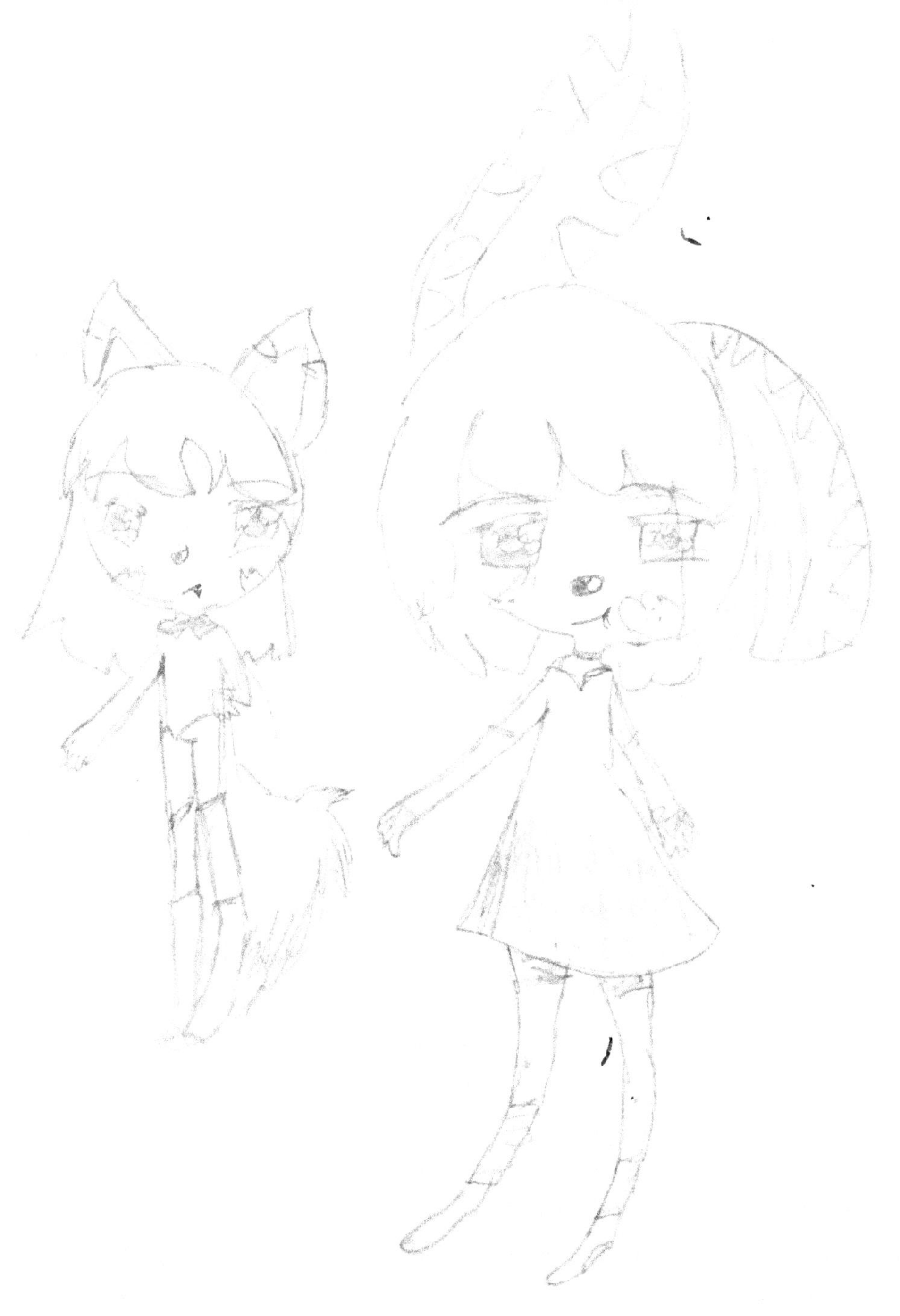

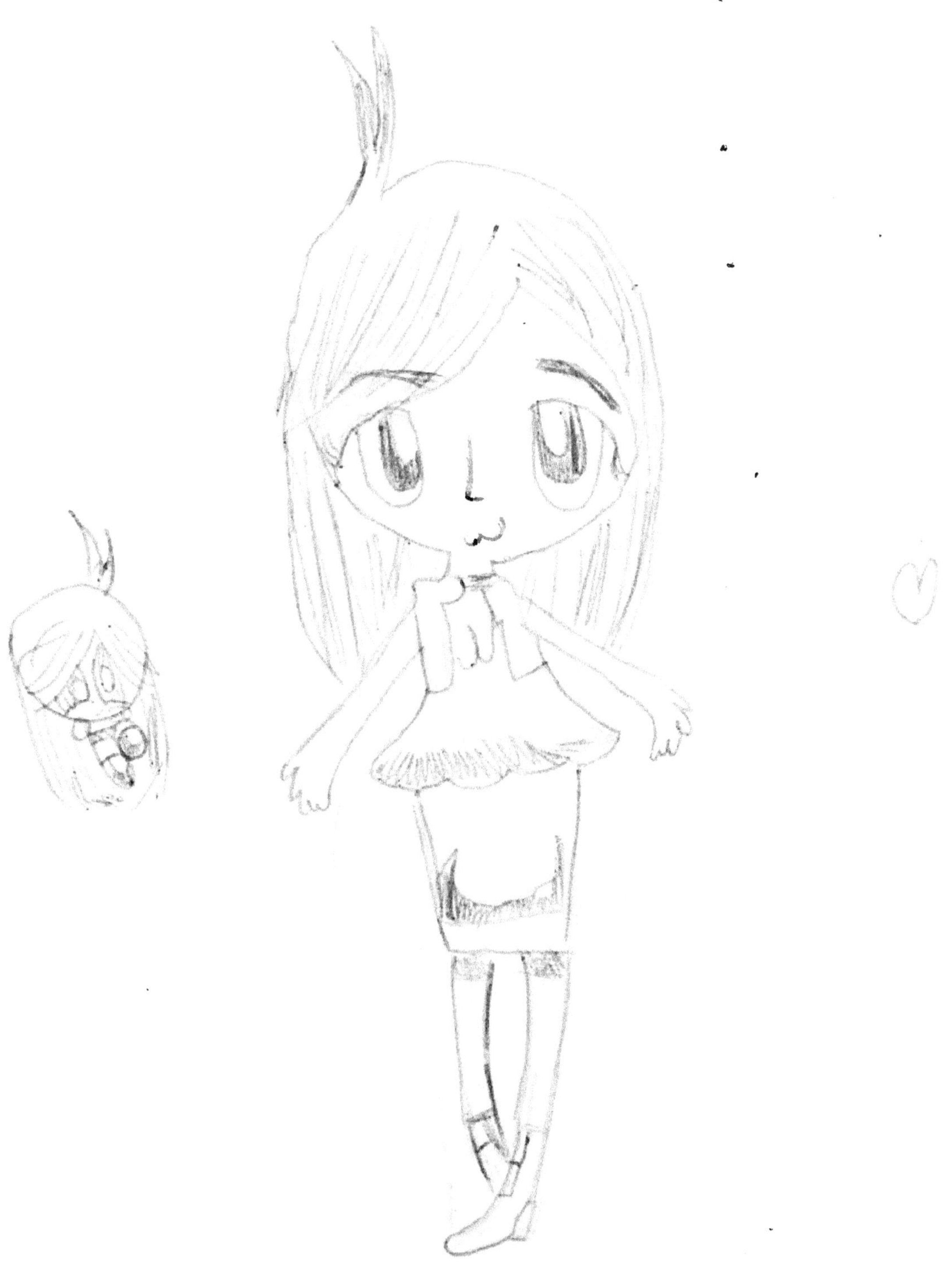

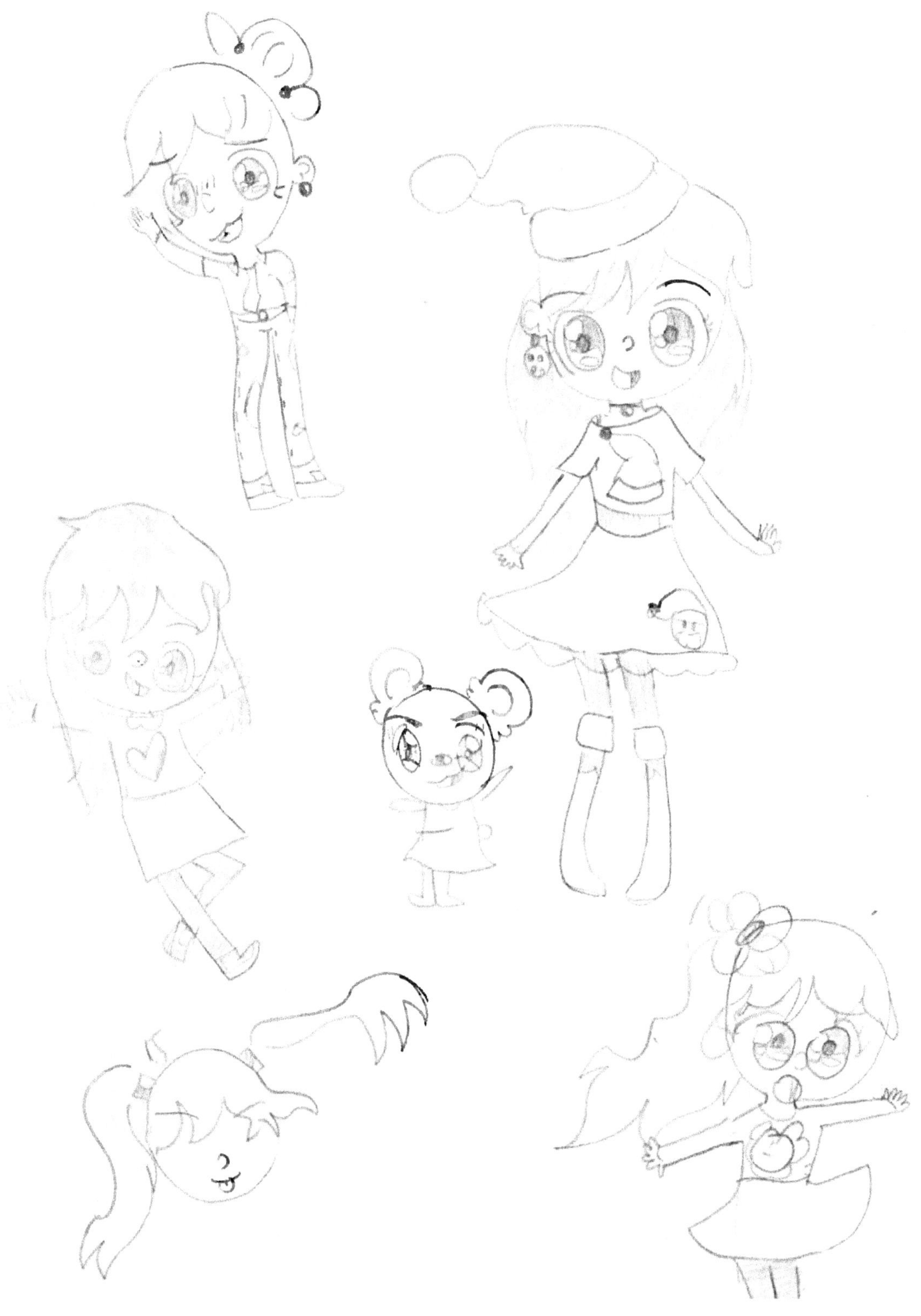

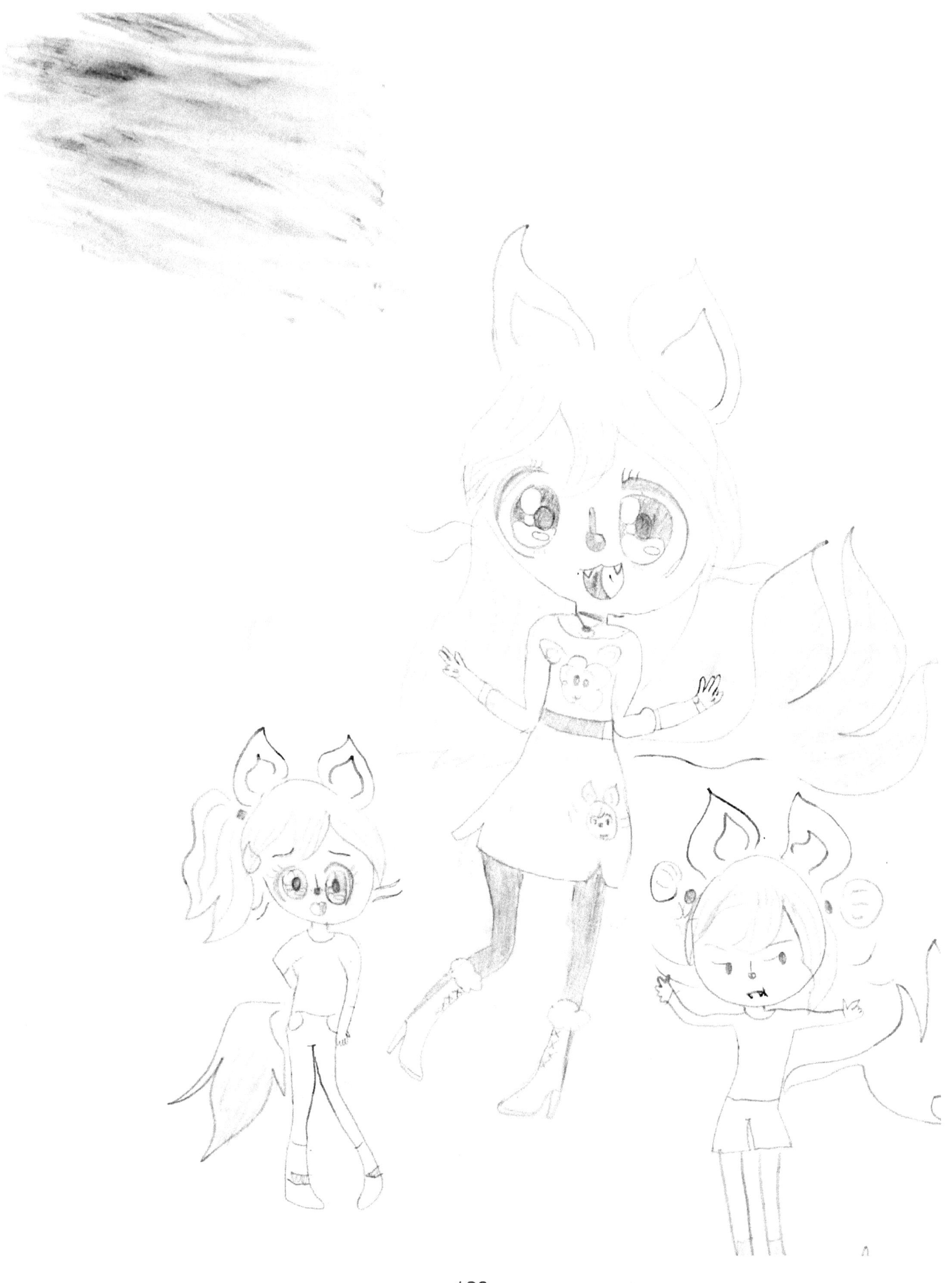

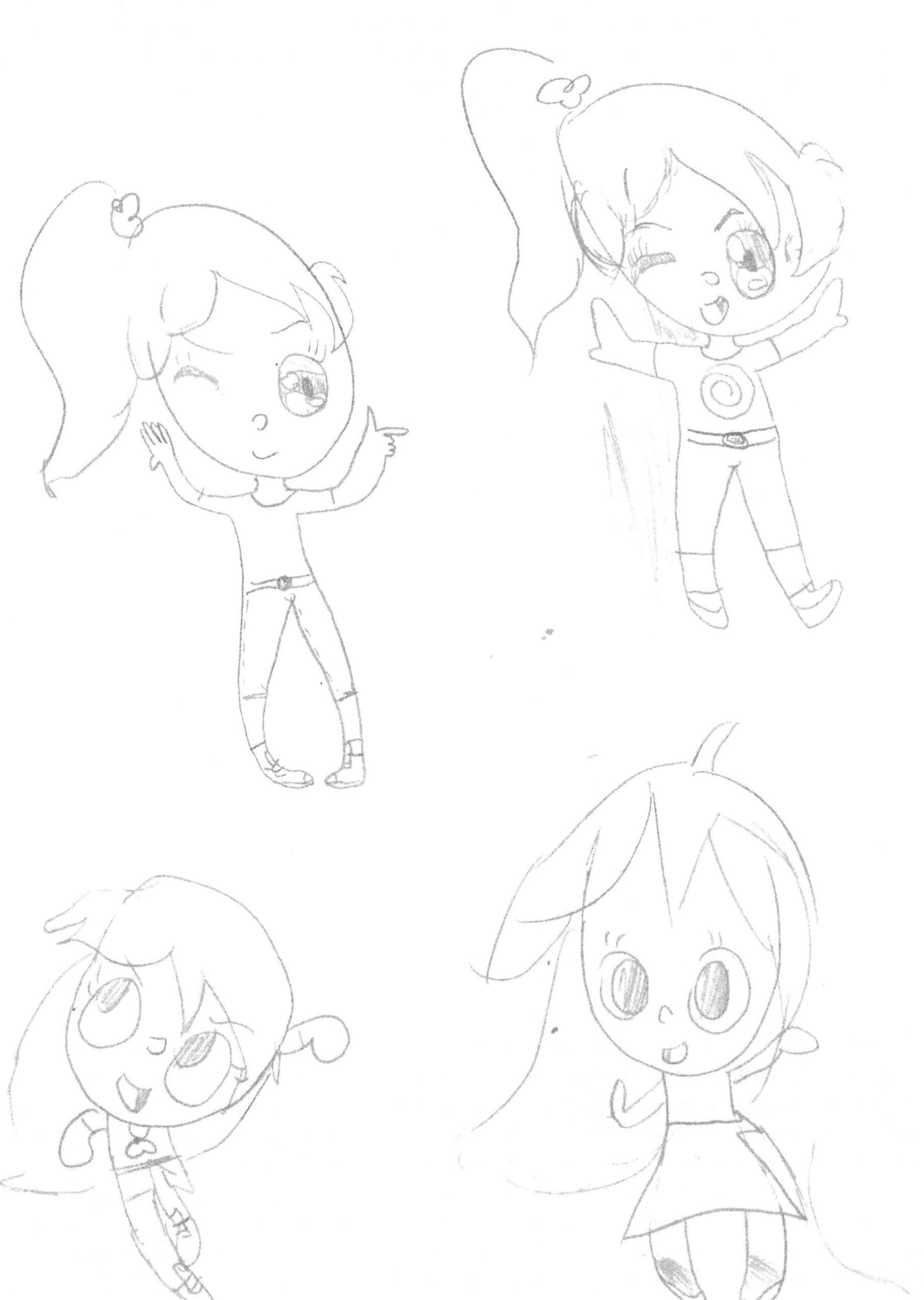

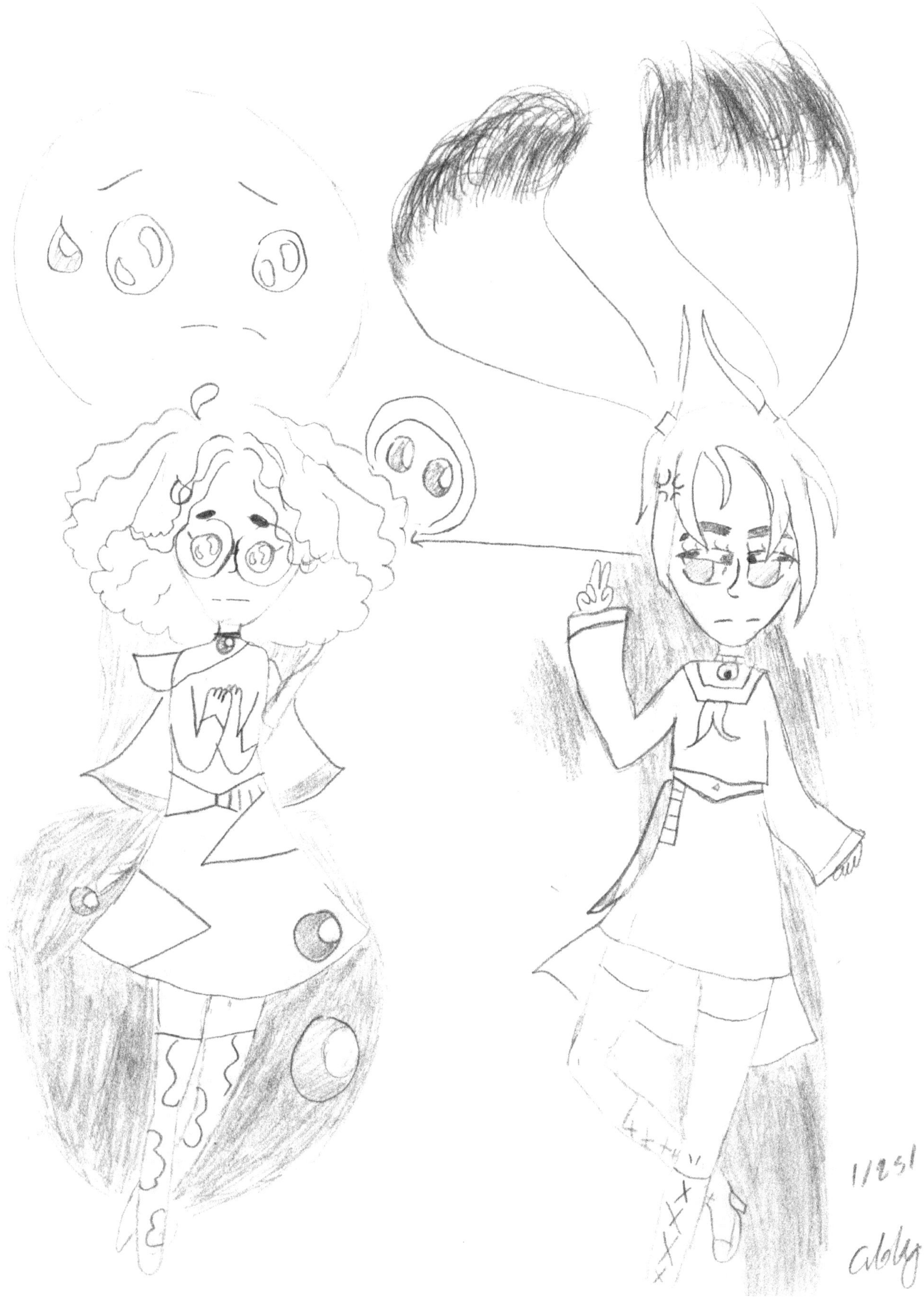

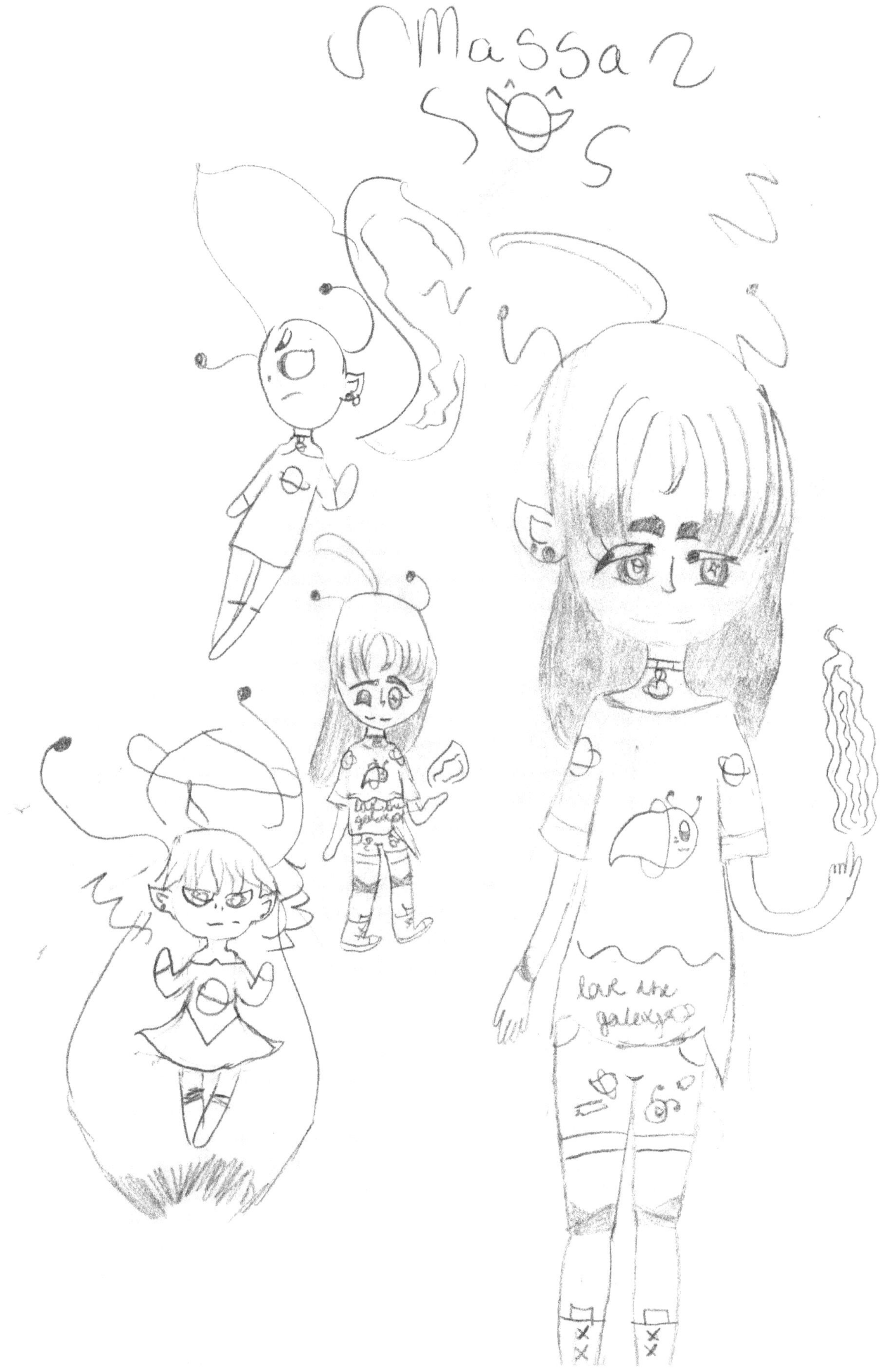
Massa
love the galaxy

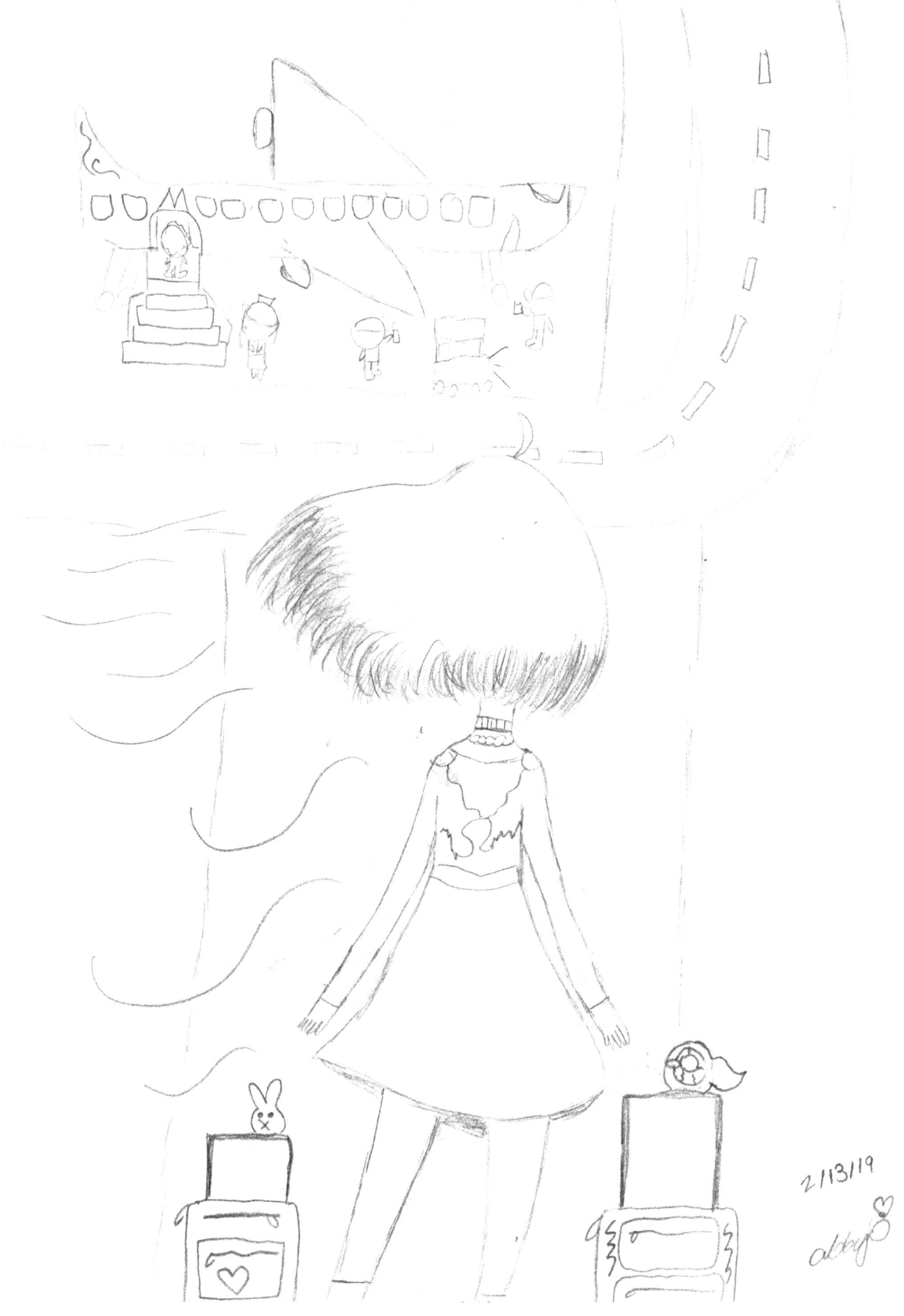
2/13/19
abby

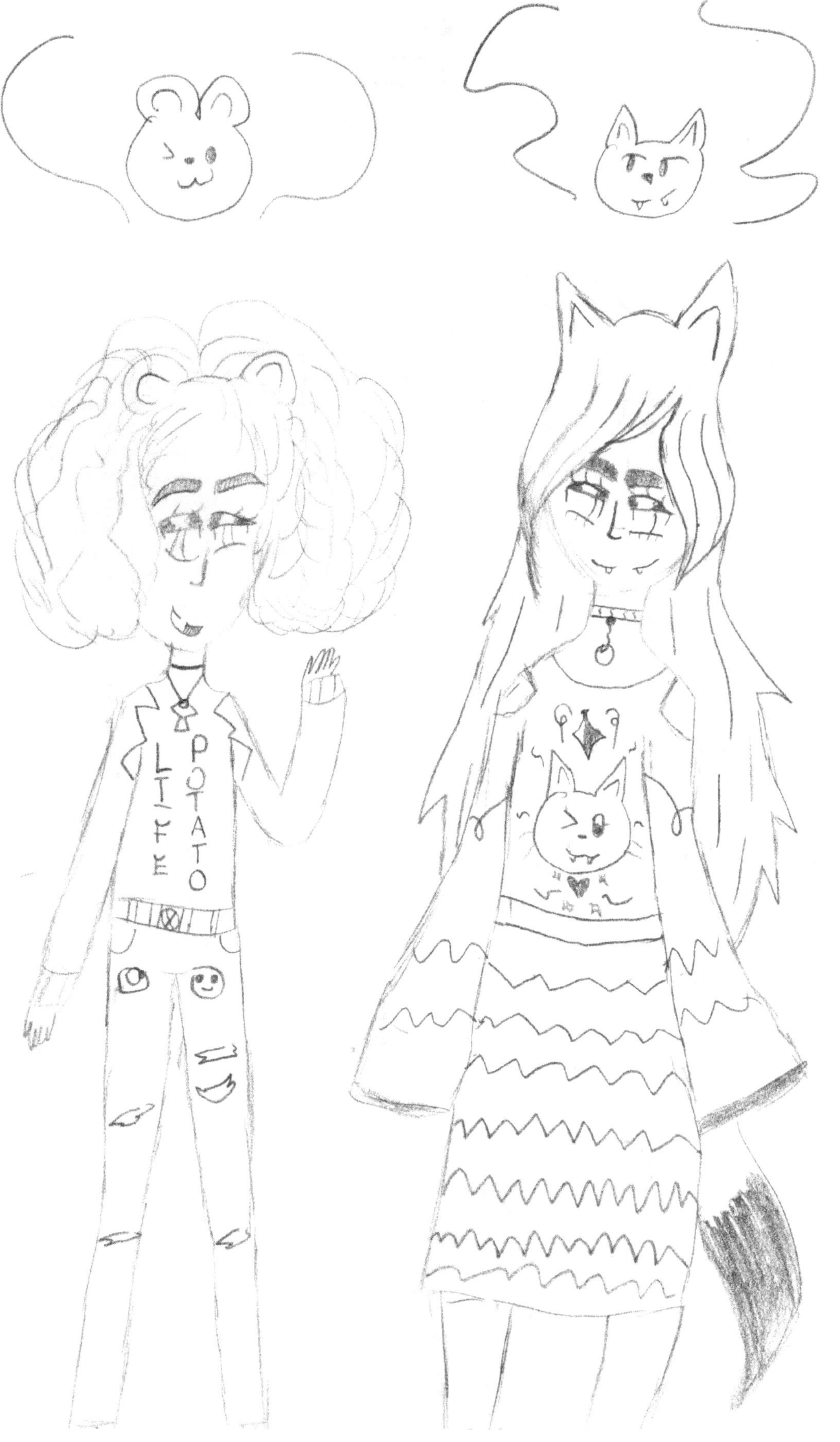
POTATO

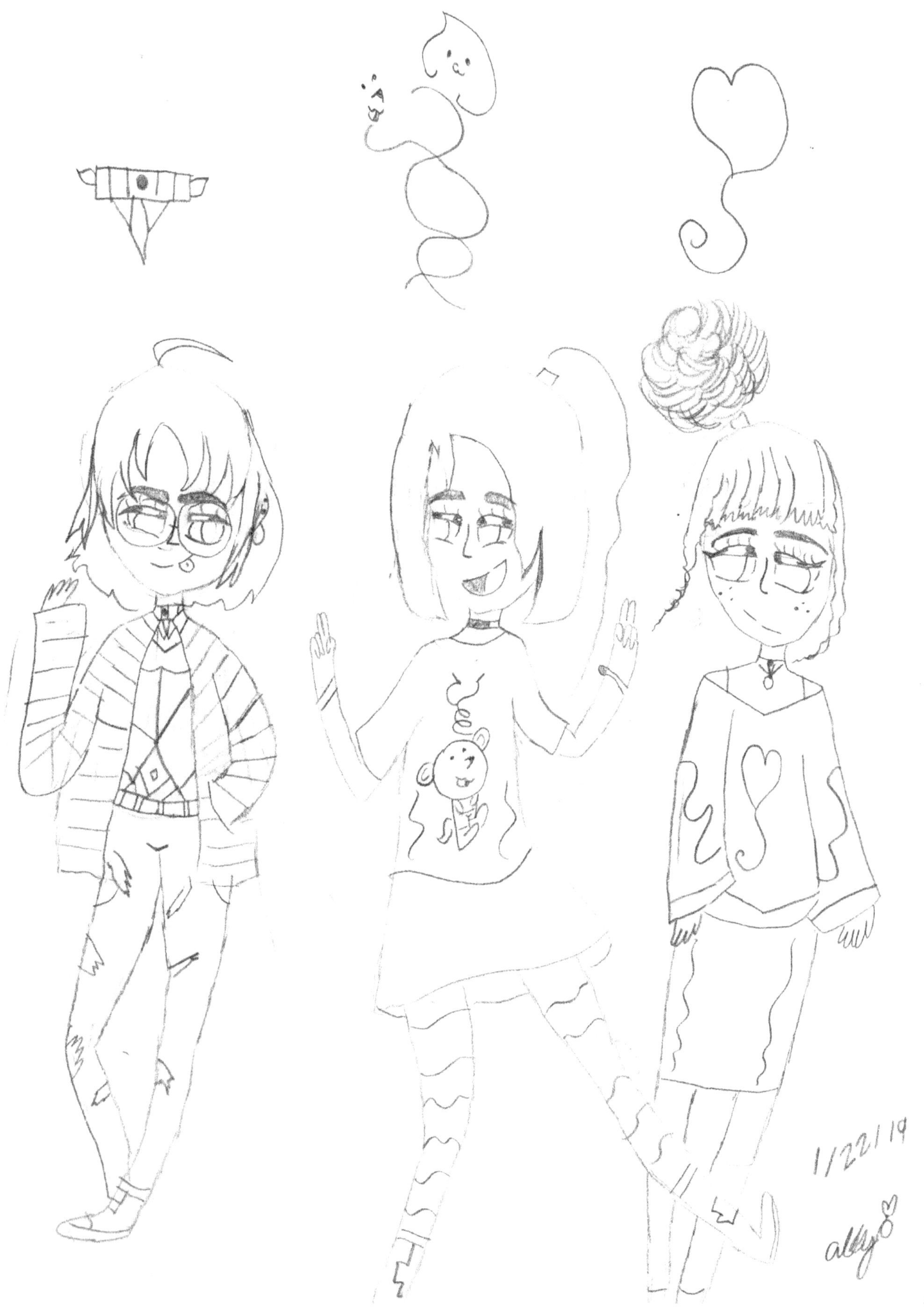
1/22/19
ally

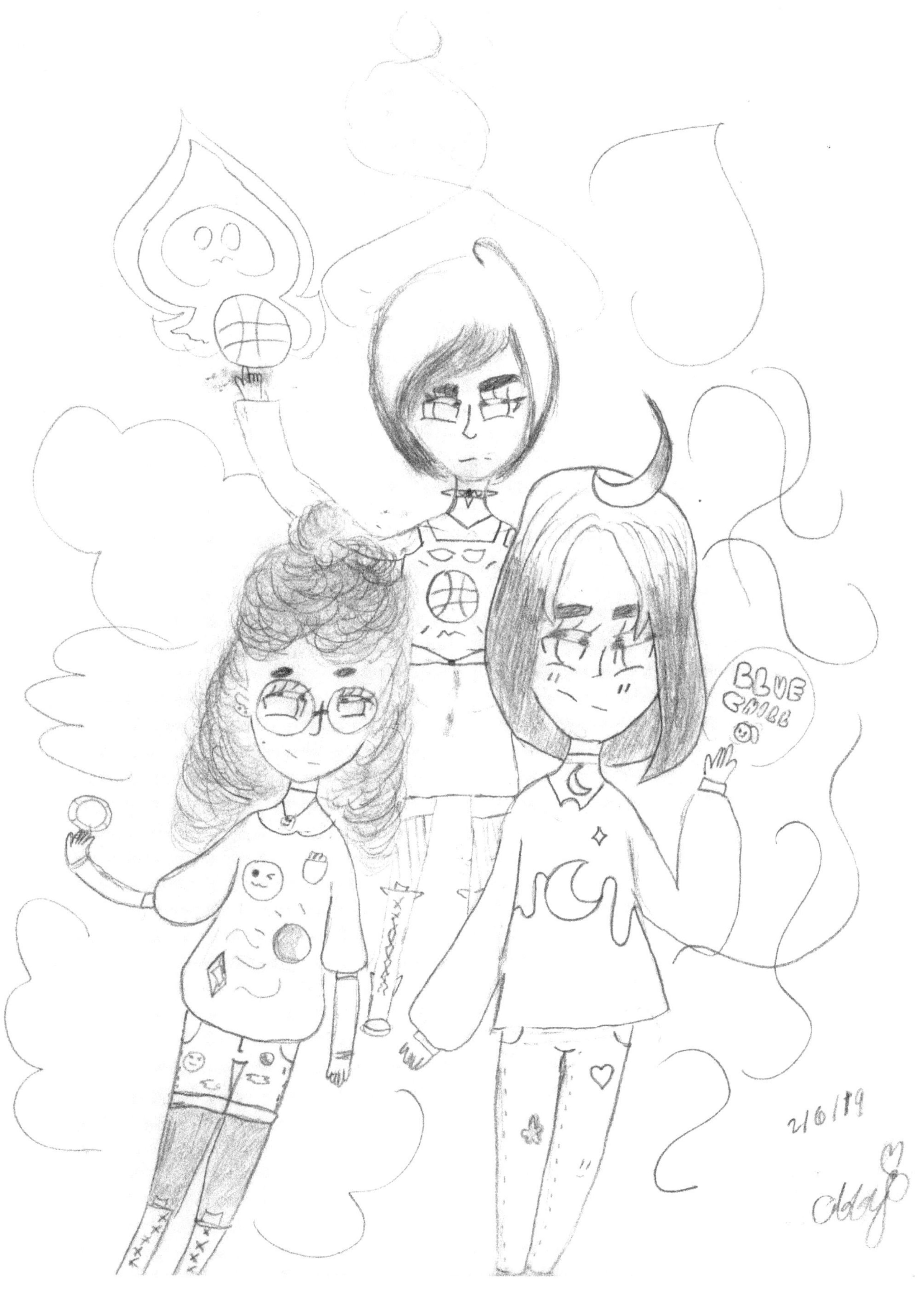
BLUE
2/6/19

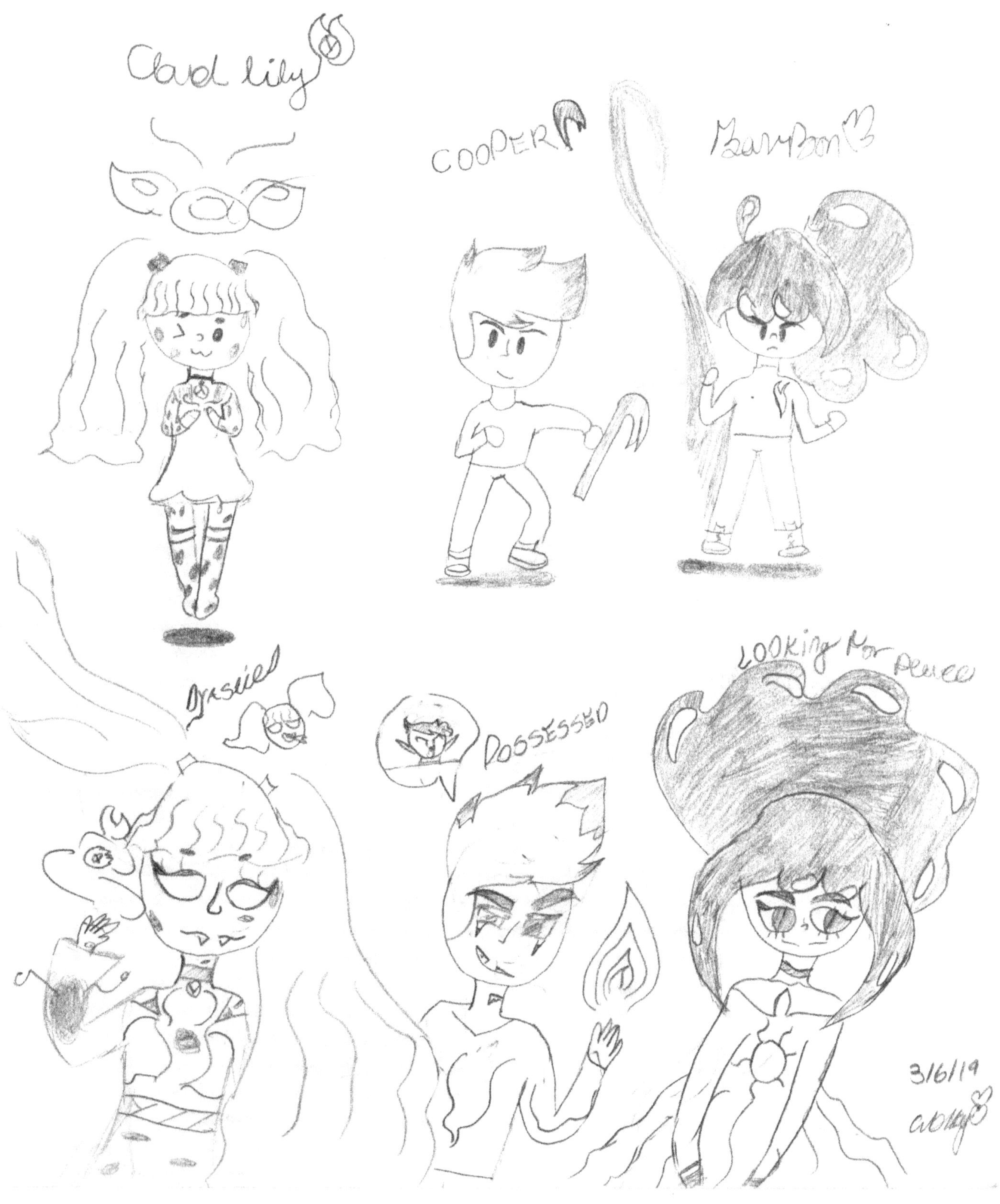
Cloud lily
COOPER
POSSESSED
LOOKing for peace
3/6/19

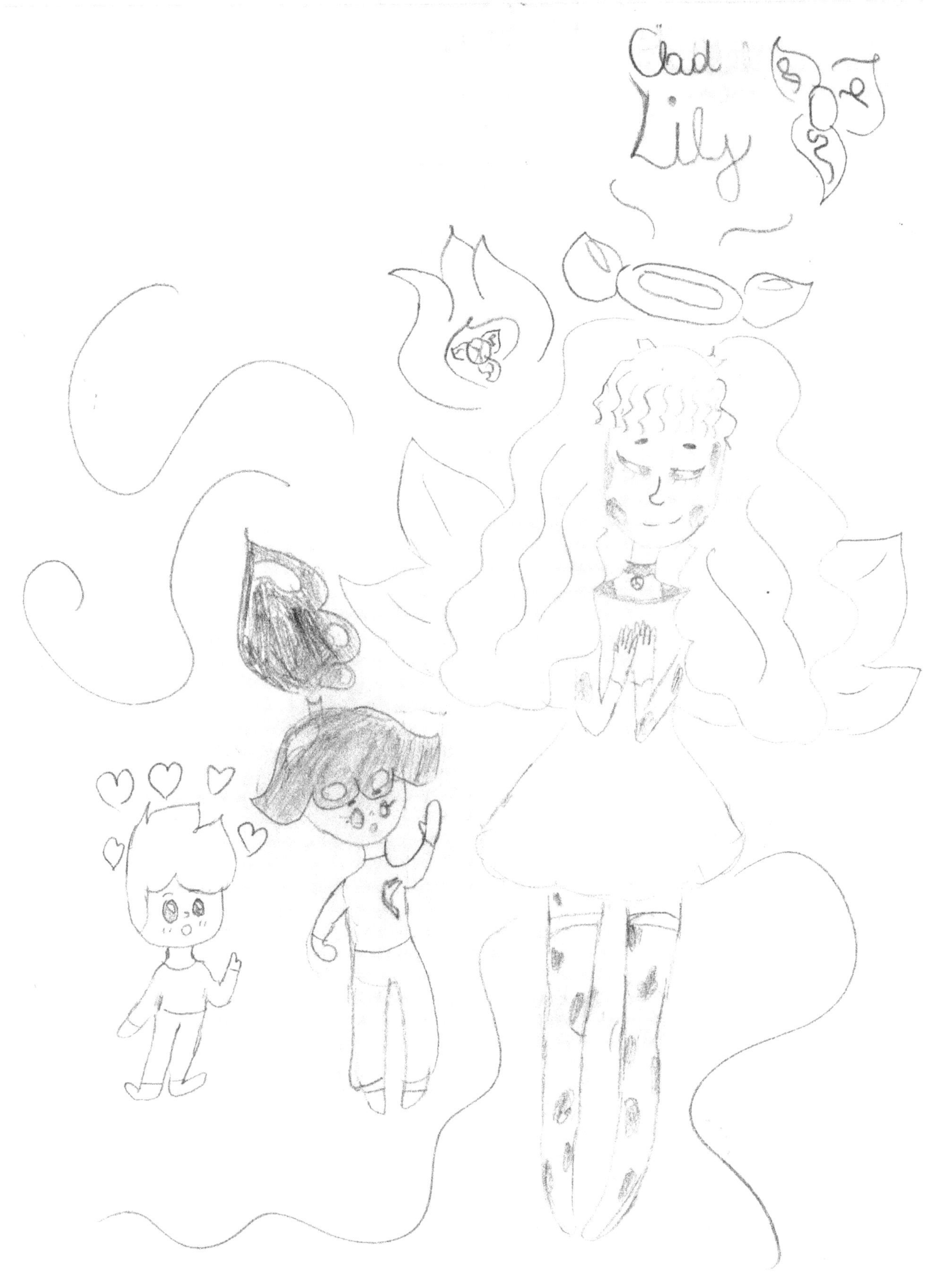
Clad
Lily

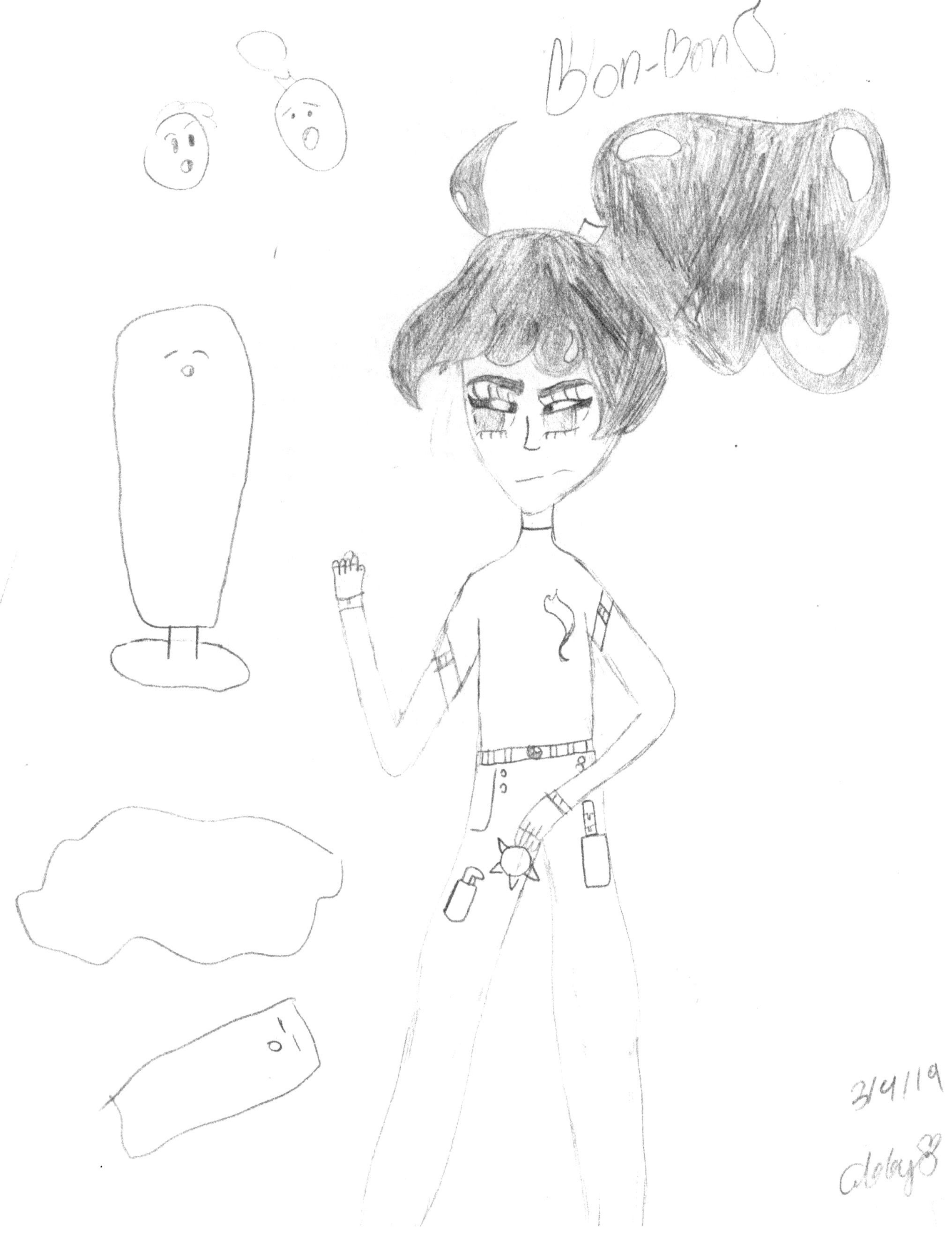
Bon-Bon
3/4/19
cldoy8

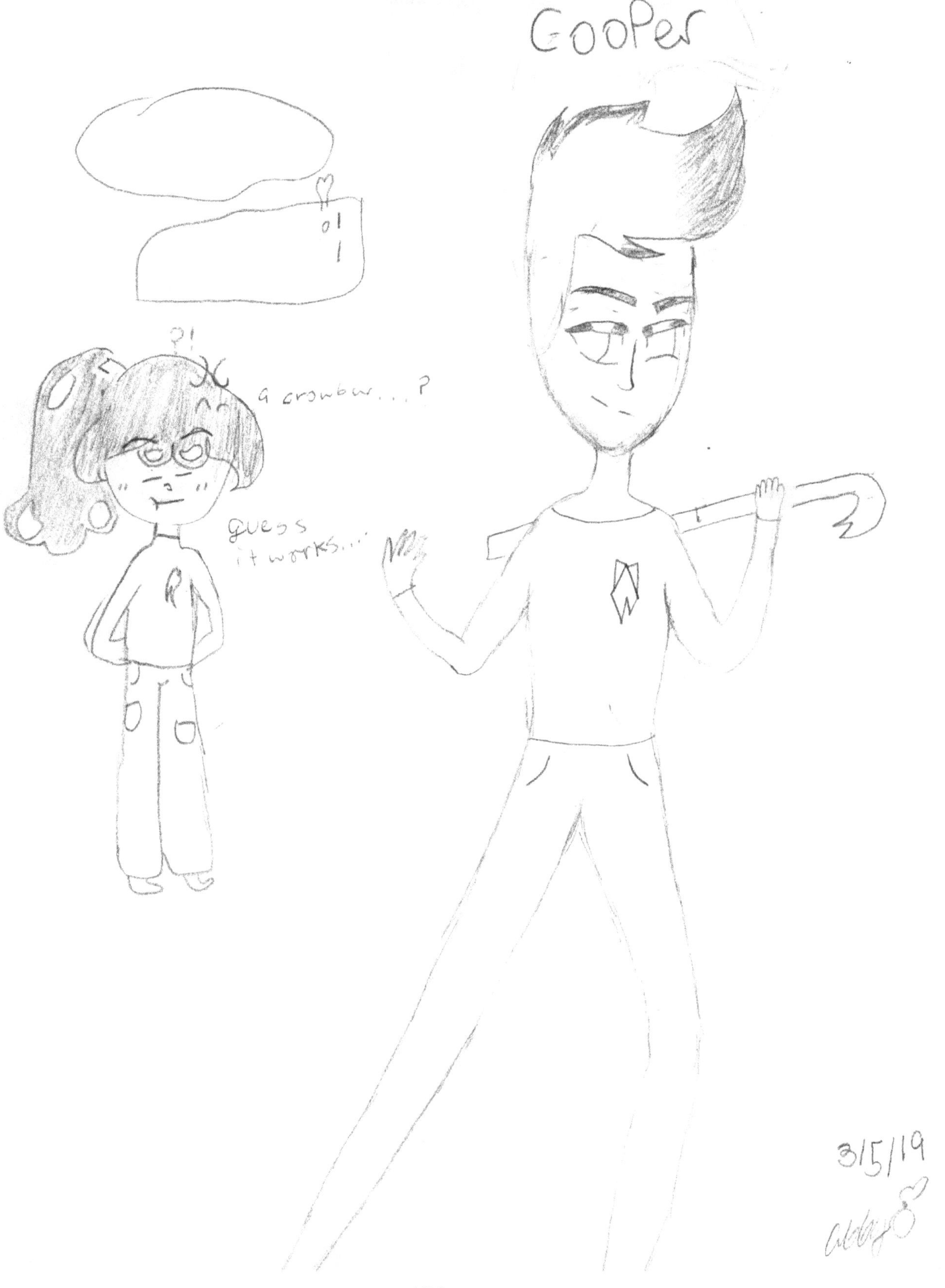
Gooper
?!
a crowbar...?
guess it works...
3/5/19

www.ingramcontent.com/pod-product-compliance
Lightning Source LLC
Chambersburg PA
CBHW081238180526
45171CB00005B/459

* 9 7 8 1 6 4 4 2 6 1 8 5 9 *